Teaching Styles and Strategies:

INTERVENTIONS TO ENRICH

INSTRUCTIONAL DECISION-MAKING

by

**Harvey F. Silver, J. Robert Hanson,
Richard W. Strong
and Patricia B. Schwartz**

**Third Edition
2003**

Published by Thoughtful Education Press, LLC
227 First St.
Ho-Ho-Kus, NJ 07423-1533
800-962-4432
www.thoughtfuled.com

© 2003 Thoughtful Education Press, LLC

227 First Street
Ho-Ho-Kus, NJ 07423
(800) 962-4432
www.thoughtfuled.com

Printed in the United States of America

ISBN 1-58284-002-4

TABLE OF CONTENTS

Acknowledgments 5

**Chapter One: Introduction, Definitions,
     & Teaching Processes** 7

**Chapter Two: Overview of the
     Mastery Strategies (ST)** 19
     Command Strategy
     Exercise-Proceduralizing Strategy
     Graduated Difficulty Strategy
     New American Lecture Strategy

**Chapter Three: Overview of the
     Understanding Strategies (NT)** 61
     Circle of Knowledge
     Compare and Contrast
     Concept Attainment
     Reading for Meaning
     Inquiry
     Mystery
     Interpretation of Data
     Application of Principles

**Chapter Four: Overview of the
     Self-Expressive Strategies (NF)** 131
     Divergent Thinking
     Metaphorical Teaching
     Inductive Learning
     Dilemma Decision-Making

**Chapter Five: Overview of the
     Interpersonal Strategies (SF)** 169
     Team Games Tournament
     Jigsaw (The Experts Strategy)
     Reciprocal Learning (Peers Coaching Peers)
     Circle Strategy
     Role Playing

**Overview of the Meta Strategies
     (Strategies for "Four"-Thought)** . . . 225
     Write to Learn (Logs)
     Creative Problem-Solving
     Knowledge By Design
     Task Rotation

References and Useful Resources 255

Additional Materials 261

ACKNOWLEDGMENTS

This fourth edition of Teaching Styles and Strategies is in response to those users who wanted a more complete narrative treatment of the strategies. This edition features rationale, procedures, sample lessons, decision-making steps, things to remember and assessment suggestions.

We're grateful to all those teachers who gave us content ideas as well as constructive feedback on the volume. We're particularly grateful to Dr. Patricia Schwartz for her work in expanding the strategies and making the document more comprehensive and internally consistent.

Harvey Silver, Ed.,
Richard Strong, MA.,
& J. Robert Hanson, Ed.
Woodbridge, NJ

1
CHAPTER ONE

Introduction, Definitions, & Teaching Processes

Introduction

Teaching strategies are nothing new. Plato, Aristotle, St. Paul and Aquinas all had their favorites. Today we hear about Skinner, A.S. Neill, Bruner, Torrance, Taba and Hunter. These teachers—and many more—have all presented instructional strategies that matched the needs of students' perceived learning strategies. These needs were all different. This is because, then and now, we all learn differently. Different cultures impose different learning requirements; needs are different. The lessons we learn are different. Thus, there is no right or wrong strategy, but rather the mismatching of strategies and learners. All strategies and their related teaching styles have their place. The key to good teaching is to see how learner and strategy best fit together. Good teaching, or fully professional teaching, means that a teacher can move from style to style, strategy to strategy, and learner to learner to create those climates and implement those strategies most conducive to learning different kinds of objectives.

Teaching Styles and Strategies is a practical directory of teaching strategies. The manual has one purpose: to enrich the practice of teaching. The use of the strategies provide no painless solutions to the mysteries of good teaching, nor does their use represent a proven pathway to teaching success. Rather, the use of the strategies allows the practitioner to create a classroom atmosphere for the achievement of specific educational goals. One strategy is not superior to any other. One strategy is not totally different from all the others. Instead, each strategy has a particular purpose, and each contains elements of both cognitive and affective functioning. The strategies may be used singly or in combination, one at a time, or many at one time. The strategies, in various combinations and sequences, represent a classroom management system.

Teaching Styles and Strategies was written with the conviction that there are a variety of ways to enrich the instructional process within the confines and existing resources of the typical classroom. The strategies proposed require no additional equipment or materials. They require no special places or physical arrangements. Rather, the strategies are ways to evoke responses in particular learning environments pertinent to the nature of the content to be learned.

Teaching Style

Teaching strategies do, however, differ from teaching styles. Anyone who teaches (or communicates in any way) has a style. A teaching style is a reflection of the individual's value system regarding human nature and of the kinds of goals and environments that enhance human learning. One's teaching style represents a conscious (or unconscious) enacting of the ways one prefers to learn and remembers being taught. It is exhibited in preferred or repeated behaviors. Some teaching behaviors are naturally more comfortable for one style than for others. Teaching styles tend to support particular kinds of teaching and their related subject matters, to the general exclusion of other styles and their related contents. No individual displays all of the characteristics of any particular teaching style, nor do the characteristics of any particular teaching style explain all of a teacher's behavior. Environmental, cultural, and inherited characteristics invariably modify an individual's behavior.

Teaching Strategies Defined

A teaching strategy is a particular set of steps to evoke from learners a specific set of desired behaviors. Teaching strategies are deliberate efforts by the teacher to vary the mode of presentation to more appropriately represent the functions (cognitive and affective) inherent in a particular learning objective. In the teaching strategies as much effort is devoted to the learner's role as to the teacher's role. In the use of the strategies, teacher and learner become a team with announced goals and clearly identified procedures for reaching these goals.

Learning Styles Defined

The 25 strategies described in this Manual facilitate one or more of the four basic teaching styles of the Thoughtful Education Model. These four styles, developed from the research of Carl Gustav Jung[1] and Isabel Briggs Myers[2], provide a framework for analyzing and categorizing teaching and learning behaviors. This categorization places a learner's dominant behaviors in one of four distinct groupings. Jung's theory argues that learning and teaching behavior is not random, but rather is a reflection of one's developed or accessible functions for perception (how data are perceived or collected), and how these same data are judged and mentally processed, i.e., how the individual comes to conclusions about the meaning and importance of specific data.

Four Jungian Functions

The two ways of perceiving or finding out about persons, places, or things are through one's senses, or on the opposite pole of the same axis, through one's intuition.

The sensing orientation focuses on things as they appear. Sensors assume that what their senses tell them is what exists. Sensing deals with shape, color, texture, and the arrangement of things. The sensor operates in the here and now.

The intuitive orientation focuses on the inner meanings and relationships of what is occurring. Intuition deals with seeing possibilities, insights, and interpretations of what might be. The intuitor operates in the near and longer-term future.

The two ways of judging one's perceptions are thinking and feeling. Thinking judgments are made on the basis of facts, logic, analysis and external evidence. Decision-making for the thinker is more logical and impersonal. Feeling judgments are made on the basis of values, personal beliefs, subjective responses, and internal evidence. Decision-making for the feeler is more personal and based on like/dislike

judgments. Jung's theory says that we tend to prefer one perception and one judgment function over their opposites. We all use all four functions, but not at the same time or with the same frequency. Preferences develop like muscles: the more they are used, the stronger they become. Preferences for perception and judgment are the comfortable behaviors we develop over time. These preferences in turn become our learning and teaching styles.

Jung's Theory of Type

Jung theorized the two sets of opposing function, i.e., sensing versus intuition and thinking versus feeling, as a picture or archetype of human behavior. The form the archetypal picture takes is that of a mandala. Each function in the four-sided mandala represents a universal characteristic found in all human behavior. The mandala, a symbolic representation of the four-fold character of life is pictured in Figure 1-1.

The pairing of the perception and judgment functions results in four different styles or types. These styles can be summarized briefly by key behaviors:

The Sensing-Thinker (ST) or Mastery learner can be characterized as realistic, practical, and matter-of-fact. This type of learner is efficient and results-oriented. They prefer action to words and involvement to theory, and have a high energy level for doing things that are pragmatic, logical and useful. ST learners prefer to perceive the world through their senses and thus live in the "here and now." They also rely on thinking to make decisions, and are concerned about logical consequences more than personal feelings. The ST learners perceive the world in terms of things tangible to the senses, rather than abstract or symbolic ideas, theories, or models. The ST learner is objective, efficient, and goal-oriented.

The Sensing-Feeler (SF) or Interpersonal learner can be characterized as sociable, friendly, and interpersonally oriented. This type of learner is very sensitive to people's feelings. They prefer to learn about things that directly

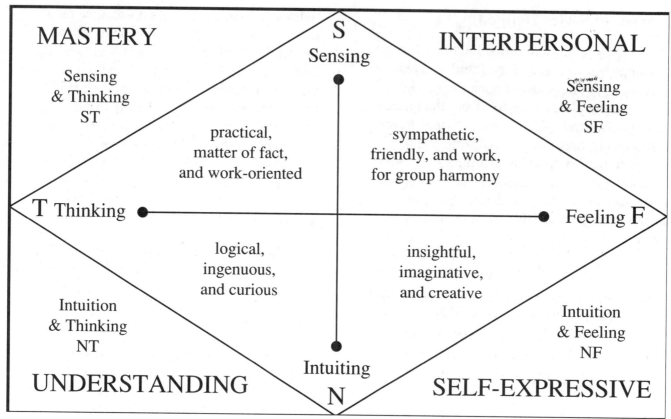

Figure 1-1

affect people's lives rather than impersonal facts or theories. The SF learners perceive with their senses and accept and use the data they find around themselves. This type of learner makes decisions based on personal feelings of like or dislike rather than impersonal logic. They focus on facts primarily in terms of people. This combination of functions produces learners who are keen observers of human behavior and who display a great deal of interest in—and empathy for—others.

The Intuitive-Thinking (NT) or Understanding learner can be characterized as theoretical, intellectual, and knowledge-oriented. These types of learners prefer to be challenged intellectually and to think things through for themselves. The NT is curious about ideas, has a tolerance for theory, a taste for complex problems, and a concern for long-range consequences. The NT learner prefers to look at the world through intuition rather than senses. They are interested in abstract ideas, possibilities, and the meanings of things beyond what is concrete and tangible. They rely on

thinking more than feelings to make decisions. As a result, their thought processes tend to be logical, analytical, often critical, and generally impersonal. The NT learner is unlikely to be convinced by anything but reason.

The Intuitive-Feeling (NF) or Self-Expressive learner can be characterized as curious, insightful, imaginative, and creative. The NF is one who dares to dream, is committed to his/her values, is open to alternatives, and constantly searches for new and unusual ways to express himself. The NF learners prefer to look at things with their own intuitions rather than using the senses, and are mainly interested in seeing possibilities beyond what is present, obvious or known. Intuition heightens their understanding, long-range vision, insight, curiosity about new ideas, interest in the future, tolerance for ambiguity, and love of books. Since this type of learner prefers to make decisions using feelings, intuition is geared toward people, values, and artistic expression.

Jung's descriptions of the four functions, and the later pairing of the functions under the direction of Isabel Briggs Myers, provides a pragmatic tool for assessing learning styles and for categorizing content to be learned in terms of required cognitive and affective functions. The Hanson-Silver instrumentation on learning and teaching styles utilizes learning behavior descriptions by paired functions, and is specifically focused on classroom practice.

Four Goals of Education

The four learning styles can be directly translated into the four basic goals of education:

Mastery: The Sensing-Thinking style is the Mastery goal. In the Mastery goal, the teacher presents information and provides practice opportunities for students to exercise new learnings. This is done in order to remember important skills and information.

Understanding: The Intuitive-Thinking style is the Understanding goal. In the Understanding goal, the teacher presents data for the students to process. The teacher probes student explanations in order to develop reasoning skills and an understanding of concepts, patterns, and proofs for ideas.

Self-Expressive: The Intuitive-Feeling style is the Self-Expressive goal. In the Self-Expressive goal, the teacher presents the students with challenges and problems to solve. The Self-Expressive goal requires students to reorganize their thinking. Self-Expressive thinking focuses on the development of creative, practical, and synergistic applications of old skills and information to new contexts and the production of original work.

Inter/Intrapersonal Awareness: The Sensing-Feeling style is the goal of Inter/Intrapersonal Awareness. In this goal the teacher presents questions or activities in which the students relate their personal experiences and feelings to some content. This goal focuses on the development of personal and social maturity, the establishment of a healthy attitude toward self and others, and the recognition of what one values.

Introversion and Extroversion

Jung identified a third dimension which describes the context within which one processes perceptions and judgments. He termed this bipolar dimension introversion/extroversion. These behaviors can also be defined as the reflective (I) or active (E) orientations to learning. Thus, in addition to an individual's preferences for certain paired functions, he/she also has a fundamental orientation or attitude toward life and learning. This attitude or value system, i.e., introversion or extroversion, determines how the individual operates ("thinks" in a generic sense), regardless of his/her perception and judgment preferences.

Introverts

The introvert or reflective learner directs mental energies inward toward issues of subjective interest. They are influenced by their own intentions, rather than by external events. Their interests tend to focus on the subjects that they can best deal with internally, reflectively, contemplatively, and in desired detail. Their focus is subjective and value-driven.

Introverts direct their mental energies inward toward issues of subjective interest. They are influenced more by their own intentions than by external events. Introverts are more involved with the meanings of their own internal images and values, and may appear less verbal than extroverts. As one result, they tend not to be joiners, not to be easily led, and more difficult to "read." They like quiet for concentration, are careful about details, and dislike broad generalities.

Extroverts

The extrovert or active learner on the opposite pole, is characterized as one who focuses psychic energies on the external world of ideas and objects. They are influenced primarily by their surroundings. Their interests have an outward movement toward people. Their focus tends to be objective.

Because extroverts operate "in the open," involved as they are with the world outside themselves, they tend to be more easily understood, more outgoing, more at ease in groups, and willing to be channeled in terms of new interest and activities. They tend to be more verbal and socially active. They like variety and action; tend to work quickly; dislike complicated details, and enjoy group functions.

Introversion/extroversion are mutually exclusive. While they cannot peacefully coexist, they do alternate in emphasis depending on circumstances. In most instances, one attitude or value system (conscious or unconscious) tends to predominate. That attitude, and its associated behaviors, characterizes how the learner prefers to think about or process information. The practical implications for teacher decision-making include the following considerations.

Introversion/reflective orientation: students prefer independent study, can process effectively working alone, tend to need quiet for concentration, and can formulate conclusions based on their own study of printed matter.

Extroversion/active orientation: students prefer to learn by doing, enjoy questions and answer sessions, appreciate working in groups or pairs, need hands-on experiences, learn through hearing themselves talk, and work well in groups.

The understanding and use of the different learning and teaching styles is essential if teachers are to become sensitive and alert to their own teaching style and to the various teaching strategies and their purposes. Clearly, there are some strategies that teachers have used all along. Other strategies may be new to the reader. We recommend them all... for the correct purpose and at the right time. Figure 1-2 (on next page) identifies major behaviors and activities for each style.

Three Basic Constructs For Teaching

Improving the quality of the teaching/learning act requires improvement in the teacher's decision-making ability; i.e., to make the best possible matches between the students' learning preferences, the content to be taught, and the strategy to be used. Making matches requires an understanding of three basic constructs:

1) A thorough understanding of the teaching/learning act;

2) An understanding of the matching process and the choices available to teachers and students; and

3) The skills to carry out the available options.

Teaching/Learning Act

The teaching/learning act (Figure 1-3) may be defined as a series of scenes or episodes taking place over time in an environment which involves an interrelationship between teacher behavior, learner behavior, and the content to be mastered. The role of the teacher in this triangular relationship is that of decision-maker.

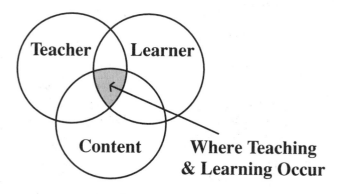

Figure 1-3

LEARNING BEHAVIORS AND ACTIVITIES BY STYLE

Mastery	**Understanding**	**Self-Expressive**	**Interpersonal**
Sensing-Thinkers	*Intuitive-Thinkers*	*Intuitive-Feelers*	*Sensing-Feelers*

Teachers may be characterized as:

Mastery	Understanding	Self-Expressive	Interpersonal
Trainers	Intellectual Challengers	Facilitators	Nurturers
Information Givers	Theoreticians	Stimulators	Supporters
Instructional Managers	Inquirers	Creators/Originators	Empathizers

Learners may be characterized as:

Sensing-Thinkers	*Intuitive-Thinkers*	*Intuitive-Feelers*	*Sensing-Feelers*
Realistic	Logical	Curious	Sympathetic
Practical	Intellectual	Insightful	Friendly
Pragmatic	Knowledge Oriented	Imaginative	Interpersonal

Curriculum objectives emphasize:

Sensing-Thinkers	*Intuitive-Thinkers*	*Intuitive-Feelers*	*Sensing-Feelers*
Knowledge	Concept Development	Creative Expression	Positive Self-Concept
Skills	Critical Thinking	Moral Development	Socialization
Procedures	Inductive Learning	Application of Knowledge	Self-Invention

Setting (Learning Environments) emphasize:

Sensing-Thinkers	*Intuitive-Thinkers*	*Intuitive-Feelers*	*Sensing-Feelers*
Purposeful Work	Discovery	Originality	Personal Warmth
Organization/Competition	Inquiry/Independence	Flexibility/Imagination	Interaction/Collaboration
Drill and Practice	Finding Proof	Creativity	Cooperation and Dialogue

Operations (Thinking and Feeling Processes) include:

Sensing-Thinkers	*Intuitive-Thinkers*	*Intuitive-Feelers*	*Sensing-Feelers*
Observing	Classifying	Hypothesizing	Describing Feelings
Describing	Applying	Synthesizing	Empathizing
Memorizing	Comparing/Contrasting	Metaphoric Expression	Responding
Translating	Analyzing	Divergent Thinking	Valuing
Categorizing	Evaluating	Creating	Supporting

Teaching strategies include:

Sensing-Thinkers	*Intuitive-Thinkers*	*Intuitive-Feelers*	*Sensing-Feelers*
Command	Mystery	Torrancial Thinking	Circle of Knowledge
TGT	Concept Attainment	Metaphorical Problem-Solving	Peer Problem-Solving
Graduated Difficulty	Inquiry	Inductive Learning	Role-Playing
Goals	Reading for Meaning	Creative Thinking	Reciprocal Learning
Surveys	Compare & Contrast	Etch-A-Sketch	Study Teams

Student activities include:

Sensing-Thinkers	*Intuitive Thinkers*	*Intuitive-Feelers*	*Sensing-Feelers*
Workbooks	Independent Study	Creative Art Activities	Group Projects
Drill & Repetition	Essays	Imaging	"Show & Tell"
Demonstrations	Logic problems	Boundary Breaking	Team Games
Hands-On Projects	Debates	Dramatics	Directed Art Activities
Competitions	Argument	Open-Ended Discussions	Personal Sharing

Assessment and evaluation procedures include:

Sensing-Thinkers	*Intuitive-Thinkers*	*Intuitive-Feelers*	*Sensing-Feelers*
Objective Tests	Open-Ended Questions	Fluency of Expression	Personal Journals
Checklists	Essays	Flexibility of Response	Oral Reports
Behavioral Objectives	Demonstration of Abilities:	Originality of Response	Ranking Procedures
Use of Mechanical Devices	Apply	Elaboration of Detail	Trained Observations
Demonstrations of Specific	Synthesize	Development of	Collection of Unobtrusive
Skills	Interpret	Aesthetic Criteria	Data
Criterion Referenced Tests	Integrate	Producing Creative	Self-Reporting
Rubrics and Standards	Analyze	Products	Surveys
	Evaluate	Projects, Exhibits	
	Think Divergently	Portfolios	

Figure 1-2

To make more of teaching/learning time, teacher decisions need to be made regarding the "scope" of instruction; i.e., Setting, Content, Operations, Process, and Evaluation. These five decision settings include:

Setting Decisions

- whom to teach
- assessment of student needs, interests, abilities and styles
- physical setting
- classroom organization
- psychological climate

Content Decisions

- what to teach
- quality, quantity
- order, sequence
- materials and equipment
- mode and media

Operational Decisions

- thinking and feeling processes
- introversion/extroversion preferences
- tasks and activities to be performed

Process Decisions

- teaching strategies to be used
- student roles, teacher roles
- implementation procedures

Evaluation Decisions

- giving and receiving feedback
- establishing criteria for successful performance (product and process)
- collecting, analyzing, and utilizing data for future learning

The Whole Pie

These five SCOPE decisions may be best understood when seen as integral to the planning, implementation, and evaluation (P.I.E.) of an instructional scene or episode. Decision-making occurs in three distinct stages:

- The first stage is **planning** for learning (decisions made prior to instruction)
- The second stage is **implementing** learning (decisions made during instruction)
- The third stage is **evaluating** learning (decisions made during and after instruction)

Thus, a description of the teaching/learning act is that: teaching behavior is a chain of decision-making—

- occurring in a series of scenes or episodes, taking place over time
- with critical variables in each scene being: teacher behavior, learner behavior, and the content to be mastered
- where decisions must be made regarding setting, content, operations, process and evaluation, and where
- decisions are made for the three steps of instruction, i.e., planning, implementation, and evaluation.

Graphically illustrated, the decision-making process appears in Figure 1-4.

Effective teaching, then is the result of making appropriate decisions on three interrelated sets of variables (Figure 1-5).

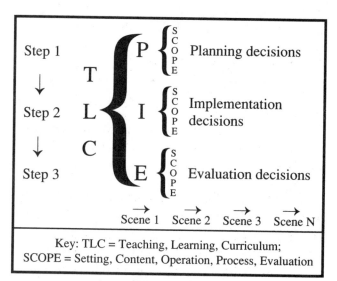

Figure 1-4

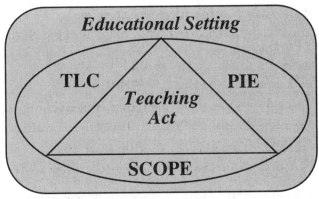

Figure 1-5

Matching Process

The Jungian-based Thoughtful Education Model provides the teacher with a framework for understanding the choices available for decision-making. This framework can assist teachers in diagnosing student learning preferences, as well as in correctly categorizing the nature of the content to be learned relative to required mental operations. As a result, the teacher can select those behaviors which are most appropriate for working with an individual student, or a group of students, to achieve a particular objective. The essence of good teaching is that of implementing teaching behavior which is congruent with the intent of the objectives to be mastered and with the student's learning styles. A shorthand method for describing the congruent teaching act is the formula $B \approx I$, or teaching behavior congruent ($\approx$) with one's intent. In other words, was the lesson taught the way you intended, based on the P.I.E., T.L.C., and SCOPE decisions?[3]

Perfection and Completion

Jung spoke of two major objectives for psychic development that have clear parallels for teaching, learning, and the matching process. He called these two objectives "perfection" and "completion."

By perfection Jung meant the need to develop one's own particular strengths or abilities to the maximum. An alternative choice is to strive after completion. This "striving-after" attempts to develop strengths across all of one's actual as well as one's potential abilities.

Basically, there are two types of matches. First, there is the matching of student learning style, content mastery, and teaching techniques based on the goal of perfection. This type of match emphasizes "congruity." Congruence occurs when the student is consistently provided with opportunities to learn in his own most preferred style. Such matches provide for approval and success.

A second matching process is based on the goal of completion. This type of matching emphasizes fluency and flexibility. Fluency occurs when the student is consistently provided with opportunities to learn in different styles through the development of different competencies. Matches that are fluent and flexible lead to the student's appreciation of alternative learning styles, as well as to the student's ability to operate in different learning styles.

Where the teacher's goal is perfection, the objective for making matches is congruence. Where the teacher's goal is completion, the objectives are fluency and flexibility.

Learner Validation

In making these matches, the teacher exercises power to approve (validate) the pupil to enhance his self-concept, and to increase his repertoire of cognitive and affective skills.

A primary teacher role, therefore, is to recognize, respect, and use the inborn drives of the learner. Accepting the learner's dependencies to operate in specific ways "validates" behavior, and contributes to freeing learners to risk behaviors in their less-developed styles. The more students are approved for the way in which they prefer to learn, the more they will be willing to risk altering those ways! For example, the Intuitive-Thinking learner should be provided with opportunities to fully exploit the strengths of the Intuitive-Thinking style, but simultaneously should be encouraged to express and appreciate his less preferred functions of feeling and sensing. By the same token, the extrovert needs to be provided with opportunities to interact, to take action, to discuss ideas, and to work with others. On the other hand, he must be encouraged to work independently, to become more self aware, to learn to be more reflective, to appreciate more of his own inner thoughts and feelings, and to commit himself to completing tasks of high personal importance. In short, Jung would say that the primary role of the teacher is to recognize the many potentialities of her students, and to consciously plan for the balanced development of each individual across each of the four styles.

Executing Teaching Strategies

The strategies described in this book are presented as decision-making tools. These decision-making tools are available to both teachers and learners. Each group of tools or strategies has a different use so teachers can better assist learners in achieving successful experiences in all types of learning situations. Each strategy has assets and liabilities. No single strategy is suitable for all content or for all types of learners.

In studying the various strategies, teachers will discover that some are variations of practices already used. As such, those strategies commonly used may also represent a particular teaching style.

Other strategies represent the need to experiment with new learning behaviors. These new or unused strategies require practice and training. As in learning anything new, some of the strategies will come more easily than others. The strategies described in this manual that are not used, or least used, may represent a teaching style opposite to your own.

Finally, the effective practice of new strategies, or new twists on familiar practices, requires both the willingness to risk and the commitment or time. The development of a complete teaching repertoire, a sign of professional maturation, comes both from experience and from the desire to make one's behavior congruent with one's teaching intent.

Teaching Styles and Strategies

Each teaching style tends to favor certain strategies to the exclusion of others. In order for a teacher to be fluent and flexible in the use of the strategies, she also needs to balance the types of presentations she makes over the four types of learning styles. It is not enough to make congruent matches. The most effective classroom management is for the teacher to be both congruent and flexible in her decision-making. Looking at the four learning styles as the four spokes of a wheel, the teacher is encouraged to "teach around the wheel;" i.e., teaching all content, as nearly as possible, in each of the four styles, and with varied mixes of strategies as they relate to each style. As flexibility is acquired, student learning becomes more powerful, meaningful, and useful.

Teacher Self-Assessment

It is true that the strategies can be effectively employed without prior knowledge of teaching styles or even of one's own learning and teaching preferences. Yet, it is generally of greater help to educators if they understand their own learning and teaching styles. Such self-knowledge allows the teacher to be more sensitive to the different learning styles of their students. Able teachers must know themselves if they are to be sensitive to their students. The teachers must be able to accept and like themselves if they are to be free to accept and like their students. Teachers must find contentment with their own natures and learning styles if they are to be able to stimulate students to search actively for theirs. As a role model for the students, teachers must enjoy the process of growth and becoming if they are to encourage students to live vigorously, enthusiastically, and without fear. Teachers, in short, must rejoice in their calling and their being. Growth and maturation are both the challenges and the meaning of life.

An understanding and appreciation of the characteristics of each of the four teaching styles serves as its own impetus for the making of better matches between content, learning styles and teaching styles.

Summary and Next Steps

These Thoughtful Education teaching strategies are presented as tools for improved classroom management and teacher practice. They are presented so that teachers can better assist learners in experiencing success in all types of content and learning situations. These 18 teaching strategies are methods for proving one's ability to work effectively with all kinds of learners. They serve as vehicles for self-discovery as they acquaint the user with instructional systems that feel most comfortable, and probably reflect one's preferred teaching style. Obversely, the strategies in non-preferred categories need to be practiced to enlarge one's own repertoire of skills, and to address learner needs previously overlooked or undervalued. The same distinction may also address content areas; i.e., certain teaching styles and strategies tend to serve certain types of instructional objectives to the possible exclusion of others. For example, a teacher that makes extensive use of sensing-thinking strategies may tend to focus her teaching on the practice, drill, and memory-based learning of factual information and skills. Such a focus tends to exclude activities oriented to self-expression and to critical and creative thinking. Or, the teacher that operates largely in the intuitive-thinking style—with its emphasis on concept formation and analysis—may tend to overlook the development of specific skills, or to involve students' feelings in a constructive and instructional way in the learning process.

In short, to work toward the goal of having each learner be an educational winner requires that instruction and related content mastery be presented using a carefully chosen group of styles and strategies specifically focused on the learner needs. Ideally, one teaches portions of the required content in each of the four styles, and with related strategies. The Thoughtful Education[4] strategies become, as it were, a "format" for the planning, delivery, and evaluation of content and learning. Teaching is both art and science, feeling and technology, perceiving and judging. As an art form, teaching requires that one be able to change roles, styles and strategies to meet the demands of students and content. As a science, the teacher must be able to diagnose learning styles, categorize content, and select from among multiple styles and strategies those combinations that make the best "matches" or fits for the class.

The teacher's ability to flex or move from role to role, and style to style, frees her from an age-old conflict; i.e., the "versus" issue, which demanded that one style be identified as best. Being freed from the constraints of custom and tradition, the teacher is now able to plan for the well-rounded intellectual and emotional diet all students need and enjoy. Good teaching represents the teacher's ability to present content across all four learning styles using as many of the teaching styles and strategies as are appropriate.

The (25) strategies that follow are not meant to be an exhaustive list. They are, however, inclusive enough to provide alternatives for each type of learner and content, and do reflect the findings of long-term and extensive research.

A fascination of teaching is experimentation. Teachers are encouraged to modify the use of the strategies to fit their particular purposes, or to mix them together as needed. More drastic modifications, however, may have a greater possibility of losing the initial power of the strategy. In any event, good teachers have been modifying and experimenting since the earliest times. These strategies, hopefully, will make our time and our teaching more effective and enjoyable.

References

[1] Jung, Carl Gustav, <u>Psychological Types</u>, Bollingen Series, Volume 6, Princeton University Press, Princeton, NJ, Second Printing, 1974. pp. 330-405.

[2] Myers, Isabel Briggs, <u>The Myers-Briggs Type Indicator Manual</u>, Consulting Psychologists Press, Palo Alto, CA, 1962. pp. 51-64.

[3] Joyce, Bruce and Marsha Weil, <u>Models of Teaching</u>, Prentice Hall Publishers, Englewood Cliffs, NJ, 1972. pp. 1-27 and sections on individual strategies.

[4] Hanson Silver Strong Learning Preferences Inventory (for student learning style diagnosis); Teaching Style Inventory (for teacher self-analysis of teaching style preferences) and Learning Style Inventory (for adult self-analysis of learning style preferences).

2
CHAPTER TWO

The Mastery Strategies

OVERVIEW OF THE MASTERY STRATEGIES (ST)

In the Mastery Strategies, the emphasis is on acquisition of knowledge and skills through practice, repetition, drill, and memorization. In the Mastery style, someone other than the learner determines the content or skills to be mastered. The teacher or curriculum guide is the primary source for establishing knowledge and skills as essential for students to learn. The content is predetermined, sequenced, demonstrated, practiced, and applied. Retention and performance are stressed. Feedback is obtained, and corrections are made where necessary.

Bruce Joyce and Marsha Weil (1972) categorize teaching which uses techniques to insure mastery as a "behavior modification" approach because the focus is on changing the external behavior of the learners by manipulating reinforcements. Joyce describes such approaches in terms of visible rather than underlying behavior.

The strategies in the mastery position are derived from the works of David Ausubel (1963), Madeline Hunter (1984), Muska Mosston (1972), and Robert Marzano; et al., (1986). The mastery strategies described in this chapter are New American Lecture, Command, Graduated Difficulty, and Exercise-Proceduralizing.

Ausubels' principles of meaningful learning and Hunter's elements of effective instruction were used to design the New American Lecture Strategy. Mosston's work as described in his book, *Teaching: From Command to Discovery* (1972), serves as the foundation for the Command and Graduated Difficulty Strategies, as well as for the Reciprocal Learning Strategy found in the Interpersonal chapter. Marzano provides the background for Exercise-Proceduralizing. These strategies move students from a highly teacher-directed and controlled learning mode to a more student-directed mode, with accompanying freedom and responsibility for learning.

Mosston provides the teacher with a "spectrum" of strategies, described as "universal styles of teaching," from which to choose. The styles described by Mosston, as with the categorization of models by Joyce and Weil (1972), have several elements in common with the four basic styles of the Hanson Silver Strong Thoughtful Education Model.

The *Command Strategy* provides the teacher with the greatest amount of control over student behavior. It is the most directive of all the sensing-thinking strategies. The primary goal of this strategy is to achieve 100% accuracy by having the students follow the teacher's directions on command.

The *Exercise-Proceduralizing Strategy* is used when you want students to master a specific skill by breaking it apart into its separate steps and then practicing it until it becomes automatic. In the Exercise-Proceduralizing Strategy, students work under the close direction and supervision of the teacher to master important skills. The first step toward mastery is to model the skill and to proceduralize it. The Exercise-Proceduralizing Strategy uses modeling, directed practice, guided practice, and independent practice to help students move from teacher dependence to learning independence.

The *Graduated Difficulty Strategy* is the last strategy to be described in the Mastery chapter. Freedom and responsibility are expanded in this strategy. Students are asked not only to make implementation and evaluation decisions, but assessment decisions as well. Students assess their own ability, select the task(s) they deem most appropriate to their readiness level, and then determine the knowledge and skills they need to move to the next level.

In the Graduated Difficulty Strategy, the teacher is still the sole source for determining content and establishing criteria for evaluation. Students choose from an array of options, prepared by the teacher, based on a sequential analysis of the content to be learned, and the degree of difficulty of the task to be performed.

The Graduated Difficulty Strategy is an excellent tool for differentiating performance levels in a heterogeneous class. It may also be used for intuitive-thinking learning tasks, depending on the nature of the activities designed and the thinking processes students are expected to employ.

The *New American Lecture Strategy* is used to provide students with information. The goal is to help students understand and remember important ideas. This strategy uses four kinds of support to make presentations more memorable: an anticipatory set or hook; an Advanced Visual Organizer; deep processing; and periodic thinking reviews utilizing questions in all four styles.

Now!

COMMAND STRATEGY
(or Simon Says)

The Command Strategy is used when you want to maintain total control of student behavior in order to achieve 100% accuracy or total control over procedures. Control is maintained by leading students through a series of steps, one-by-one, on command. The teacher is the sole decision-maker about content, process, organization, standards, discipline, and all related issues.

The Strategy at Work

In Dr. Santiago's eighth grade math fundamentals class, students have studied squares and square roots, and are ready to learn the procedure for finding the square root of any number. Dr. Santiago has broken down the procedure into steps which can be presented as a series of discrete directions.

Sample Lesson I:
Finding Square Roots

Say: "Today we are going to learn a procedure for finding the square root of any number. Your work with squares and roots will become much easier when you remember these steps. Because this is a new procedure with a number of steps, I am going to use the Command Strategy to teach it to you."

Dialogue:

Teacher: "What's my role in the Command Strategy?"

Students: "You tell us what to do one step at a time."

Teacher: "And what is your role?"

Students: "We listen carefully to the directions but do nothing until we hear the command signal."

Teacher: "The command signal today is 'square root!' What is the command signal?"

Students: "'Square root.' Whenever you say 'square root,' we follow your directions just as you directed us to do."

Teacher: "Good. When I give the sign, I want you to sit up straight in your seats, put your hands on your desk, and place your feet flat on the floor."

"That's our 'Command position.'—'square root!'"

"Fine." (Writes problem on the board).

$$\sqrt{841}$$

"Copy the problem on your paper.—'square root!'"

"Count off with me from the right, separating your number into pairs with small vertical lines like this:"

"Notice we have one pair (41) and one line digit (8). Under that first number (the 8) write the closest perfect square that is less than that number.—'square root!'"

(Teacher circulates to check and support.)

"Congratulations. You all wrote:"

$$\sqrt{8\ [41}$$
$$4$$

"Now write the square root of 4 directly above the 8 on the line:—'square root!'"

"Fine. Now you should have this written on your paper."

$$\overset{2}{\sqrt{8\ [41}}$$
$$4$$

"If that is not what you have, correct it now.—'square root!'"

"Now double that square root and write the answer off to the left like this:"

$$\sqrt{8\ [41}$$
$$4$$

"Write the 4 double here. —'square root!'"

"Subtract the 4 from the 8.—'square root!'"

$$\overset{2}{\sqrt{8\ [41}}$$
$$4\quad\underline{-4}$$
$$4$$

"Bring down the next pair of numbers.—'square root!'"

"Good. Now we divide our doubled square into this number. 4 goes into 44 eleven times. Since we can only use single digit numbers, 9 is as close as we can get. Write the 9 next to the 4.—'square root!'"

"Good. Multiply this new number by 9.—'square root!'"

$$\begin{array}{cc} 4\,9 & \overset{2}{\sqrt{8\ 4[1}} \\ \underline{\times\,9} & \underline{-\ 4} \\ 441 & 4\ 4\ 1 \end{array}$$

"Subtract this new number from 441.—'square root!'"

$$\begin{array}{cc} 4\,9 & \overset{2}{\sqrt{8\ 4[1}} \\ \underline{\times\,9} & \underline{-\ 4} \\ 441 & 4\ 4\ 1 \\ & \underline{4\ 4\ 1} \end{array}$$

"Your answer should be zero so write 9 in the line over the 41 in the problem.—'square root!'"

```
         2 9
  4 9    √ 8 4⌐1
  x 9    − 4
  441      4 4 1
           4 4 1
```

"This completes the problem. Read your answer aloud.—'square root!'"

29

"Congratulations. Stand at ease! You've solved your first square root problem. Are you ready for some practice?"

The Command Strategy has evolved from attempts to develop an efficient system for sequencing tasks and shaping behavior. The Command Strategy provides the teacher with total control over a specific teaching/learning activity. In this strategy, the teacher is established as the sole decision-maker about content, process, organization, standards, discipline, and the like. In the Command Strategy, the teacher makes all of the decisions about planning, implementation, and evaluation. Students follow all of the teacher's instructions on command.

In recent years, the Command Strategy has come under attack. The controversy stems from the supposed contradiction between American educational philosophy and its practice. Inherent in American educational philosophy is the recognition of the uniqueness of the individual, while the underlying foundation of the Command Strategy is a rigid set of uniform behavioral standards applied to all. The strategy is based on a belief that the person in authority knows more, and knows it better, and that the student must obey and follow the teacher without doubt, question, or change.

No apology is necessary for the use of the Command Strategy. There are times when insisting on conformity to rigid standards is as appropriate and educationally useful as is responding to each student individually. Each teaching strategy has its own assets and liabilities. Knowing what the Command Strategy can and cannot do is central to making an informed judgment about when its use is educationally sound. The issue need not—indeed, should not—be an either/or.

Activities that are serialized and subject matter that has finite and correct procedures are especially well suited to the Command Strategy. Reviewing and practicing safety procedures, lab procedures, conducting an orchestra, organizing students, drilling number facts, teaching arithmetic algorithms, and learning game rules are examples of situations in which the Command Strategy is appropriate and highly efficient. Command Strategy content is factual, concrete, immediately verifiable and easy to correct. The focus is precision, correctness and sequence.

The Command Strategy establishes clear objectives to be reached by all students. It develops externally observable group discipline. It guarantees that everyone participates, and distinguishes those who cannot participate from those who can. On the other hand, the Command Strategy involves students at a rote level. It impedes independence, and it does not take into account the individual differences of students, such as their rate of performance, level of ability, and so on. As a consequence, some subject matter; e.g., seeing connections, making applications, seeing alternatives, making choices, etc., clearly requires other teaching strategies.

Of equal concern in using the Command Strategy is classroom tone. A lighthearted tone turns the Command Strategy into an enjoyable follow-the-leader game, and is especially suited to review situations and for work with young children. A businesslike tone signals serious matters such as learning the long division algorithm or the procedure for finding square roots. A markedly stern, harsh, and humorless approach coupled with the rigid demands of the Command Strategy itself, however, can make some students uncomfortable, and may terrify others. Properly used, the Command Strategy will increase focus and insure success.

How To Plan Lessons Using The Command Strategy

To use the Command Strategy with your students, first select the content to be taught. The Command Strategy is best suited for teaching content which has right or wrong answers, which follows a sequential procedure, and in which safety or order is important. The Command Strategy is best used when the task is sufficiently difficult for students to need to follow directions in order to be successful.

Keep in mind that the Command Strategy need not always be used for a whole lesson. You might use it as an introductory part of a lesson to be followed by related activities. You might use it as a regular warm-up or review to help students internalize a particular skill and make its procedures automatic. You might use it, as needed, as one aspect of a classroom management scheme which allows you to move children and furniture quietly and efficiently for large and small group activities. It can be effectively used to introduce students to rules and procedures for the use of supplies—scissors, artists' knives, Bunsen burners, power tools, and the like—prior to an activity in which you want them to use this equipment safely but independently.

When you have selected the content, look at the task and break it down into steps. Consider the number of steps you need, the amount of explanation required for each, and how meaningful each step will be to the students. Write out the directions as a list or flow chart. Then try to follow them exactly as written to make sure that they are crystal clear and complete. The set of directions you will use for the Command Strategy should not require any further explanation by you. Students should be able to listen and do, listen and do in the manner of the game, "Simon Says." They should be able to give their full attention to performing the task by following your directions without being distracted by the need to question or explain.

The last planning step is to select your command signal. You may keep the same signal for a period of time, or change it regularly; each method has advantages and disadvantages. Using a food word such as "popcorn" or "cookie" with young children can be reinforced by bringing in the food as a treat at the end of the week. Some teachers have their students choose their own command word for the week.

For some older students, "cute" command words will be inappropriate; nevertheless, some consistent command word, perhaps "go" or "okay" should be used to trigger the response. Keep in mind in your planning that the objective of the strategy is to focus all of the student's attention on correctly completing a sequence of directions.

Putting The Command Strategy To Work In Your Classroom

Your role in a lesson using the Command Strategy is to set the scene and deliver the content. In setting the scene, you will designate students' location, posture, movement, appearance, deportment, and so on. You need to explain to your students that, for this lesson, your role is to make all of the decisions for them, and that their role is simply to follow all of your directions on command.

Establish the command word which will signal student response. Make sure that all of the students understand that they are to listen carefully to each direction as you give it, and then wait until they hear you say the command word. Students should respond as one on hearing the command word.

Define the goal and objectives of the lesson, and demonstrate the task to be covered. Make your demonstration as clear and precise as possible; it will serve as the standard for acceptable behavior. An effective technique for demonstrating a skill is to first perform the complete skill, and then to break it down into smaller parts. In this way, the Command Strategy serves the function of a still-frame camera, enabling the student to view the skill one step at a time.

When you are ready to begin, specify how the work is to be done and how much time you will allot for completion of each step after the command word has been given. As students perform each step, check to see that it is done properly, and give feedback in the form of brief, positive corrections where needed.

How To Evaluate The Command Strategy

You alone are responsible for evaluating students during and after the lesson. Feedback should begin during the setting of the scene and continue throughout the performance of the task in order to establish and reinforce the value system of the Command Strategy. Provide both corrective and value feedback to each student on completion of each step. Corrective feedback needs to be used because you must insure that each student is completing each step in the process correctly. Value feedback such as "That's good," or "I see you understand," or "You're really listening carefully" should be used to reinforce appropriate role behavior.

Make sure that all students have completed the assigned direction satisfactorily before issuing another command. Such watchfulness guarantees that everyone will keep up with the pace of instruction and will complete the activity successfully.

Summary

When to use it:
When you want students to follow a set of procedures with 100% accuracy.

How to use it:
1. Break the task down into simple commands;
2. State the command as an imperative;
3. Give the command signal;
4. Observe and evaluate each student performing the command;
5. Return to step 2 until all steps have been done; and
6. Have students review steps and repeat process on their own.

How to evaluate it:
1. Are all students following commands?
2. Are all students completing the activity successfully?
3. Can they repeat the process on their own?

Things to remember:
1. Keep commands short and to the point;
2. Before beginning, practice the commands using humorous examples, a la Simon Says;
3. Check students' work and make corrections after each command regarding task and role; and
4. Coach students, as necessary, when they repeat a step in the process.

Sample Lesson II: First Day of School— Beginning Printing

The Story of Nixo
Ms. Ali planned to use the Command Strategy for an introductory writing lesson on the first day of school. This lesson would give her children a good start toward proper letter formation; it would also allow her to observe students' listening skills and their ability to follow verbal directions.

Anticipatory Set:
Ms. Ali said, "We are going to tell a story together. It is the story of Nixo. As I tell you the story, I will tell you to draw some things on your paper. I will use a code word to tell you when to begin. The code word is "popcorn." Listen carefully to the story; and to what I tell you to do, but don't do it until I say, "popcorn!"

Procedures:

After Ms. Ali had distributed lined paper to the class, she went to the easel to draw lines which illustrated what the children would draw as she told the story.

Ms. Ali said, "And now the story begins...

1. This is Nixo.

A row of Nixos would look like this:

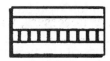

Draw a row of Nixos. "Popcorn!"

2. Soon, Nixo meets a soldier. He is tall and stands very straight. He looks like this:

A row of soldiers would look like this:

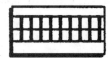

Draw a row of soldiers. "Popcorn!"

3. Soon, it starts to rain. Draw the rain. It looks like this:

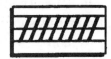

"Popcorn!"

4. Nixo goes to the soldier's tent, and the soldier's tent looks like this:

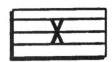

A row of soldier's tents would look like this:

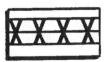

Draw a row of tents. "Popcorn!"

5. The soldier gives Nixo a ball. Draw a row of balls. They look like this:

"Popcorn!"

6. The soldier gives Nixo a nickel, too. Draw a row of nickels. They look like this:

"Popcorn!"

7. The rain stops. Nixo says good-bye to the soldier and walks home. Draw Nixo walking home. He looks like this:

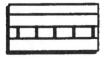

"Popcorn!"

8. Let's write Nixo's name across the page. It will look like this:

"Popcorn!"

EXERCISE-PROCEDURALIZING STRATEGY

The Exercise-Proceduralizing Strategy is used when you want students to master a specific skill by breaking it apart into its separate steps and then practicing it until it becomes automatic.

The Strategy at Work

Mr. McDermott used the Exercise-Proceduralizing Strategy to teach his fifth graders how to simplify fractions to find the equivalent fraction in lowest terms. His first step was to break the skill down into meaningful steps. To do this, he developed the following list of steps:

1. Find as many factors of the numerator as possible.
2. Find as many factors of the denominator as possible.
3. Find the largest factor which appears on both lists (the greatest common factor).
4. Use the greatest common factor to divide the numerator.
5. Use the greatest common factor to divide the denominator.
6. Check by listing the factors of the numerator and denominator of the new fraction. If none of these factors match, you have the lowest terms fraction.
7. If one of the factors of the new numerator matches a factor of the new denominator, use this factor to divide again.

When Mr. McDermott taught his lesson on simplifying fractions, he first had his class make equivalent fractions for $1/2$ and $1/3$. The class developed the following sets of equivalent fractions:

$1/2$	$2/4$	$3/6$	$4/8$	$5/10$	$6/12$	$7/14$	$8/16$	$9/18$	$10/20$
$1/3$		$2/6$		$3/9$	$4/12$		$5/15$	$6/18$	

He lined the equivalent fractions up on the blackboard as shown above and then asked whether these fractions could be added. Sonia replied that they could be added because they had the same denominators. Mr. McDermott asked Tom, Alice, and Juan to come to the board to add the fractions. When the answers, $5/6$, $10/12$, and $15/18$ had been written, he asked the class to use their paper fraction strips showing sixths, twelfths, and eighteens, and to work in their problem solving groups to determine which answer was the solution for the example $1/2$ plus $1/3$. After some discussion, the small groups agreed that the answers were all correct because they were names for the same amount.

Mr. McDermott then explained that for quizzes and tests, it was easier to check answers if everyone used the same equivalent. By custom, he said, the equivalent fraction commonly used as the "correct answer" was the lowest terms equivalent fraction, in this case $5/6$.

Having established a purpose for learning how to simplify fractions to their lowest terms, Mr. McDermott proceeded to model the skill with the fraction $12/18$. As he did each step on newsprint, he explained and wrote the directions for the step in words next to it. When he had completed the first three steps, finding the factors and the greatest common factor, he asked the students to read what he had written and then write down the next three steps. When he had completed the next two steps, dividing the numerator and denominator by the greatest common factor, he again asked them to read and write. He repeated this request after the checking step.

To move the modeling phase into the Interpersonal style, Mr. McDermott then asked his students to work in pairs, with one student giving the directions and the other working out the example he had just done on the board.

Next, Mr. McDermott told the class that they would all do one example together. Using the fraction $18/24$, Mr. McDermott asked specific questions to lead all of his students step-by-step through the process. The students did the work on paper folded in half lengthwise. On one side, they wrote the work step-by-step; on the other, they wrote the directions for the steps in words. As they did so, they referred to Mr. McDermott's listed procedure. Mr. McDermott made sure that each student was able to demonstrate what to do.

When the class had finished this directed practice, Mr. McDermott provided three examples to be done as guided practice. While the students worked independently on these examples, Mr. McDermott moved from student to student, responding to requests for help, monitoring student work, and coaching where necessary.

Mr. McDermott planned to spend a brief time the next day reviewing the procedure for simplifying fractions and providing guided practice. After the second session of guided practice, he planned to ask students to do two examples independently for homework. For these two examples, students would be required not only to show the steps, but also write out the procedure in words. Subsequently independent practice would be brief, but distributed over a period of time, with students working toward a goal of at least eight out of ten fractions correct each time. In two weeks, Mr. McDermott would begin to include simplifying fractions in his regular weekly review quiz.

The Exercise-Proceduralizing Strategy

In the Exercise-Proceduralizing Strategy, students work under the close direction and supervision of the teacher to master important skills. The first step toward mastery is to model the skill and to proceduralize it. Proceduralizing a skill or process establishes a sequence of steps which students can learn to perform automatically.

The Exercise-Proceduralizing Strategy uses modeling, directed practice, guided practice, and independent practice to help students move from dependence to independence. A skill is selected, its steps are analyzed and written out, and the skill and written procedures are presented to students in meaningful chunks. The teacher leads students step-by-step through directed, guided, and independent practice to rehearse, clarify, and routinize the skill.

The goals of the Exercise-Proceduralizing Strategy are:
1. To help students learn to routinize a skill or process through proceduralizing it and practicing it;
2. To help students learn how to recognize skills and processes which can be proceduralized; and
3. To help students learn to proceduralize skills and processes independently.

The steps in the Exercise-Proceduralizing Strategy are:
1. Select a skill at the correct level, analyze its steps, and present it to students in meaningful chunks;

2. Model the skill by demonstrating the steps; describe what the students have to do and how they go about doing it by describing the thinking needed to perform the skill;

3. Lead students through Directed Practice, assisting them to identify and write the sequence of steps necessary to perform the skill;

4. Before engaging students in Guided Practice, have them read over the procedure they have written and visualize themselves performing the skill;

5. Engage students in Guided and Independent practice to rehearse, clarify, and develop independence in performing the skill;

6. Monitor and adjust throughout the process when necessary; discard written description of steps only when procedure becomes automatic; and

7. Have a performance to test student acquisition of the skill.

How to Plan Lessons Using The Exercise-Proceduralizing Strategy

When you are planning a lesson using the Exercise-Proceduralizing Strategy, consider first the skill you want the students to master. Select practice items to use for modeling the skill, and for student practice. It is essential that items chosen for practice be at the level for the students. The instructional level needs to be not too easy, resulting in boredom, and not too difficult, resulting in confusion. When you are establishing examples at the correct level, keep in mind that you want work sufficiently challenging to stimulate student interest, and sufficiently manageable to guarantee student success.

X-ray the skill you have chosen. Identify the steps needed and the decisions you have to make in order to do the skill. Your aim is to make the skill breakdown as meaningful as possible for the students, and to model proceduralizing for them. Write the steps down, read them over, visualize yourself performing this sequence, do several examples using the procedure you have written, and revise it as needed.

Determine how to explain to your students the purpose for learning the skill. Plan to set the stage in your lesson by introducing the skill in terms of some larger context. For long division, for example, you may construct a real-life story requiring its use. In home economics, where you want students to learn how to thread a sewing machine, or in art, where you want students to learn to use a print-making technique, you need to display a finished product. To teach students how to use scale on maps to figure distance, you might set a task requiring students to plan a trip. When students are about to learn how to move a Logo turtle, show them a finished computer design or picture made with Logo procedures.

Rehearse the way in which you will demonstrate the skill aiming to develop a clear, precise model for students to emulate. How will you explain what to do and how to do it? What specific focusing questions can you ask to help students understand the procedure? How can you design your questions so that you talk to all four styles in the course of your demonstration?

As you plan, keep in mind that you want students not only to learn the skill, but also to begin to master the process they will use to proceduralize skills on their own. Proceduralizing is an intricate process; much teacher-directed practice will be needed before students will be ready to proceduralize independently.

Select items to use for Guided Practice, and, later, for Independent Practice. Plan a practice schedule which provides for massing practice into many short sessions, and then distributes practice sessions over time.

Establish the way in which you will evaluate student progress. You want your students to separate practice from performance in their own minds. You want them to feel comfortable practicing and making the inevitable mistakes. You want them to be motivated to prepare to demonstrate that they have attained the skill.

Be sure that students will know when and how they will be tested and what criteria they will need to meet to be considered successful.

Putting the Exercise-Proceduralizing Strategy to Work in Your Classroom

When you are ready to implement the Exercise-Proceduralizing Strategy, begin by establishing the purpose for which students will learn the skill. Demonstrate a clear model. Identify the steps and explain them by appealing to all four styles of learning. Make sure students are able to identify the steps and describe the process.

When you have provided a model, you want your students to engage in Directed Practice. If the skill is to be written, have your students work on paper which they have folded in half; as they do each step, have them write in their own words the procedure they used for step one, step two, and so on. Direct them through each step, one at a time, rather than allowing them to proceed on their own through an example. A lesson in a practicing and proceduralizing dictionary use might begin like this:

Find the meaning(s) of the word sandwich.

Sandwich is in the "S" section.

Step one: look at the first letter of word to find which section it's in.

Remember that Directed Practice is a rehearsal. Use specific focusing questions to direct students through the steps and to help them recall and write the sequence of steps that make up the procedure for the skill.

Once the students have completed Directed Practice successfully, they are ready to clarify the skill through Guided Practice. Provide additional examples at the appropriate level which cover the scope of the skill taught. Before your students reach the level of routine, they will be slow to complete the skill and should not be hurried. Monitor students as they work, and provide coaching whenever necessary. Encourage students to request help.

The purpose of independent practice is to instill confidence. At this point, you want to shift decision-making about method of practice, organization, materials, and evaluation to students. Prior to assigning independent practice, evaluate student needs as they have become apparent through the monitoring and coaching phase, and determine whether to make adjustments in instruction. Then assign additional examples to practice independently, making sure that practice activities are varied and that they represent an assortment of learning styles and strategies. Make sure that the practice schedule falls into short periods, distributed over each item. Establish criteria so that students can monitor their own progress. Evaluate practice to assure that its many forms meet the students' needs.

Evaluating the Exercise-Proceduralizing Strategy

After students have completed the schedule for independent practice, you are ready to assess what they know and what they need to know. Administer some test of performance for which you have established criteria for success. Make sure that the performance covers the content taught and practiced. Record student progress in a way which involves students. Provide feedback to all students, and adjust your teaching based on the results.

As students begin to use proceduralizing and become more familiar with it, remember that breaking a procedure into component parts is a sophisticated skill. Do not rush to assume that students are ready to proceduralize a skill by themselves. Look for evidence that they have begun to recognize skills that can be proceduralized. Depend more and more on them to identify and verbalize the sequence of steps, but only gradually shift responsibility to them for proceduralizing independently.

Summary

When to use it:

When you want to present a specific skill to your students and have them practice it to be able to perform it successfully.

How to use it:

1. Select a skill at the correct level, analyze its steps, and present it to students in meaningful chunks;

2. Model the skill by demonstrating the steps; describe what the students have to do and how they go about doing it by describing the thinking needed to perform the skill;

3. Lead students through Directed Practice, assisting them to identify and write the sequence of steps necessary to perform the skill;

4. Before engaging students in Guided Practice, have them read over the procedure they have written and visualize themselves performing the skill;

5. Engage students in Guided and Independent practice to rehearse, clarify, and develop independence in performing the skill;

6. Monitor and adjust throughout the process when necessary; discard written description of steps only when the procedure becomes automatic; and

7. Have a quiz to test student acquisition of the skill.

How to evaluate it:

1. Do the students know what they have to do and how to do it?

2. Can the students perform the skill independently?

3. Are the students able to make appropriate decisions which demonstrate that they are taking more responsibility for learning the skill throughout the process?

4. Do students value practice and use their time wisely to prepare for performances?

5. Have students developed a level of automation which allows them to discard their written description of steps?

Things to remember:

1. Distinguish between practice and performance; i.e., quizzes for self-assessment versus tests for evaluation and grades;

2. Identify student roles at each level of practice;

3. Help students move from dependence to independence;

4. Mass the practice in the beginning, and distribute it in smaller segments over time; and

5. Practice small meaningful chunks often rather than large practice chunks infrequently.

Sample Lesson I: English Literature— How to Build a Theme

Mr. Strong wanted his eighth graders to be able to identify the theme of a poem. To help them, he proceduralized by breaking the process into a series of steps.

Objectives:

Mr. Strong's eighth graders would be able to build a theme for a poem by following a written sequence of steps until the process became automatic.

Anticipatory Hook:

Mr. Strong started his discussion of "building themes" by asking his students if they had ever built something. After asking them to take a minute to visualize what they had built and how they had gone about building it, he asked them to make a list of what they thought it would take to "build" something. The discussion elicited a number of ideas such as a plan, tools, and materials to build with.

Procedures:

Mr. Strong reminded his students that when they go "theming," they look for themes, big ideas that can hold together all the details in a work. He asked them to write the definition of thematic unit that they had agreed upon the day before. The students wrote, "A thematic unit is a noun or noun phrase that describes a universal notion in a work of art."

Mr. Strong explained that he was going to teach his students a procedure—a sequence of steps to follow—to build the theme of a poem, and then he would give them ample opportunity to practice building themes with poems. He wrote on the board, "How to Build a Theme," and, under it, the poem which follows. To the left of the poem, he wrote the steps, one by one, discussing each, and asking students to write in their learning logs their responses to each step. After the students had written their responses, the class discussed the possibilities, and chose a class response, which Mr. Strong wrote to the right of the poem. The finished model looked like this:

HOW TO BUILD A THEME

STEP ONE
Read the poem and look for thematic units.

STEP TWO
Look for a connection among the thematic units—one you can state as a sentence.

STEP THREE
Collect evidence (particulars) from the poem that support your theme. If you can't find any (or enough), try to build another theme.

The
locust tree
in flower
among
of
green

stiff
old
bright

broken
branch
come

white
sweet
May

again

STEP ONE
Thematic units:
OLDNESS (Age)
stiff old broken
branch
NEWNESS/SPRING
sweet May again

STEP TWO
The newness comes out of the oldness.

STEP THREE
"Out of oldness comes newness"
The poem is in a line, oldness at the top, newness at the bottom. Check thematic units. The old is green, the new "May" is white like a flower.

When his students were satisfied with the theme for this poem, Mr. Strong presented another, which the class did under his direction. Again he wrote out the steps as the class used them. He ended the Direct Practice by asking, "What do you notice about the steps in theming?"

Guided practice took place using another poem, together with the Peer Reading Strategy. As pairs of students worked together, Mr. Strong circulated to monitor and coach the steps where needed. After sufficient guided practice over several lesson periods, Mr. Strong began to assign independent practice in building themes for poems.

Do a report on one of the major lung diseases.

Describe how the lungs function.

Draw a diagram of the lungs. Label the parts.

1. Easy level—match pictures, numbers, times on a clock face, etc. with the Spanish word or phrase;

2. More difficult level—match the Spanish word or phrase with a Spanish synonym or definition;

3. More difficult still—match the Spanish word or phrase with a Spanish antonym;

4. Most difficult level—provide the Spanish word or phrase, Spanish synonym or definition, or Spanish antonym for a picture, Spanish word or phrase, etc.

As Ms. Tenorio introduces new vocabulary from each lesson, she adds to her already large collection of practice exercises at the various levels. She makes copies of each exercise with answers on the back for self-checking, files each exercise separately in a folder, and keeps folders in separate boxes marked levels 1, 2, 3 and 4. The boxes are on a table; on the bulletin board behind the table are thumbtacked sample packets for students to browse through when making a selection. Each student has a record sheet on which to keep track of practice exercises done and scores attained.

Every second Monday in Ms. Tenorio's Spanish I classes is Review Day. On this day all students are involved in Graduated Difficulty exercises which review the current unit of study. Students who finish early are encouraged to use their records sheets to help them decide which previous units of study to review and at what level of difficulty.

While students work on their selections, Ms. Tenorio circulates and observes. Fifteen minutes into the period, Ms. Tenorio begins holding brief conferences with students to discuss the choices they have made.

GRADUATED DIFFICULTY STRATEGY

In the Graduated Difficulty Strategy, students are provided with an instructional program which includes an array of options from which to choose. Options are based on a sequential analysis of the subject matter to be learned and the degree of difficulty of tasks to be performed. Students are responsible for assessing their own abilities and for choosing the task and level of performance they consider best suited to them.

The Strategy at Work

Ms. Tenorio frequently uses the Graduated Difficulty Strategy for her beginning Spanish students. The work sheets she makes generally follow this pattern:

The Graduated Difficulty Strategy

The Graduated Difficulty Strategy involves students in the assessment of their own abilities, and encourages them to make responsible choices of tasks and levels of performance within an instructional program. The Graduated Difficulty Strategy is based on the philosophy that students are unique in their interests, abilities, achievement, and ways of functioning as learners; that students should learn to make decisions for themselves, especially in regard to their instructional programs; and that subject matter can and should be individualized.

In order for the Graduated Difficulty Strategy to be effective, the teacher must have trust in the students and their ability to make judgments about themselves, to work independently for prolonged periods of time, and to identify and correct their own mistakes. Like any of the other teaching strategies, Graduated Difficulty requires that students be trained in the various roles in order to perform each task. The time invested in setting up the Graduated Difficulty program will be paid back several-fold when students become independent learners, are self-motivated, and are working at an individually appropriate level and pace.

The Graduated Difficulty program provides teachers with an excellent diagnostic tool for differentiating performance levels in a heterogeneous class. It frees teachers from constantly having to provide stimuli for students to work and provides them with more time for individualized contact with students.

The Graduated Difficulty Strategy is used when teachers want their students to take responsibility for assessing and practicing previously taught information skills. In the Graduated Difficulty Strategy, teachers design three levels of the task to be practiced, each with a different degree of difficulty. Each level of the task should require a great amount of independence and should allow for students to check their own work. Students decide the level at which they will work, carry out the task, proof and correct, and finally reflect on their own decision-making process. Teachers observe student performance and confer with students about their choices.

The goals of the Graduated Difficulty Strategy are:

1. To provide an opportunity for students to succeed by encouraging them to select their own appropriate level of performance and to work at their own pace;

2. To help students practice previously taught information and skills;

3. To help students explore their own decision-making processes; and

4. To help students improve their decision-making abilities.

The steps in the Graduated Difficulty Strategy are:

1. Determine what is to be taught;

2. Provide options on three levels of difficulty for student selection;

3. Encourage students to select the level with which they feel most comfortable;

4. Prepare criteria for evaluation;

5. Circulate and observe the performance of students;

6. Acknowledge performance of students, and invite students to change their choices if necessary;

7. Guide student self-assessment by asking questions focused on criteria and student performance; and

8. Record student self-evaluations to improve decision-making and task management.

How to Plan Lessons Using the Graduated Difficulty Strategy

When you design the instructional program to be used with the Graduated Difficulty Strategy, you must include several tasks, a range of performance for each task, and a set of objectives defined in behavioral terms for students to accomplish. The tasks must require a high degree of independent performance and must allow for students to check their own work and progress. Design charts or record cards for students to use so that their progress will be visible to both them and you.

To use the Graduated Difficulty Strategy, choose subject matter that allows you to easily distinguish degrees of difficulty, and where answers are convergent—yes or no, right or wrong, and having only one correct answer. Mathematics, grammar, spelling, geography, and science all have lists of straightforward skills that can be segregated according to difficulty. In mathematics, for example, multiplication skills might be represented by work sheets on multiplying by one, two, or three digits. Determine at least three levels of difficulty, but be aware that you may have more than three levels.

Determining the level of difficulty is a combination of qualitative and quantitative considerations. Qualitative decisions are more difficult and subjective. One qualitative concern might be the level of questioning; i.e., from simple recall to analysis, or from literal to interpretive comprehension. Detail, complexity, and aesthetics are all examples of quality criteria. Quantitative decisions are concerned with the number of items or pages to be done, the time allowed to perform the task, the number of repetitions, the percent of correct responses, etc.

Consider your students' learning styles and design their options accordingly. Plan for a clear explanation of the program, its tasks, and performance criteria, so that students can move through the instruction in an effective and efficient manner. Will your students need freedom to move about and to gather materials to accomplish certain tasks? If so, structure your classroom, materials, and equipment so students can manage their own instruction. Establish specific parameters within which students may choose the location in which they wish to work, their starting and stopping times, their pace and rhythm, and so on. Since students will finish their tasks at different times, decide what you want those who finish early to do with their time. Plan for student conferences to discuss their choices and self-assessment.

Putting the Graduated Difficulty Strategy to Work in Your Classroom

Your role in implementing a lesson using the Graduated Difficulty Strategy is to be available to students, to observe, and to give assistance and support to those who request it. Spot-checking performance violates the trust that needs to be established for this strategy, and should be avoided. Specific time should be set aside for conferencing with students about their choices and progress.

Encourage students to choose the level they feel will make them most comfortable. Provide time for them to look over all three (or more) levels. Make them responsible for assessing their own abilities. When your students choose the right level, they will succeed more often and will have the confidence to challenge themselves with higher levels of difficulty. Since the Graduated Difficulty Strategy is based on the philosophy that students are unique, set the expectation that they can and should learn to make decisions for themselves and be able to learn at their own pace. Let them know that you trust them to be able to make judgments about themselves.

When your students have made their choices, circulate and observe them at work on their tasks. You want students to discover for themselves how they work and to decide for themselves what consequences their decisions have for their progress. Be available to give assistance and support where necessary. Observe your students' choices and their manner of working. This is a wonderful time to acquire information about students because you are not occupied with intervening in students' choices or tasks.

During the strategy, create a climate that is relaxed and where students feel free to monitor their own learning and progress. If students ask for direction or coaching help, it is time for you to reinforce their role as decision-makers. Students may want to change their choice, sometimes more than once; invite students to change their choices as they go along. Students may have initially been incorrect in their assessment of the difficulty of the chosen level. Make sure that your students know that you expect them to decide for themselves if and when further placement is needed.

Expect students to identify and correct their own mistakes. Answer sheets must be available so that students can check their work and progress. Students should know how and where to record their progress. Records of progress should be readily visible to both you and the individual student, although there is no need to make these records "public."

Set aside specific time for conferencing. Encourage students to arrange for their own conferences as desired. Set an expectation that they will decide when they need assistance or clarification. In these conferences, spend some time discussing student choice(s) and student assessment of progress. How did an individual student feel about the choices made? What constitutes a "good" choice for this student? How does a student determine "more difficult" or "less difficult?" What evidence can this student present regarding progress? What does this student see as coming next; what is this student's view of individual needs?

How to Evaluate the Graduated Difficulty Strategy

During the strategy acknowledge students' performance. Provide feedback to them regarding their ability to operate independently and to be self-directed, to assess and evaluate their own performance, and to perform the necessary tasks appropriately. Expect students to evaluate their own performance in relation to the subject matter and to the criteria which you have established. Expect them to confer with you about the adequacy of their self-assessments.

To bring closure to this strategy, lead a discussion on student choices and what students discovered on the basis of them. Maintain a neutral demeanor throughout, always permitting and encouraging students to make their own discoveries. Make sure to keep a record of the self-evaluations of students so that you can become more aware of how they learn and their levels of comprehension.

Summary

When to use it:

When you want students to take responsibility for assessing and practicing previously taught information and skills.

How to use it:

1. Determine levels of difficulty of content;

2. Prepare options at different levels of difficulty for student selection;

3. Provide answer sheets for immediate feedback; and

4. Confer with students about their choices and their self-evaluations.

How to evaluate it:

1. Are students making choices appropriate to their learning needs?

2. Are students completing one level and choosing to go on to the next higher level?

3. Are students correcting their work and learning from their mistakes?

Things to remember:

1. Provide students with three or more options at different levels of difficulty from which to choose;

2. Do not penalize students for the level they select; and

3. Help students to remember that tests for evaluation and eventual grading will cover all levels.

Sample I: Levels of Difficulty

Adding and subtracting decimals

Level I
Directions: Solve the following problems
1. 4.76 + 3.03
2. 6.5 + 2.7
3. 3.25 + 4.82
4. 26.02 + 15.98
5. 8.065 + 2.122
6. 2.7 - 1.4
7. 6.54 - 1.65
8. 12.5 - 11.4
9. 9.45 - 8.96
10. 26.8 - 10.8

Level II
Directions: Solve the following problems
1. .42 + .06 + 1.11
2. 16.4 + 6.5 + 20.6
3. 4.4 + 30.6 + 11.2
4. 5.9 + 18.1 + 19.5
5. 7.11 + .64 + 1.02
6. 20.48 - 16.6
7. 31.51 - 16.6
8. 4.768 - 0.23
9. 26.075 - 2.651
10. 16.58 - 0.49

Level III
Directions: Solve the following problems
1. 6 + 4.2 + 9
2. 5.106 + 4 + 1.5
3. 2 + 10.01 + .006
4. 19.5 + 21.1 + 21
5. 1.6 + 16 + .016
6. 28.1 - .008
7. 19.5 - 6.274
8. 36 - 44
9. 12.1 - 0.101
10. 16 - 8.94

Answers:

Level I	Level II	Level III
1. 7.79	1. 1.59	1. 19.2
2. 9.2	2. 43.5	2. 10.060
3. 8.07	3. 46.2	3. 12.016
4. 42.00	4. 43.5	4. 61.6
5. 10.187	5. 8.77	5. 17.016
6. 1.3	6. 3.68	6. 28.092
7. 4.8	7. 14.91	7. 13.226
8. 1.1	8. 4.538	8. 35.56
9. .49	9. 23.424	9. 11.999
10. 16.0	10. 16.09	10. 7.06

Adapted from Bloomfield T.E.S.S. Project lesson

Sample II: Graphing

Level I:
Directions: Count and color in the fruit on the graph.

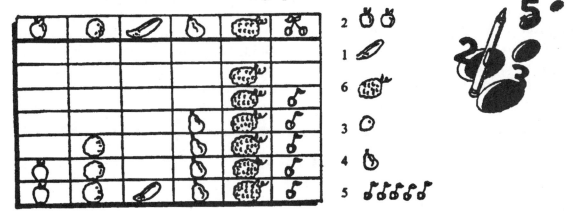

Level II:
Directions: Draw the fruit on the graph and then color in the fruit.

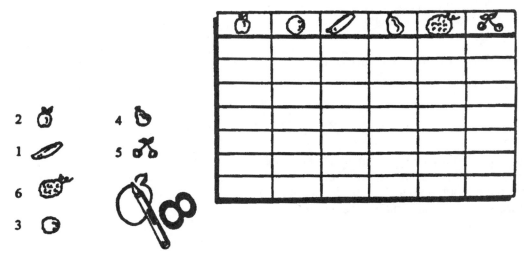

Level III:
Directions: Count each set of fruit. Draw the fruit on the graph and color in the fruit.

Adapted from Bloomfield T.E.S.S. Project lesson

Sample III: Choose Your Poem

Sometimes the best way to evaluate how well we have learned something is to choose our own assessment task. That's exactly what we're going to let you do. You will be asked to develop an interpretation for one of the following pieces of literature. Level I is the easiest, Level II is a little more difficult and Level III is challenging. Feel free to work at whatever level feels comfortable to you, but make sure you at least look through each before making your decision. You may use your organizer to guide you or you may use a blank "How to create an Interpretation… Study Guide" page, which can be found on page 34. When you are finished, complete the questionnaire on page 33.

LEVEL I:

There were the roses in the rain.
Don't cut them, I pleaded.
   They won't last, she said
But they're so beautiful
   where they are.
Agh, we were all beautiful once, she
   said,
and cut them and gave them to me in my hand.

William Carlos Williams

LEVEL II:

They asked me once my thoughts on infinity and I told 'em
with all I had to think about, infinity was not on my list
of things to think about. It could be time on an ego trip,
for all I know. After all, when you're pressed for time,
infinity may as well

not be there.
They said, to them, infinity is
time-released time.

Frankly, infinity doesn't affect
me personally one way or the other.

You think too long about infinity, you could go
stark raving mad.
But I don't ever want to sound negative about going crazy.
I don't want to over-romanticize it either, but frankly,
goin' crazy was the best thing that ever happened to me.
I don't say it's for everybody;
some people couldn't cope.

from "The Search for Signs of Intelligent Life in the Universe," by Jane Wagner

---

LEVEL III:

That time of year thou mayst in me behold

When yellow leaves, or none, or few, do hang

Upon those boughs which shake against the cold,

Bare ruin'd choirs, where late the sweet birds sang.

In me thou see'st the twilight of such day

As after sunset fadeth in the west,

Which by and by black night doth take away,

Death's second self, that seals up all in rest.

In me thou see'st the glowing of such fire,

That on the ashes of his youth doth lie,

As the death-bed whereon it must expire,

consum'd with that which it was nourish'd by.

   This thou perceiv'st, which makes thy love more strong,

   To love that well which thou must leave ere long.

Shakespeare

NEW AMERICAN LECTURE STRATEGY

The New American Lecture Strategy is designed to help students remember subject matter delivered in an organized format by a lecturer. New content is presented by the teacher who has systematically planned for: 1) the establishment of an anticipatory or mental set; 2) the presentation of a visual organizer for recording and analyzing information; and 3) the use of questions in the four styles for processing and elaborating on the information to be learned.

The Strategy at Work

For a seventh grade social studies lesson introducing students to the location and geography of ancient Egypt: The valley of the Nile River, Mr. Shevchenko prepared a lesson using the New American Lecture Strategy.

Mr. Shevchenko believed that his lesson on the geography of the Nile River Valley provided an opportunity to teach a procedure his students would be able to use to study any content. To introduce his students to the New American Lecture Strategy, and to set expectations for student involvement, he made an overhead transparency of the following procedures:

1. take notes to summarize important points of a lecture or reading

2. organize the notes into small "chunks"

3. ask a question which requires that you reflect on a "chunk"

4. stop to memorize each "chunk" before going on to the next

5. check to see how successful you have been at learning each "chunk" by trying to reproduce it exactly in writing

Mr. Shevchenko pointed out that, once learned, this procedure can be used independently as a study strategy for any type of material which must be memorized: facts, rules, algorithms, chronology of historical events, etc. "In fact," he said, "a lesson I have planned for later in the week will give you an opportunity to work independently to apply this technique for organizing and memorizing a reading assignment on the history of Ancient Egypt."

Mr. Shevchenko had prepared a transparency of the blank organizer for use with an overhead projector, and now distributed a copy of the blank organizer to each student. As he presented information, he recorded key ideas on the transparency and gave students time to record those same key ideas on their organizers. He interrupted the presentation regularly with questions or brief activities that required the students to connect their experiences with the new information, deep-process the information to make it vivid, or elaborate on the information by responding to it in one of the four styles. He also provided time within the framework of the lecture for students to actually study the information and reproduce exactly what they had recorded on their blank organizers.

To begin filling in the organizer, Mr. Shevchenko established an anticipatory set by asking his students to close their eyes and imagine the following scene:

You are to imagine yourselves examining a wall painting in the tomb of a wealthy Egyptian. The painting shows men harvesting grain in time to the music of a flute, fattened cattle, geese and crane, loaves of bread, baskets of fruit, a line of fishermen hauling in a net full of fish, servants brewing beer made from a mash of dates and grain, jars of wine made from grapes, and the owner of the tomb trapping ducks and other waterfowl in a reed-filled marsh. All of the people shown in the painting are wearing lightweight clothing made of linen. Sandals, baskets, ropes, nets, and small boats in the painting are all made of reeds.

Mr. Shevchenko had borrowed some reproductions of tomb art similar to what he had described. He had his students open their eyes and look at these reproductions.

Mr. Shevchenko then asked the students to write down as many of the items of food, drink, clothing, and so on that were included in the wall paintings. He asked his students to speculate about what the wall paintings might tell us about the life of ancient Egyptians. He gave his students a chance to share their ideas with a neighbor, and then made a class list. Students suggested that the ancient Egyptians were farmers and fishermen, and that there might have been crafts-people who made baskets and sandals, that they hunted water birds, that they made useful things out of marsh reeds, etc. They speculated that the wealthy Egyptian's life was different from the workers' lives.

Mr. Shevchenko distributed blank maps showing the Nile River. He located the Nile River on a world map and discussed its location relative to the continent of Africa, the Atlantic Ocean, the Mediterranean Sea, and the Red Sea. He had his students find and label the Mediterranean Sea, the Red Sea, the rocky barren desert on both sides of the Nile River, and the cities of Aswan, Thebes and Memphis on their blank maps.

Mr. Shevchenko asked his students to place their lower arms with fingers of their hands outstretched next to their maps. He said, "How is your arm and hand similar to the map of the Nile?" The students said that the river from Aswan to Memphis is like their arm from elbow to hand, and that the river separates into many branches north of Memphis just as their hand separates into fingers. Mr. Shevchenko told them that the area north of Memphis is known as the Delta, and it is very wet and marshy. He pointed out that the Nile does not begin in Aswan, and suggested that looking at their arm from shoulder to elbow might give them a clue as to where the Nile begins. He continued to have students use their arms as a metaphor for the Nile, making sure that they could imagine the river flow from the mountains (their shoulder) down over six waterfalls called cataracts to Aswan (their elbow) to Memphis (their hand) to the Delta (their outspread fingers). He had his students draw arrows on their blank maps showing the flow of the Nile from south to north.

Under Mr. Shevchenko's direction, the students filled in the first box on their blank organizers with three important facts about the locations of the Nile River. Mr. Shevchenko then asked, "The Ancient Egyptians used boats on the Nile River as a convenient way of getting from place to place in Egypt. Travel on the river was easier if the boat was going downstream because the boat would be carried by the flow of the water. To go upstream, Egyptians used sails and oars. If you were traveling from Thebes to Memphis, would you float or use sails and oars? If you were going from Memphis to Thebes, would you float or use sails and oars?" After discussion, he asked the students to write the answer to the question about the Nile's path underneath the first box.

Mr. Shevchenko stopped here to have students study, cover, and reproduce on another sheet of paper the filled-in part of the organizer. After they compared their effort with the original, he had them circle the appropriate evaluation statement.

Mr. Shevchenko continued, "Every year, in spring, constant heavy rains fall in the mountain areas where the Nile's sources are located." He asked the students to imagine lakes and rivers, located on their shoulders, filling to overflowing from the heavy rains. "What will happen to all of the water? What will the water pouring down from the mountains to the level land which is Egypt carry with it?" He explained that this yearly flooding happened slowly over a period of four months, covering all of the land on either side of the riverbanks with deep water and rich black soil for that whole time. Beyond the flooded area was barren desert. The Egyptians developed their calendar around the flooding which was so predictable: a four-month season of flood, and two other four-month seasons for growing crops. The Egyptians learned to bring water from the Nile to these fertile fields by digging a system of canals and ditches to irrigate the good growing land.

Mr. Shevchenko helped students to fill in the second box on their organizer with the effects of the Nile River on the land of Egypt. He then had his students stop to reflect on the advantages and disadvantages of the flood season: he asked them to consider the effect of flood time on farming, housing, transportation and work time. He gave students a minute to jot down an answer to the questions on the organizer about advantages and disadvantages of having four months when the land on either side of the Nile River was completely under water. He had students share answers with a neighbor, and then make a class list of responses. The students' discussion brought out the facts that houses and buildings had to be carefully planned to be out of the flooded areas, and that farming could not be done during four months of the year. On the good side, farmers had free time for these four months, and could work on special projects. Mr. Shevchenko told them that the pyramids and temples were built during flood seasons, and boats with cargoes of heavy stones or huge statues could float much closer to the desert areas where they would be set up.

Mr. Shevchenko stopped again to have students study, cover, and reproduce the organizer and to circle the appropriate evaluation statement.

Mr. Shevchenko asked the class to look again at the list of things they learned about the Ancient Egyptians through thinking about the wall painting in the wealthy man's tomb. "How many of those things were affected in a positive way by the Nile River?" He asked. Students saw connections between the Nile and—

Rich soil for growing crops. The evidence included:
men harvesting grain—grown in rich soil
fattened cattle—ate the grain
loaves of bread—made from grain
baskets of fruit—grown in rich soil
servants brewing beer from dates and grain—from rich soil
wine made from grapes—from rich soil

River habitat for wild animals used for food. Evidence:

fishermen hauling net of fish—good habitat in Nile

geese and cranes—good habitat on the Nile

ducks and other waterfowl in a reed-filled marsh—reeds plentiful in marshy delta

Wild and cultivated plants growing abundantly. Evidence:

clothing made of linen—made from plant called flax

sandals, baskets, ropes, nets, and small boats made of reeds—papyrus reeds grew wild in marshy delta

Students also connected the boats with the use of the Nile as a transportation route.

Mr. Shevchenko helped his students to fill in the third box on their organizer with the things they could think of as gifts of the Nile River. He then asked his students if they ever doodle… do they make sketches or designs, or write words in silly or funny or unique ways in the margins of their papers? He asked them to take a few minutes to design some doodles on the margins of their organizer to help them remember the important ideas about the Nile River. After they had had some time, he asked students to share their ideas for doodles.

Mr. Shevchenko stopped again to have students study, cover, and reproduce the entire organizer and to circle the appropriate evaluation statement. He surveyed the class to find out how many students felt that they had improved in their ability to recall the information on the organizer even though there was more to remember this time than in the previous two.

Mr. Shevchenko had his students place their completed organizer and map in their portfolios so that it could be referred to as needed. He asked his students to expand their doodles to make a visual representation of the importance of the Nile River. The requirements for the representation were that it should include the words NILE RIVER, a map sketch of the Nile, and designs representing the Nile's gifts.

The Land of Ancient Egypt

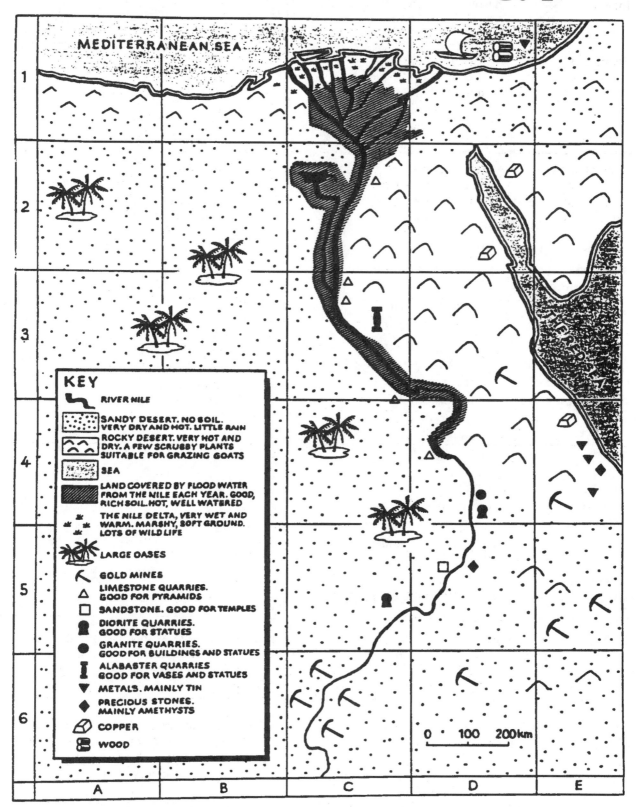

Matrix Organizer

VISUAL ORGANIZER

Sub Topics	Topics Ancient Egypt: The Valley of the Nile	
	Nile River	Nile River Basin
Resources	Mode of transportation flooding replenishes soil marshes rich in waterfowl, reeds for baskets, papyrus for paper	Papyrus (paper) reeds (baskets) rich soil from "inundation" (annual flood) flax
Technologies	Fishing nets; boat-building (fellucas) irrigation (dikes, cisterns)	cultivation Hieroglyphics flax to linen (to hold water from floods) stone work (temples, statues) tool-making basketry domestication of animals brick-making (houses)
Food Sources	Fish Geese & ducks	farming (two crops per year) cattle (meat, milk, skins) grains (bread, feed, beer) grapes (wine) berries, other fruits goats (milk, meat)

QUESTIONS FOR PROCESSING INFORMATION

Describe ancient Egyptian life from the items found in the wall paintings.	Cover up and retrieve as much information as you can from the organizer. Make a doodle to help you remember those things you forgot.
Explain the positive and negative effects of the Nile River on the life of the Egyptians.	Use your arm and hand as a metaphor to describe the Nile River. What part is from your arm to elbow? From your elbow to your hand? What do your separated fingers represent?

The New American Lecture Strategy

The New American Lecture Strategy, adapted from David Ausubel's theory of "meaningful verbal learning," is used when you want students to understand and remember important information. At a time when lecturing is being challenged by many educational theorists, Ausubel contends that expository teaching for the acquisition of content is a valid and essential method of teaching. Ausubel argues that the lecture need not be passive or one-way. Student participation, he says, can be enhanced by the use of appropriate principles of learning that can guide teachers in making more effective presentations.

One of Ausubel's principles of "meaningful verbal learning" is the establishment of an anticipatory set to connect the learner's prior knowledge and experience with what is to be learned. This link is developed through an introductory bridging activity which helps secure student attention and establish the purpose of the lecture.

When lecturing on the discovery of America, for example, the teacher might begin with the hook, "Have you ever done something and not received the credit?" This question can lead into the lecture's objective: to provide students with the necessary information to enable them to make a decision as to who really discovered America, and who should get the credit. The introductory activity raises a question in the student's mind and helps to transfer prior feelings to the information being presented.

Another principle in delivering an effective lecture is the use of an Advance Organizer. An Advance Organizer is a visual representation of essential information supplied in the lecture. The Organizer helps students see how the lecture connects the information being presented and how it organizes the content. As a student, how often have you taken notes feverishly on a lecture, and then spent two or three hours organizing the lecture notes? The Advance Organizer allows students to record, process, review, and retrieve the information with less effort and more success.

To understand the function and value of an Advance Organizer, consider two drawers in your kitchen: a silverware drawer, and another drawer used for gadgets and "junk." Looking for something in the "junk" drawer is inevitably time consuming and frustrating. Retrieving something from the silverware drawer, on the other hand, is effortless because of its structure and organization. The Advance Organizer allows students' memories to work much like the silverware drawer, organizing and retrieving information with ease and accuracy.

A third principle of "meaningful verbal learning" is elaboration through questioning. Elaboration ensures effective processing of information. Questions are used throughout the lecture to help students process the information being received; students are asked to compare and join new ideas, existing ideas, and information to form new understanding. Four types of questions should be used, each type drawing on a different style of thinking and learning. Students must be asked to remember, reason, reorganize, and relate personally to the information, and should be given time to process information covertly and to verify their answers. Participation can be maximized by having the students visualize and think through their answers, write them on paper, and discuss them in small groups in intervals of three to five minutes.

When these principles of "meaningful verbal learning," i.e., bridging, organizing, and elaborating are applied effectively, the lecture becomes a powerful two-way communication strategy in which all students are engaged at all levels of thinking.

The New American Lecture Strategy reworks the older and more traditional form of the lecture in order to meet the following goals:
1. To increase student participation;

2. To teach study skills such as note-taking and memorizing;

3. To permit the teacher to monitor students' understanding at frequent intervals, and adjust the presentation to their needs; and

4. To take into account the variety of student learning styles and modalities in the class.

The steps in the New American Lecture Strategy are:
1. Select the content to be learned; determine main idea and supporting details;

2. Make an Advance Organizer;

3. Order facts to fit the memory;

4. Establish an "anticipatory set;"

5. Present information using a visual organizer;

6. Facilitate active learning by asking frequent questions in the four styles for elaboration;

7. Have students make an active summary; and

8. Provide feedback regarding role and task, during and after student performance.

How to Plan Lessons Using the New American Lecture Strategy

When you begin to plan a New American Lecture Strategy, first select the topic and identify the purpose of your lecture. Then determine the content to be provided. Jot down all the information to be covered in the lecture. Look for relationships between the various bits of information. What ideas unite the facts? What big idea holds them all together?

In working with the content of your lecture, try to identify the knowledge hierarchy on which it is based. Ausubel believes that all academic disciplines have a structure of concepts—the cognitive structure. These concepts, he contends, are hierarchically organized. Each discipline is made up of a pyramid of concepts that are linked together with the most concrete concepts at the bottom and the more abstract concepts at the top.

Two techniques that you can successfully use to help identify your topic's cognitive structure are "mind mapping" and "inductive learning" (concept formation). To use either, begin by brainstorming words, phrases, and jottings to generate a pool of ideas and information about the topic. If you are using "mind mapping," draw lines between these ideas to demonstrate how they are generated and connected. If you are using inductive learning (concept formation), transfer the words, phrases, and ideas onto individual index cards or slips of paper, and move them around to form groups; then label each group to form a conceptual hierarchy.

Working to organize the topic in this way, you will identify the main ideas, subtopics, and details to be presented. Moreover, you will begin to identify categories which you will be able to use to chunk information.

Your next step is to determine what type of Advance Organizer you will use to record the information. An Advance Organizer is a visual representation of all essential information; it often has a triangular or pyramid form. Many Organizers look like this…

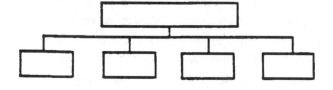

…although other shapes are possible. The selection is dependent on the type of information being presented and the objective being accomplished. There are a number of different Organizers:

- Matrix Organizers help organize information into categories which are useful for making comparisons.

- Conceptual hierarchies branch from a general to a specific layout in a hierarchical structure.

- Flowcharts organize information in a step-by-step fashion. Acronyms provide clues which assist in the organization and retrieval of information, e.g., H.O.M.E.S. (The names of the Great Lakes).

- Diagrams or visuals assist the learner as the picture becomes a visual memory.

Any of these formats can be used. Display your blank Advance Organizer where everyone can see it and where you can fill it in as you move through your lecture. Or, plan to use an overhead projector; use an already filled-in organizer, but display only the area under discussion. Distribute blank copies to your students to be completed during the lecture or encourage them to copy your blank organizer.

Next, order the facts to fit the memory. Make sure that important bits of information get repeated three times. Formulate the questions to be used for bridging and elaboration. Have students verbalize the information.

Bridging Questions build on students' personal knowledge and attempt to link their prior knowledge and experience to the new information being presented. To develop an effective bridge, ask yourself "What is the lecture about, and how does it relate to what my students know and have experienced?" The questions you develop need to draw on personal experience and feelings.

Elaborating Questions help students make connections between prior learning and new learning and help them to form new understandings. Four types of questions can be used:

- Remembering Questions in the Mastery position ask students to remember new information.

- Reasoning Questions in the Understanding position ask students to make connections between and among ideas presented.

- Reorganizing Questions in the Self-Expressive position ask students to speculate and form new structures.

- Relating Questions in the Interpersonal position ask students to personalize new information.

Elaboration Questions should be used throughout the lecture.

Decide what Bridging and Elaboration questions to use for review and where in the lecture those questions will be placed. You want to plan to stop lecture every five to seven minutes to ask students one or more review questions. These questions, together with frequent requests from you for student summaries, anchor the key points in student memory. Plan to move at a moderate pace. You need not cover the entire Advance Organizer in one class period. It is better to deliver a memorable half-lecture than a forgettable whole lecture.

Putting the New American Lecture Strategy to Work in Your Classroom

Begin your lecture by establishing the anticipatory set. Then use the organizer to present information, stopping frequently to ask questions for student processing.

As you say what needs to be said, add new information to the Advance Organizer. Give students time to copy it and encourage them to reread what they have just written. Waiting five to eight seconds before going on helps content become fixed in short term memory.

The sequence of information is important. Information you present at the beginning of a lecture is generally easiest to remember. The greatest difficulty occurs with information presented in the middle of the lecture. These facts tend to become confused with previous data. Possible solutions to the retention problem might be to change the position of the most important or most difficult material; to learn the material in sequence, and then repeat it again at the end; or to review the difficult parts, thereby placing the difficult material in a summary position.

Consider, too, that it is easier to remember something when it stands out in some way from the rest. Recalling a list of ten three-letter nonsense syllables is less difficult if the syllables in the middle are written in another color, or in bigger letters. Vividness attracts attention because it differs from what was expected.

Current brain research reminds us that anything novel elicits an altered reflex in our brain and causes us to turn our attention to the thing which differs. Examine the sequence and content of the lecture to see how and where to increase vividness, interest, or novelty. You need not do this in Broadway production style; an eye-catching photograph, a colorful graph, a riddle or play on words may do the trick. The essence is to try to change the quality of attention when you want your students to focus on a more difficult aspect of the lesson.

Invite active participation during the lecture. One of the easiest ways to do this is to incorporate student writing into your lecture. Have students jot down answers to your questions and discuss them with a neighbor before you call on anyone. Ask students to describe how the new material relates to their existing knowledge about the subject. Ask students to provide additional examples of the concept or proposition being discussed. Ask students to verbalize the essence of the material, to translate it into their own terminology, or to apply their personal frame of reference to it. Ask students to examine the material from alternative points of view, or to correlate the material to contradictory material, experiences, or knowledge.

Encourage a critical thinking approach to enhance the active participation of your listeners. Encourage your students to recognize assumptions or inferences in the presentation; to judge and challenge these assumptions; and to resolve contradictions among them.

Where you want students to remember the specifics from their Advance Organizer, stop at the halfway point and ask your students to memorize exactly what is on their copy. Give them a few minutes of concentrated study time; have them turn their Organizer over and reproduce as much as they can remember on another sheet of paper. Then have them compare their Organizer with what they remembered. Discuss what gave them trouble. Repeat the process at the end of the lecture.

During the lecture, your students' role is to listen, to act on ideas and information presented, and to compare and contrast new data with existing knowledge. They should work to internalize new data so that they can make coherent "I" statements about the new learning; i.e., "I learned that the human body is made up of seven interdependent systems consisting of…" Students are expected to participate actively by answering questions, taking notes, outlining materials, analyzing teacher inferences and assumptions, and asking questions.

The last step of the lecture is one which must be done by your students. Ask them to make an active summary. Summaries should be both written and oral. Have your students present their summaries first in a small group, and then have some students share their summaries with the whole group.

How to Evaluate the New American Lecture Strategy

Your evaluation of the effectiveness of your lecture takes place both during and after the presentation. Focus on assessing both student involvement and understanding of the new materials.

During the presentation, observe student behavior. Make judgments about what is being heard, the pace and rhythm of the presentation, and the spacing of difficult material. Determine student understanding by asking and inviting questions, observing student note-taking, reading facial and body language, and heeding the general appearance of alertness.

When the lecture is completed, measure comprehension by testing, assigning papers, asking questions, and having discussion sessions on what has been learned. Ask students to critique the lecture and to make suggestions. Give successful students an opportunity to share methods of active listening, note-taking, and study that work for them when information is presented in a lecture mode.

After the lecture strategy on a given topic has been completed, consider using several related activities. One idea is to have students complete their own Advance Organizers based on your questions. Another is to have students complete an Advance Organizer based on a reading assignment rather than a lecture. A third option is to have students read an assignment, and then create an original Advance Organizer for the information contained therein. A fourth possibility is to ask students to use the New American Lecture Strategy to prepare and deliver a lecture themselves.

Summary

When to use it:

When you want your students to remember and understand important facts, ideas, and information.

How to use it:

1. Select a topic; identify important information; and develop a focusing activity to engage students;

2. Design the topical question; e.g., Who really ought to get credit for discovering the New World?;

3. Design a visual organizer for storing information;

4. Design questions in four styles for the learners to answer about the information;

5. Present key ideas and have students record them on their organizer;

6. Have active participation—every 3–5 minutes; and

7. Ask questions and secure closure.

How to evaluate it:

1. Are the students able to recall what they have learned?

2. Does their ability to sustain attention develop over time?

3. Can they develop their own organizers to present information?

4. Can they answer, in writing, the topical question?

Things to remember:

1. The human mind can store seven (7 plus or minus 2) bits of information for approximately 18 seconds in short term memory;

2. The human mind must process information regularly and verbally to make it memorable; and

3. The basic principles of memory are:

   a. connecting—building a bridge between experience and new learning through discussion

b. organizing—visual organization for retrieving

c. deep-processing—making information vivid using all the senses

d. elaboration—asking questions in all four styles: remember, reason, relate, and reorganize.

New American Lecture: Sample Advance Organizer for Making Plurals (Matrix)

When You Have	Here's What You Do	Examples...
regular plurals	add "s"	car = cars girl = girls
words ending in s, x, z, sh, and ch	add "es"	church = churches box = boxes buzz = buzzes
y after a consonant	change y to i, add "es"	fly = flies party = parties
f or fe	usually add "s" sometimes f or fe changes to ve	roof = roofs chief = chiefs leaf = leaves knife = knives
o after a vowel	add "s"	radio = radios video = videos
o after a consonant	check dictionary very rare	

Adapted from New Brunswick Lesson Plan Project

STATES OF MATTER (MATRIX)

	Solids	Liquids	Gases
Molecular Movement	Molecules are packed closely together and vibrate.	Molecules are further apart—still attract one another, vibrate and move away.	Molecules are furthest apart—have no attraction, move very fast.
Shape	Has a definite shape	Depends on shape of container	No particular shape
Change	Increase in heat	Melting	Evaporating, boiling
Process	Freezing Solidifying	Condensing	Decrease in heat

IDENTIFYING SUBSTANCES
(Flow Chart)

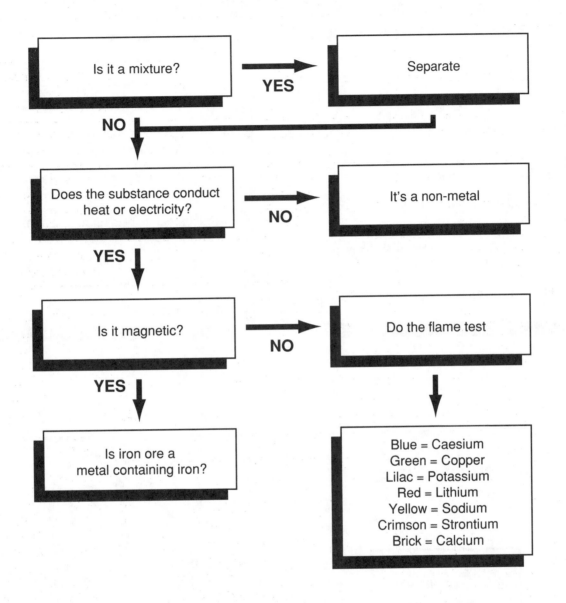

Is it a mixture? — **YES** → Separate

NO ↓

Does the substance conduct heat or electricity? — **NO** → It's a non-metal

YES ↓

Is it magnetic? — **NO** → Do the flame test

YES ↓

Is iron ore a metal containing iron?

Do the flame test ↓

Blue = Caesium
Green = Copper
Lilac = Potassium
Red = Lithium
Yellow = Sodium
Crimson = Strontium
Brick = Calcium

WAS CHRISTOPHER COLUMBUS A SUCCESS?

GOALS

Globe was round; could be circumnavigated

Look for safer, faster route to West Indies

Open/expand merchant trade with Japan, China, India

Bring back gold/silver fund Spanish army navy warfare and trade protection

Expand Christianity and acquire converts

ACCOMPLISHMENTS

Found you could sail west and not fall off earth; didn't circumnavigate.

Establish Europe to West Indies route; but not to East Indies.

Aroused curiosity in circumnavigation and Western route.

Took back proof of discovery; natives and tobacco plants, but no riches.

Started European exploration.

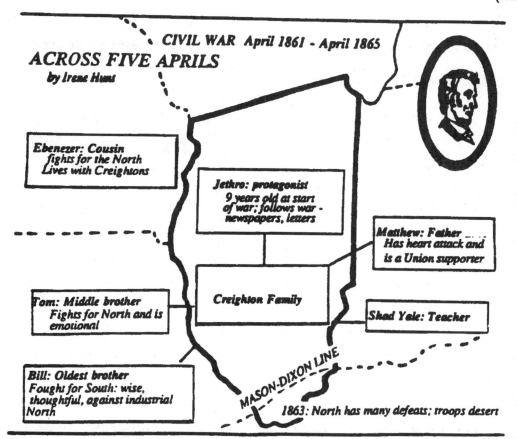

HUMAN DIGESTIVE SYSTEM

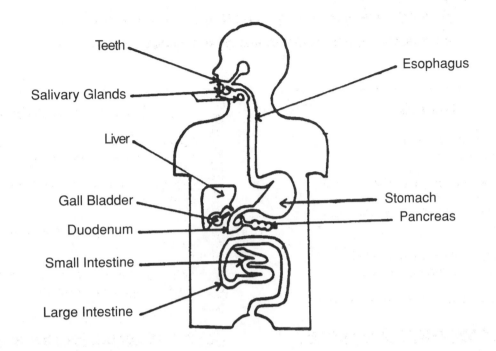

Teeth

Salivary Glands

Esophagus

Liver

Gall Bladder

Duodenum

Small Intestine

Large Intestine

Stomach

Pancreas

(COMPARATIVE)

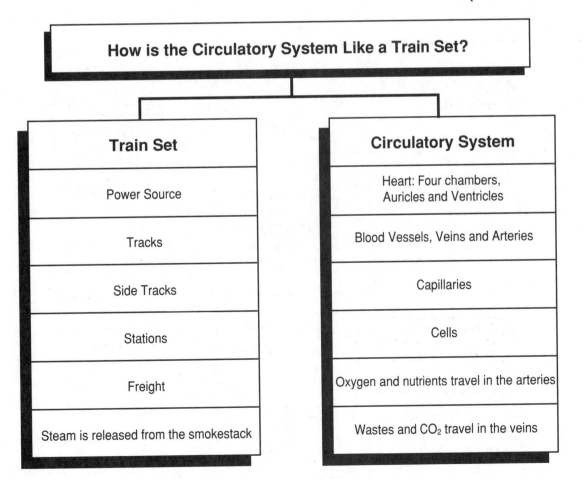

How is the Circulatory System Like a Train Set?

Train Set	Circulatory System
Power Source	Heart: Four chambers, Auricles and Ventricles
Tracks	Blood Vessels, Veins and Arteries
Side Tracks	Capillaries
Stations	Cells
Freight	Oxygen and nutrients travel in the arteries
Steam is released from the smokestack	Wastes and CO_2 travel in the veins

Teaching Styles And Strategies

3

CHAPTER THREE

The Understanding Strategies

OVERVIEW OF THE UNDERSTANDING STRATEGIES

The goal of the Understanding Strategies is to develop students' analytical thinking abilities and to encourage them to formulate concepts and generalizations. Students working in the Understanding Strategies process data and reflect on their own thinking. In the Understanding Strategies, students are asked to observe and describe data, compare and contrast, identify patterns, formulate concepts, and generalize conclusions. Teachers using the Understanding Strategies create discrepant events or provide data fields for students to interpret and analyze. In the Understanding Strategies, teachers facilitate students' thinking and challenge the quality and depth of their responses. Unlike the Mastery Strategies, where the teacher leads and directs, the Understanding Strategies require the teacher to probe, ask questions about students' answers, clarify, and maintain a high level of curiosity and interest in how students think, reason, and how they organize their thoughts.

In the *Understanding Strategies*, the teacher respects and encourages a variety of answers or responses to questions of possibility or probability. Diversity of thought is valued over convergence on a single response or correct answer. Students are made aware that there may be several answers, all equally well-reasoned. The Understanding Strategies encourage students to focus on the reasonable, analytical, and conceptual processes involved in thinking and problem solving. The focus is on the thinking processes themselves—application, interpretation, synthesis, analysis, divergent construction, and evaluation—and on being able to defend the path taken to reach conclusions.

Effective teaching methods in these strategies include the use of "devil's advocate," the asking of "why" and "what if" questions, the setting up of debates, and the development with students of criteria or standards for making judgments about how best to evaluate solutions. The teacher assists and challenges students to understand answers, and, more particularly, to explicate the process by which answers were reached.

The strategies in this section are based on the work of Jerome Bruner, Richard Suchman, Hilda Taba, and David Ausubel. Each strategy is designed to increase students' thinking abilities as well as to accelerate the acquisition of knowledge.

The *Circle of Knowledge Strategy* is designed to insure effective discussion through high levels of participation, a high degree of focus, and a high level of thinking among students. In using this strategy, the teacher designs key questions—a focusing question and several sparking questions, encourages students to internalize the question, uses a variety of techniques to help students show response, and orchestrates discussion through the use of a variety of recognition techniques. Students participate actively in discussion, use evidence to support arguments, develop solid explanations, and describe relationships between and among key ideas.

The *Compare and Contrast Strategy* helps students describe simple, complex, and abstract objects and ideas in terms of their similarities and differences. In this strategy, teachers help students recall the important characteristics of key ideas, discriminate and make careful observations, and see patterns and relationships. Students are asked to use similarities and differences according to given criteria such as function, location, size, shape, and components, to describe objects and to produce clear explanations based on observed characteristics.

The *Concept Attainment Strategy* is based on the research of Jerome Bruner and his associates (1968), about the ways individuals acquire concepts. In using this strategy, teachers select the concept to be studied and prepare examples of what the concept is and is not. Examples are presented to students as yes or no items. Students must compare and contrast attributes of the positive and negative examples, hypothesize the essential attributes, test their hypotheses, and articulate the concept.

The *Reading for Meaning Strategy* requires the students to become problem-solvers in reading, to interpret what they read, and to find the main ideas. Problem-solving in reading demands that students identify and analyze difficult passages, form hypotheses, and share ideas with others. In this strategy, teachers develop Mastery (or literal) statements based on the essential information from a difficult passage which students will need to know in order to be able to identify the main idea. Students read the Mastery statements first, and then read the passage to determine which Mastery statements paraphrase information from the text. Next, teachers present students with interpretive statements which focus on Understanding issues of the passage. Students are required to interpret the text, use inference, and recognize main ideas. Assignments can be extended to include statements from all four styles.

The *Inquiry Strategy* is based on the research of Richard Suchman (1966). In this strategy, teachers design a discrepant event, or prepare a contradictory or puzzling statement. Students collect data by asking yes or no questions and generate a hypothesis explaining the meaning of the discrepant event. Both the Concept Attainment and Inquiry Strategies serve as a form of guided discovery using yes and no feedback to assist students in arriving at correct responses to the inquiry.

The *Mystery Strategy* involves content that we want students to learn, presented as a mystery to be solved. The content or event can be a question to be answered, a riddle to be solved, unusual phenomena to be explained, or a secret to be discovered. Students continuously evaluate by reflection on how they analyzed and interpreted data, how they inferred points, and how logic was used to solve the mystery before them.

To enhance thinking abilities, Hilda Taba (1971) has developed three strategies—Inductive Learning (originally named Concept Formation), Interpretation of Data, and Application of Principles. To allow teachers greater flexibility in determining their uses with students, we have separated Taba's three-part process. The first of these strategies—Inductive Learning—may be found among the Self-Expressive Strategies. The other two are described here.

The *Interpretation of Data Strategy* asks students to analyze data to determine relevant points, generate possible causes and effects for the data, and then draw conclusions about the data. Teachers provide the data for students to interpret, prepare questions for their analysis, and report on the thinking processes being demonstrated.

The *Application of Principles Strategy* assists students in applying generalizations to the explanation of new phenomena, or predicting consequences from established conditions. Teachers act as facilitators. Students are required to design experiences which support their generalizations.

CIRCLE OF KNOWLEDGE STRATEGY

The Circle of Knowledge Strategy is designed to ensure effective discussion through high levels of participation, a high degree of focus, and a high level of thinking among students.

The Strategy at Work

As part of the study of the development of medicine through time in his ninth grade World History classes, Mr. Lehmann planned a lesson using the Circle of Knowledge Strategy. Prior to this lesson, Mr. Lehmann's students had learned about medical techniques used in prehistoric times, and had read brief explanations of the Chinese theory of Yin and Yang, a balance between these two opposites being required for good health; astrology, as conceived by the Chinese, the Babylonians, and the Greeks, with its study of the effect of heavenly influences on various parts of the body; and the Greek theory of the four humours, which could be unbalanced by the weather or the wrong foods and cause illness.

Mr. Lehmann wanted his students to consider the question, "Why did these ancient peoples believe that their methods worked when modern-day medical experts insist that they don't?"

To provide background for the focusing question, Mr. Lehmann had his students read the following review statement:

"During prehistoric times, people developed medical techniques that included the use of healing herbs, trephining, obstetric techniques for helping women give birth and helping their babies survive, and the use of bandaging for cuts and fractures.

The Chinese theory of Yin and Yang, astrology (the influence of the stars), and the Greek theory of the four humours all represent attempts of ancient peoples to develop natural explanations for the causes of disease. Their theories are the beginning of formalized scientific thought.

These early medical theories were accepted by doctors over a period of 2,000 years. However, modern day medical theorists have, for the most part, refuted the theories of the ancients.

How can you explain this? Why did the ancients believe that their methods worked when modern-day medical experts insist that they don't?"

After his students has a chance to read the statement of the problem, Mr. Lehmann asked them to recall a time when they were sure that they knew the explanation for something that had happened, and then discovered that something else was the true reason. Mr. Lehmann wrote this sparking question, devised to motivate his students to explore the focusing question as well as to provide them with information on the question's meaning, on the board. To give them time to internalize the question, Mr. Lehmann asked the students to sit back quietly and visualize an incident, and to try to form a clear image of what the question asked them to do.

After a few moments of silence, Mr. Lehmann asked the class to jot down in their notebooks a brief description of a time when they are sure that they knew the explanation for something that had happened, and then discovered that something else was the true reason. This was a preparation time, he noted, a time for them to pull their thoughts together. He then divided the class into clusters of three students to share the responses. After a short wait, Mr. Lehmann asked the students to consider together why they believed something that turned out later not to be true, and to make a list of their explanation.

Having completed this "kindling" of ideas, Mr. Lehmann moved his students into a circle to begin the discussion of the focusing question, "Why did these ancient peoples believe that their methods worked when modern-day medical experts insist that they don't?" To orchestrate student participation, he used a variety of recognition techniques, including volunteering, random calling, student calling, round robin, and surveying and sampling. The feedback he provided to students ranged from silence to probing, from acceptance to correction, from requesting clarification to encouraging exploration. Throughout the discussion, he recorded responses and asked students to summarize what had been said thus far.

Before the class ended, Mr. Lehmann asked his students to consider the question, "What have we discovered?" The students decided that there were several possible explanations: that modern doctors might be wrong because of incomplete data; that the old theories might have been partly correct, and so were helpful to patients; that the theories, while wrong, made doctors observe their patients with such care that doctors could treat them properly; that some patients get better no matter what, so it appeared that the theories were right; that the patients had faith in the doctors and their theories, and this faith had a positive psychological effect that aided the patients in their recovery.

Mr. Lehmann ended the lesson by asking his students to write for homework their answer to this question: What do we still need to know?

The Circle of Knowledge Strategy

Discussion, one of the most powerful teaching strategies in our teaching repertoire, is unfortunately also one of the most fragile. No strategy is more involving, and yet none suffers as much from students who choose not to participate. No strategy is more likely to lead students to new and original insights, and yet none can so easily become confused or bogged down in trivia.

Effective discussions are characterized by three essential criteria:

1. *High levels of participation:* In effective discussions, everyone has a role. Everyone may not participate equally, but everyone has the sense of having contributed to the exploration of an important issue. The challenge of participation is "Will my learners answer my question? Will they respond?"

2. *High degree of focus:* In effective discussions, there is a clear goal, and discussants move toward it deliberately. Digressions may be tolerated, sometimes even encouraged, but, in the end, there is a clear demand that wandering thoughts move back to the goal of the discussion, and to conclusion. The challenge of focus is "Will my learners be able to follow the thread of our discussion? Will they remember what we are talking about?"

3. *High level of thinking:* In effective discussions students engage regularly in hypothesizing, synthesizing, analyzing, verifying, and evaluating data. Effective discussions are constantly spinning off examples of the upper levels of Bloom's Taxonomy (1956). These higher levels of thought can be achieved not because students have received specific instruction in these skills, but because, as the cognitive scientists say, the human mind is "hard-wired" to perform these operations. Effective discussions evoke high levels of thinking. The challenge of higher level thinking is "Will my learners be willing to think about their answers in sufficient depth? Will their answers be original and well thought out?"

Good discussions don't just happen; they are made, or more precisely, they are planned. In order to achieve the criteria, students and teachers need a wide battery of skills. The Circle of Knowledge Strategy describes a set of moves that teachers can make to encourage the development of those skills which make discussion effective.

The goals of the Circle of Knowledge Strategy are:
1. To help students participate actively in discussion;
2. To help students use evidence to support an argument;

3. To help students develop solid explanations;

4. To help students follow the course of discussions; and

5. To help students describe relationships between and among key ideas.

The steps in the Circle of Knowledge Strategy are:

1. Design key questions—the focusing question and the sparking questions;

2. Encourage students to internalize the question;

3. Use a variety of techniques to help students show response;

4. Use communications in small groups;

5. Orchestrate discussion through the use of a variety of recognition techniques;

6. Use Q-SPACE to shape discussions;

7. Record responses;

8. Summarize frequently; and

9. Establish reflective disclosure.

How to Plan Lessons Using the Circle of Knowledge Strategy

We plan for effective discussions by selecting or designing kindling questions—a single focusing question, and one or more sparking questions. Any healthy discussion needs to be a discussion about something. It needs a topic and a question. A general discussion is not likely to be as productive as a discussion about a specific issue. The focusing question describes the specific issue we want to explore. The focusing question is, in effect, the instructional objective for a discussion. This question actually describes the goal being addressed.

Effective focusing questions are clear. They also tend to be divergent. They invite the use of facts rather than the simple recollection of facts. Two examples of effective focusing questions are: "Was Hamlet a true hero?" and "Is there a real and equal balance among the three branches of the federal government?" Such questions tend to evoke solid responses.

The sparking question is the anticipatory set to an effective discussion. In general, focusing questions are too broad to be approached effectively. Once the focusing question has been laid out, the teacher needs one or more questions that not only motivate learners to explore the focusing question, but also that elicit data related to the question's meaning. In the case of Hamlet, the sparking questions might be: "What are the names of some heroes you know?" "What are some characteristics that these heroes have in common?" "What do you remember about Hamlet?"

Some examples of focusing and sparking questions are:

Spelling — focusing—"Are there any spelling patterns that can help us spell commonly misspelled words correctly?"

sparking—"What are some words you commonly misspell?" "How are these words similar?" "Can you form any groups from these words that are similar in some way?"

Reading — focusing—"What is the main idea of this (story, paragraph, essay, etc.)?"

sparking—"What word or words are mentioned frequently in this piece?" "What kinds of thing does the author say about these words?"

Sparking questions are designed to build bridges between students' prior knowledge and experience and the focusing question. By making contact between the content of the focus question and the lives and knowledge of the students, sparking questions play an important role in igniting student interest.

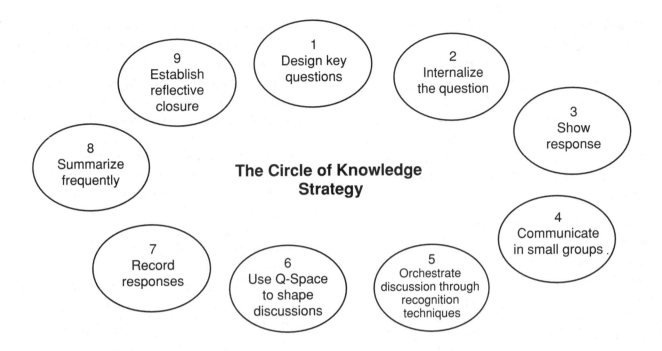

The Circle of Knowledge Strategy

1 Design key questions

2 Internalize the question

3 Show response

4 Communicate in small groups

5 Orchestrate discussion through recognition techniques

6 Use Q-Space to shape discussions

7 Record responses

8 Summarize frequently

9 Establish reflective closure

Putting the Circle of Knowledge to Work in Your Classroom

When you put the Circle of Knowledge Strategy to work in your classroom, you need to use the following techniques:

- encourage students to internalize the question;

- use a variety of techniques to help students show response;

- use communication in small groups;

- orchestrate discussion through the use of a variety of recognition techniques;

- use Q-SPACE to shape discussions; and

- record responses and summarize frequently.

Encourage your students to internalize the question. The most common cause of thoughtless answers in discussion is student impulsiveness. When students leap toward an immediate answer, they most frequently stumble on one that is routine, shallow, or unrelated to the question. Thoughtful discussion requires students to stop and think about the question. Teachers help students to do this by writing the question on the board and asking their students to say the question quietly to themselves, and

to take time out to visualize either information related to the question or possible answers.

After announcing and writing the focusing question, write your first sparking question. Don't let students answer the question immediately. Ask them to visualize the question first to form a clear image of what the question asks them to do. This procedure helps them to internalize the question.

Use a variety of techniques to help students show responses. Ask your students to show their responses in writing or in pictures. The internal speech we use when we are formulating a thought within our own minds and the external speech we use in communicating with others differs widely. Internal speech is more concentrated, charged with possible meanings, and less focused than the more sequential and ordered talk we use with others. Once the students have taken time to think, ask them to share their responses in writing or sketches. Remember that this is a preparation time. Communicate the clear message to students that this is their time to assemble their resources so that they can do well in the discussion that is to follow.

Frequently students flounder in discussion, not because they have not thought, but because they have not pulled their thoughts together. Giving them paper, and asking them to jot down some notes to themselves, to draw a sketch that illustrates their answer, or, for the very young, to "write" or scribble what comes to mind when they hear the question, are ways to get students to show their response to the question they have internalized.

Use communication in small groups.
Your next step is to encourage your students to communicate in small groups. Practice may not make perfect performance, but it nearly always makes for better performance. If we are going to ask students to participate in class, it seems only fair to let them practice first. Encourage students to share their answers with a neighbor or a small group and to explore the ways in which their answers are similar or different. Give them a specific task to accomplish such as "Talk with the people at your table, and make a list of how your responses are similar and different."

These three steps—1) internalizing the questions, 2) showing responses, and 3) communicating in small groups are sometimes called "kindling." Kindling is also an important aspect of the Write to Learn Strategy, and is often used to establish an anticipatory set for any strategy. In the same way that we kindle a fire with little pieces of fuel, we kindle a discussion with little pieces of thought: questions, images, notes, and a few spoken words. Once a fire is kindled, it needs to be sustained by careful tending. In building a fire, this means the careful adding of fuel; in a discussion, it means controlling and shaping the ways in which students add their thoughts to the group conversation.

Orchestrate discussion through the use of a variety of recognition techniques. One of the thorniest problems you will face is the coordination of your students' responses in a discussion. If you stay too long with one student, others may tune out; if you attempt to involve everyone, the discussion can easily lose its focus in a flurry of disparate responses.

To orchestrate the discussion so that most students feel involved and still keep the conversation on track, you need a wide variety of recognition techniques. You can significantly increase the level and quality of participation by skillfully applying these six techniques:

1. Volunteering (raised hands) should be used when the question is difficult and you don't want to put a particular student on the spot.

2. Random calling (you select the students) should be used when you want to increase tension in the group; when you want everyone to know that they are all expected to have an answer; when you know through observation that a particular student has something to offer; when you want to keep a record to make sure that everyone had a chance to say something.

3. Student calling (one student addresses a question to another) should be used when you want to increase interaction among students; when you want students to stop talking to you and start speaking to each other.

4. Round robin (every student has a turn to talk) should be used when you want to know that everyone will have an opportunity and a responsibility to speak; it is especially useful when your students may feel tense about sharing.

5. Surveying (everyone shares a response at once through raised hands or other signs) and sampling (you ask the same question of a number of students in turn to get a sample of students' responses) should be used when you want your students to see where their classmates stand on a particular issue.

6. Redirection (you redirect a student's question to another student or to the group as a whole) should be used when you want your students to explore a student-raised proposition that moves the discussion forward and keeps it on track.

The important thing about this list is its variety. Restricting a discussion to volunteers or to students you have selected is like restricting a painter to black and white. By using a variety of recognition techniques in a discussion, you can move from mere question and answer drills to genuine conversations.

Use Q-SPACE to shape discussions.

- Question
- Silence and Waiting Time
- Probing
- Accepting
- Clarifying and Correcting
- Elaborating and Extending

Your feedback in a discussion will give shape to the lesson. Remember that every answer is a gift. Use silence and probing to increase the sense of challenge in a discussion, to keep your students on their toes, and to provide practice and guidance in the always difficult skill of looking for proof. Use clarification and correction judiciously to keep the amount of interaction to a minimum and increase the precision of students' responses; remember that, when you use this technique, student answers will tend to be more brief, and the discussion will take on more of a question-and-answer drill-session feeling. Use acceptance and exploration to increase the quantity and diversity of students' answers, to help students feel comfortable about sharing, and to build a pool of responses you can use for later reflection.

Record responses and summarize frequently. One thing that makes discussions difficult is keeping track of what was said. Lectures keep us on track through the force of their narration and the clarity of their structure. Since a discussion is made up of the contributions of many, its structure is often harder to see. To establish and maintain focus, you need to record, restate, and summarize.

To record a discussion, jot down students' key ideas on the board, an easel, or an overhead projector. Draw lines between statements to suggest relationships of agreement or disagreement. Recording slows the pace of discussion, sometimes a plus, since it gives students more time to think. At times, however, recording hinders the excitement of a discussion. If this is the case, wait a while before recording, and then use the process of recording to review the ground covered.

To clarify and focus a discussion frequently ask students to restate what previous speakers have said.

To summarize a discussion, stop every five minutes or so and ask students to paraphrase what they and others have been saying. Good recording aids students in this process. In addition, you may summarize, although this is usually more effective if you do it as a question: "Do I hear you saying…?" After soliciting several summaries, help your students combine these into a group summary. Be sure to record all group summary statements.

How to Evaluate the Circle of Knowledge Strategy

In classrooms we want discussions that provide students with an opportunity to practice thinking about some content and to establish a clear point or issue that can be applied in other circumstances. In reflective closure, ask students to use the discussion records to think back on the content of the discussion. You may decide that it is appropriate to have students first copy these records into their notebooks as they would the notes from a lecture. Then ask them three questions: What have we discovered? How have we discovered it? What do we still need to know? This reflective process thrusts students into an evaluative role where they are required to examine the strengths and limitations of their work in discussion, and to raise the question(s) the class still needs to address.

Summary

When to use it:
When you want to increase student participation to synthesize their ideas; when you want students to listen to the point-of-view of others in order to reinforce their ideas and to generate new questions about what they are learning.

How to use it:

1. Establish Focusing and Sparking Questions;

2. Have students think about an answer, or, if possible, visualize one (a covert response which allows students to internalize the questions);

3. Have the students write down, demonstrate, role play, or construct answers individually (This allows students to pull their thoughts together and to assemble their resources prior to sharing);

4. Set up small group discussions to share ideas;

5. Ask students to explain and critique their responses in the small groups;

6. Lead large group discussions using a variety of student recognition techniques: volunteering, random calling, student calling, round robins, surveying, sampling, and redirection;

7. Ask students to state their positions, support other positions, critique positions, and summarize their positions; and

8. Use Q-SPACE techniques: silence, probing, acceptance, clarifying, and elaboration to increase the quality and depth of student responses.

How to evaluate it:

1. Are students able to work covertly in organizing their ideas and overtly in sharing them clearly and forcefully?

2. Are small groups on task?

3. Are students able to explain and critique?

4. Has student participation increased?

5. Have students raised new questions about what they are learning?

Things to remember:

1. Have students respond in both words and drawings—(words, pictures);

2. Provide sufficient time for both covert and overt thinking;

3. Record positions on the board for students to better visualize the structure of the argument;

4. Summarize regularly to keep focus; and

5. Have students assess the quality of the discussion.

Sample Lesson I:
The Steps in the Process of Long Division

Mrs. Janetzki wanted her fifth graders to review and lock in their understanding of the steps in the long division algorithm.

Objectives:

Mrs. Janetzki wanted her students to be able to describe and use the appropriate steps to solve a long division example.

Anticipatory Set:

Mrs. Janetzki explained to her class that she wanted to make a peanut butter and jelly sandwich for her lunch, but that she wasn't sure she remembered how. She asked the students to take a minute and write a set of directions for her to follow. When the students had done so, she asked them to cluster in groups of four to compare their lists for accuracy. "You know," she said, "I can only do exactly what you tell me, so I'm really depending on you."

When the students finished their comparison, Mrs. Janetzki called on a group to read their directions while she followed them. All went well until the group said, "Put the peanut butter on the bread." Mrs. Janetzki stacked the two slices and placed the unopened jar of peanut butter on top. To much hilarity, the group corrected their directions to include opening the jar, and using a knife to spread peanut butter on one slice.

Procedures:

Mrs. Janetzki explained to the students that they had just seen a good example of the importance of clear, complete, and accurate steps in a set of directions. She then told them that she wanted them to focus on the question, "What are the steps in a long division process?" She wrote this focusing question on the board.

As the first sparking question, Mrs. Janetzki wrote three long division examples on the board, and said "What are some things you have to do in all these examples?" She wrote the sparking question on the board next to the examples, and suggested that the students do all three examples while keeping a list of steps, not necessarily in order. Before she allowed them to begin work, she asked them to take a minute to think about the sparking question, and to develop a clear image of what the question was asking them to do.

When her students had finished working independently on their responses, she grouped them as before and had them share their lists, underlining any directions that appeared on all of the lists and adding any directions they agreed had been forgotten.

Next Mrs. Janetzki asked her students, "In what sequence do you have to do these steps?" She asked the groups to continue to work together to place the steps in order, and gave them a fourth example that they could use to check their final directions. As the students worked, she circulated, listening in on conversations and noting the wording being used.

When the students had completed these preparations for discussion, Mrs. Janetzki led them in answering the focus question, "What are the steps in a long division process?" She used a variety of recognition techniques, such as random calling and surveying, based on her observations of the students working together, to maintain the focus of the discussion. To assist her students in developing a sharply honed description of the steps in the long division process, she carefully recorded response and asked for frequent student summaries.

For homework, Mrs. Janetzki assigned her students a long division example with a remainder. She asked them to show their work to solve the example on the left-hand side of the page, and to list the steps they followed on the right-hand side.

Sample Lesson II—Persuasive Writing

Mrs. Lite wanted her students to understand the elements of persuasive writing.

Objectives:
For students to be able to apply persuasive writing techniques to issues that they felt strongly about.

Sparking Activity:
Mrs. Lite asked her class if they ever had to convince someone to do something they didn't want to do at first. She asked them to review the experience in their mind and to loosely list the techniques by which they tried to convince the

person to change their mind. She then asked her students to discuss their experiences and to prepare a more formal list of approaches they used.

After the students finished their sharing, Mrs. Lite explained that people used oral discourse and the written word to persuade others to believe, feel, or behave in a specific way. She said that "Today, we are going to discuss one of the most effective persuasive speeches of the century, Dr. Martin Luther King's 'I have a dream' speech. In his speech, Dr. King used a number of significant elements of effective persuasive writing."

Focus Question:
Mrs. Lite distributed copies of Dr. King's speech and had her students read it. She then had them form small groups of five or six to discuss why they believed the speech was such a good example of powerful and effective persuasive writing.

During the class discussion, she posed the following questions: What comparison or metaphors did Dr. King use in his speech? Which did they believe were the most powerful and why? What word or phrases were used repeatedly and why? What effect to you think these words had on the listeners? What feelings or emotions did these words trigger? Did you consider the speech angry or sad? Why? What evidence do you have to support your position?

As the groups discussed the speech, Mrs. Lite compiled a list of key elements of persuasion on the board:

evokes emotion

speaker/writer feels strongly about the topic

use of metaphor

use of personal pronouns—I, we, you

repetition and alliteration which create rhythm and a dramatic mood

After the discussion, Mrs. Lite had her students find other examples of persuasive writing and determine if they contained many of the same elements of Dr. King's speech. She asked her students to construct a speech of their own about a point or issue they felt strongly about, using many of the elements they had identified during the discussion.

COMPARE AND CONTRAST STRATEGY

The Compare and Contrast Strategy helps students develop the ability to describe simple, complex, and abstract objects in terms of their similarities and differences. Students will be able to use similarities and differences according to given criteria, and to produce clear explanation based on observed characteristics.

The Strategy at Work

To help his students discriminate more clearly between the inch ruler and the centimeter ruler, Mr. Barnes planned a lesson using the Compare and Contrast Strategy. He wanted his fourth grade math class to become aware of the similarities and differences between these two rulers through the collection and comparison of descriptive data.

In his lesson, Mr. Barnes explained that he wanted the students to work in pairs to closely examine two rulers, to see how they were alike and how they were different. He gave each pair of students an inch ruler showing eighth-inches and a centimeter ruler.

Mr. Barnes encouraged his students to look carefully at the inch ruler. He asked them to work with their partners to write three good observations about the markings on the inch ruler. The students shared their descriptions with the whole class, while Mr. Barnes recorded their observations on a large sheet of paper. He then repeated the process with the centimeter ruler. The recorded observations were prominently displayed for reference.

Mr. Barnes distributed a three-column organizer and helped the students begin to list information, first for the inch ruler, then for the centimeter ruler. When the observed data for the two rulers had been entered, he asked the students to work again in pairs, but this time to focus on the ways in which the markings on the two rulers were similar. He encouraged them to look at these important characteristics of an inch ruler and of a centimeter ruler to find ways in which the rulers were similar.

The first part of the finished organizer looked like this:

ONLY THE INCH RULER	BOTH	ONLY THE CENTIMETER RULER
• Has 12 Parts	• Divided into parts	• Has about 30 parts
• Each part has 8 smaller sections	• Each part divided into smaller parts	• Each part has 10 smaller sections
• Each part is divided by lines that are not the same length	• Can be used to measure lengths	• One line that is longer than the rest divides each section in half
• Measures in eighths	• Rulers are the same length	• Measures in tenths
• Measures in fourths	• A longer line in between numbers marks the half	
• One line that is long; rest divides each section in half		

When the chart had been completed, Mr. Barnes asked his students to use it to decide whether an inch ruler and a centimeter ruler were more alike or more different, and why. For homework, he asked them to write a paragraph answering the question: Which would you rather be, an inch ruler or a centimeter ruler? Why?

The Compare and Contrast Strategy

The Compare and Contrast Strategy is nothing new. Since ancient times teachers and writers have juxtaposed two or more objects or ideas as a means of seeing both more clearly. Noting similarities and differences is an essential operation of human understanding.

Comparing and contrasting is the foundation of serious thought. With the ability to recognize similarities and differences, we become capable of classifying, analyzing, and using data appropriately. Development of comparative thinking moves through the following stages:

1. The ability to describe objects in terms of their similarities and differences;

2. The ability to use similarities and differences in terms of given criteria, such as function, location, size, shape, and components, to describe objects; and

3. The ability to formulate criteria, and to describe objects in terms of the specific similarities and differences that fit those criteria.

In order to use comparing and contrasting, students must learn to observe carefully, describe accurately, compare, contrast, formulate appropriate criteria, and reach conclusions that are supported by the evidence. The skill becomes more difficult as more complex and abstract objects are introduced. It is easier to compare two colonial buildings than it is to compare the French and American Revolutions. When two objects are very similar; i.e., an orange and a lemon, it's harder to see their differences; when two objects are very different; i.e., a chicken and an egg, it's harder to see their similarities.

Opportunities for comparing and contrasting in schools include the study of forms of government, geometric shapes, historical events, characters in a story, methods of transportation, elements in the periodic table, experimental designs, works of art, parts of speech, and mathematical proofs, which can all be compared and contrasted in diverse ways, using various criteria. Comparing and contrasting provides a form for many types of writing.

The goals of the Compare and Contrast Strategy are:
1. To help students recall the important characteristics of key ideas;

2. To help students discriminate and make careful observations;

3. To help students see patterns and relationships; and

4. To help students develop clear explanations based on observed characteristics.

The steps in the Compare and Contrast Strategy are:
1. Provide a clear purpose for the comparison;

2. Make sure students have immediate sources of information to draw on in making their comparison;

3. Identify the criteria students can use to make their comparisons;

4. Provide an organizational structure to guide students' insight; and

5. At the conclusion of the comparison, help students see whether or not they have achieved their purpose.

How to Plan Lessons Using the Compare and Contrast Strategy

The first step in planning the lesson is to decide the ultimate purpose. Deciding what you want your students to learn sets your destination so that you can properly plan your lesson. For example, if you are studying parts of speech, you might want your students to be able to differentiate a noun from a verb. Knowing this basic purpose helps you to decide what the final application will be, perhaps separating a list of words into a noun group and a verb group.

Once you know your purpose and final activity, you can begin to decide on the information which will move your students to the final activity. The most often used sources of information are films, readings, paintings, photographs, and class notes. The critical point is to select sources which contain all of the facts you want your students to use. If one source does not provide all the data, add appropriate information in some form. For a unit on reptiles and amphibians, a primary teacher might have her students observe a real frog and a real snake, and then view selected film segments showing lizards and salamanders.

Present students, as often as possible, with actual objects to study; i.e., physical objects, pictures, diagrams, maps, specific paragraphs. Make sure that the items you have selected for comparison are appropriate to the student level of comprehension. Each item will need to be described separately, either by the students or in a teacher presentation. Plan to use at least two items, passages, objects, etc. The nature of the items for comparison may vary widely, but the more observable items are, the more successful the strategy.

Once you have selected your sources of information, consider what criteria you wish to use. Anything can be described endlessly unless you provide a set of criteria to limit and focus the search. What aspects of the information do your students need to focus on? If you wish your students to compare an ameba and a paramecium, you might ask them to describe

these two organisms in light of only two criteria: locomotion and sensory stimulus. Make sure that your selected sources enable students to find data on the criteria which provide your focus. Alternatively, plan to have your students generate the criteria.

Lastly, design a visual organizer. One possibility is to use a Venn diagram. A Venn diagram consists of two overlapping circles; the differences for each object are recorded in the far left and far right portions of each circle while the similarities are recorded in the overlapped, or middle, portion. The great advantage of a Venn diagram is that it provides a visual reinforcement of the logical structure of comparison.

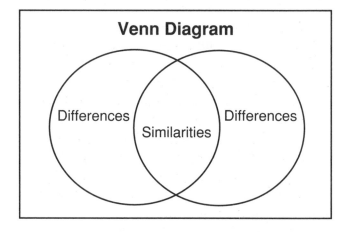

Another possibility is the side-by-side diagram. This type of visual organizer lists the criteria in the far left column, the unique aspects of the two items next to each other, and the similarities on the far right.

	Differences Sedimentary Rocks	Differences Metamorphic Rocks	Similarities
What are the characteristics?			
What kinds exist?			
How is it formed?			

A third possibility is a steeple diagram (shown at right), which is similar in effect to the side-by-side but visually emphasizes the similarities rather than the differences.

You can vary a visual organizer to accommodate any type of information. These three types are only suggestions. If you are artistic, you may wish to reinforce the topic in your visual organizer; a lesson comparing and contrasting the structure of predator birds with waterfowl might feature the outline of an eagle on one side, the outline of a duck on the other, and a large feather in the center for recording similarities.

Putting the Compare and Contrast Strategy to Work in Your Classroom

This strategy is probably the fastest one you can use in your classroom, and it is vital to slow it down so that there is sufficient time for items to be observed in detail—touched, tasted, smelled, heard, and watched. This beginning stage is the comprehension stage. Ask students to describe, one at a time, the objects which they will compare and contrast; do not be satisfied with brief initial descriptions. Record what they say on the blackboard, on an overhead projector, or on newsprint. This slows the process down somewhat, but it also helps to focus later discussion. If you have particular criteria in mind, you may ask your students to focus on them at this point. If you want your students to include particular criteria against which to compare and contrast when you ask them to generate criteria later, use your recording to cluster their descriptive statements.

Either you or the students need to generate criteria against which the items or contents are to be compared and contrasted. If students are doing the job, help them generate as many criteria as possible. Criteria generation can be done orally. Leave blank space on your visual organizer to list the criteria you finally choose to focus on. Some criteria generated will be obvious and concrete. Abstract criteria take longer to generate, but the time is an investment that will pay off handsomely in future exercises.

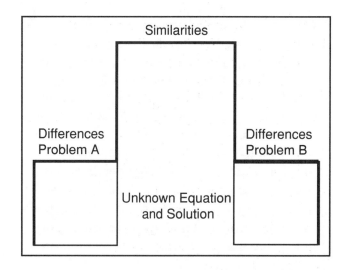

Each student is to have a compare and contrast organizer to complete. Once students have described the items, ask them to compare or contrast. If the objects are very different, begin by talking about the similarities. If they're very similar, begin by talking about the differences. Give feedback that emphasizes both extending responses; i.e., "Good, what else?" and "Anyone have another?"; and probe responses that concentrate on relating similarities and differences to specific criteria.

If you decide to ask your students to work on the organizer independently, plan to include some small group sharing (three or four students together) prior to a whole class discussion. As a whole group, explore whether the students got a clearer picture of the relationship between items, whether any cause and effect relationship was noted, or which of the similarities and differences are more important and which less.

Toward the end of the sharing process, talk with your students about how they listed similarities and differences. Ask them to talk or write about how they formed new insights and ideas about the contents as a whole. Encourage them to draw a conclusion about whether the items were more similar or more different, and what the consequences of their answers might be. Ask them how the use of this strategy shed new light on this content or subject.

How to Evaluate the Compare and Contrast Strategy

Evaluate students' thinking in terms of their ability to describe, their ability to compare and contrast, and their ability to relate similarities and differences to some predetermined criteria. Can the students now generate additional examples of their own? What generalizations can they make about these kinds of items? How can they apply what they have discovered about these items to other items in the same category? Can the students generate their own criteria for application to a new set of items?

Summary

When to use it:

When you want students to see the differences or similarities between two or more ideas, objects or materials and to draw conclusions as a result of their examination and discrimination.

How to use it:

1. Present the objects (ideas, examples, skills, things, feelings, situations, or procedures) to be examined;

2. Let the students describe them one at a time;

3. Compare the objects and generate a list of similarities;

4. Contrast the objects and generate a list of differences;

5. Identify the criteria that were important in comparing and contrasting;

6. Summarize the significant similarities and differences; and

7. Formulate conclusions about similarities or postulate causes and effects of differences.

How to evaluate it:

1. Are the students able to discriminate between the objects more clearly?

2. Are the students able to use different criteria for making comparisons and contrasts?

3. Are students able to identify and describe significant relationships?

Things to remember:

1. Students must be able to comprehend and describe the objects or ideas before they compare and contrast. Ask: What do you see? Remember? Know?;

2. Different criteria will determine if the object is similar or different. A mouse is different from an elephant in size, but similar in that they have four legs; and

3. When comparing two things which are very much alike, it is usually easier to describe their similarities and harder to describe their differences. The opposite is true for two things which are very different.

Sample Lesson I: The Heart and Lungs

THE HEART

The human heart pumps blood to all parts of the body. It is a large hollow muscle. Tubes called arteries carry blood away from the heart. The heart is fist-sized and lies near the middle of the chest toward the front. You can feel the lower, narrower end beating. The heart is enclosed in a sac or pericardium. A muscular wall or spetum divides it length wise. There are two chambers on either side, the upper being the atria which collect the blood from the veins, and the lower, the ventricles which pump blood into the arteries. The ventricle walls are muscular. The right one pumps blood only to the lungs; the left one pumps blood to the entire body. Regulators or valves control blood flow and are called the tricuspid, mitral, semilunar and aortic valves. Blood flows to the heart through coronary arteries. The two sides of the heart relax and fill at the same time. The blood in the circulatory system is always under pressure depending on the amount of blood in the system, strength and rate of contraction, and elasticity of the arteries.

THE LUNGS

Humans have two lungs. They are large, pyramidal organs made up of spongy masses and are suspended in the chest cavity. The pleura is a thin, elastic membrane which covers them. Air enters the body's air passages and enters the lungs through two bronchi found midway on the lungs within tubes or bronchioles which open into a tiny alveoli or air sacs. The alveoli contain a network of capillaries through which blood flows. The alveoli form grape-like clusters around the bronchioles called lobes. Two lobes make up the left lungs, and three the right. The lungs stretch like balloons when filled with air. Lungs give the blood its oxygen supply. They also remove carbon dioxide from the blood. As the blood circulates, it gives nourishment to the tissues, gives up oxygen, and absorbs carbon dioxide. It then returns to the lungs for more oxygen.

DIFFERENCES	SIMILARITIES	DIFFERENCES
1. Physical description:	1. Physical description:	1. Physical description:
2. How it works:	2. How it works:	2. How it works:
3. Its importance to the body:	3. Its importance to the body:	3. Its importance to the body:

Yes.

No.

Yes.

No.

Yes.

No.

CONCEPT ATTAINMENT STRATEGY

In the Concept Attainment Strategy, students are presented with a sequence of examples that are alike in some ways and different in others. The students are asked to formulate a concept by making decisions about what attributes belong in what categories. Attributes lead to a definition of the concept in question.

The Strategy at Work

Mrs. Silver used the Concept Attainment Strategy to introduce a new concept to her students. She began by having a discussion about how "Encyclopedia Brown" uses clues to solve mysteries. She said that "Today, I'm going to present you with some clues. Some are labeled 'YES'—that means they represent the idea I'm thinking of. Others are labeled 'NO'— that means they will be put into a different 'NO' pile. They may have some of the characteristics of my idea, but not all of them. Your job, like Encyclopedia Brown's, will be to use all the clues I present to you to determine the essential characteristics of my idea."

She went on to explain what essential characteristics were by talking about chairs. She asked her class to decide what all chairs have in common. After much discussion, they agreed that a chair has a seat for one, a base/ legs, a back, and its function is for sitting.

She began by providing her students with four pictures. Two were put in the "YES" pile and two in the "NO" pile. The students examined the four clues and generated a lot of possible characteristics of the "YES" pile. Mrs. Silver asked "What's the same about the 'YES' examples that are different than the 'NO' examples?"

The students agreed that the "YES" examples all carried people and went up and down in the air. The "NO" examples went up and down in the air, but didn't carry people.

Mrs. Silver then showed a picture of a building with an elevator. The students were somewhat confused whether this was a "YES" or a "NO" example. One student said it was a "YES" because it carried people and went up and down. Another said it was a "NO" because it did not move through the air. The class agreed that it did move, but did not fly. Mrs. Silver said the example was a "YES."

After examining two more pictures, one of a boy on a stationary bicycle, a "NO" example; and another on a regular bicycle, a "YES" example, the class began to narrow in on what they believed were the essential characteristics: moving people from place to place in the air or on the ground.

When Mrs. Silver showed a bird carrying a worm, the students revised their attributes to moving thing from one place to another. One student said, "Is this idea called 'transportation'?" That was what was meant by things that carry things from one place to another. Their one

definition now went beyond the examples of car, boat, bus, plane, and train. With their attributes, they could now clearly understand why a ski lift or an elephant carrying a log were good examples of transportation as well.

The Concept Attainment Strategy

The Concept Attainment Strategy is designed to help students acquire new concepts, enrich and clarify their thinking about previously acquired concepts, and advance their abilities to think conceptually.

The Concept Attainment Strategy is one of several teaching models developed from the work of Jerome Bruner and his associates as a result of research into the process by which individuals acquire concepts. Bruner contends that in order to cope with our diverse environments, individuals engage in the process of grouping information into categories based on common characteristics. For example, a child learns from experience that objects which have four wheels and an engine, travel on roads, and transport people, belong to a category called "cars."

Concepts have three basic elements: examples, attributes, and attribute values. Examples are instances of the concept; attributes are the basic characteristics of the concept; and attribute values are the specific content of the characteristics. The attributes of a basketball are its shape, size, weight, material, and texture. The attribute value for a basketball's shape is round. Most attributes

of a particular concept have a specific range of acceptable values. The attribute value for the attribute, "color" for the concept, "apple," varies from red to green to yellow; however, blue is out of the acceptable range for the attribute value. What makes one concept different from another is the combination of attributes and their values. A basketball and volleyball have roughly the same shape, but differ in size, color, and texture. The distinguishing attribute and its values are called critical attributes. If any one critical attribute is missing from an object, then that object represents another concept.

It is relatively easy to identify critical attributes when discussing an object such as a basketball. Identifying the critical or essential attributes in abstract or complex concepts such as culture, democracy, and leadership, however, may be quite difficult. The same is true for concepts implying relationships, such as punishment, which have several attributes, each of which has some kind of relationship to the others. In a relational concept, it is the particular relationship the attributes have to one another rather than their presence that forms the concept.

When students learn a concept, they must know its essential characteristics, those attributes and values which distinguish it from other concepts. Students must be presented with a variety of examples before they will be able to deduce the essential attributes of a concept. It is not possible to teach a concept through only once instance or example. Consider this: The teacher shows the student an example and a non-example of a square.

Example   Not an example

When the student is subsequently presented with the following, he responds:

Square   Not a square

The criterion the students mistakenly used to discriminate a square from a non-square was shadowing, not shape. To learn the concept the student needs to examine a set of positive examples and a set of negative examples. The examples should be constructed or chosen so that all of the positive examples have the essential characteristics, while the non-examples possess either none or only some of the essential characteristics.

Concept learning involves double discrimination. Students must discriminate relevant characteristics based on yes examples, and at the same time, discriminate relevant from irrelevant characteristics on both examples and non-examples.

In the Concept Attainment Strategy, students are presented with data which depicts an idea or concept. The data is presented in the form of positive examples and negative examples. Students are asked to identify the idea or concept common to all of the positive examples, and to formulate a rule or definition of the concept according to its essential attributes.

The goals of the Concept Attainment Strategy are:

1. To help students observe attributes;
2. To help students compare and contrast attributes in positive and negative examples;
3. To help students generate and test hypotheses;
4. To help students identify the concept;
5. To help students define the concept according to the essential attributes; and
6. To help students generate additional examples.

The steps in the Concept Attainment Strategy are:

1. Select a concept and generate a list of positive and negative examples for the concept;
2. Review the examples to develop a list of the essential characteristics;
3. Arrange examples into a sequence for students;
4. Present examples, and lead students to identify the concept according to its steady attributes; and
5. Encourage students to test their ideas by generating new examples.

How to Plan Lessons Using the Concept Attainment Strategy

The first steps in planning instruction using the Concept Attainment Strategy are to identify the specific concept you wish to teach; to select and prepare positive and negative examples of the concept; and to analyze the concept for its essential attributes. Positive examples must contain all of the attributes of the concept. Examples need to be labeled positive or negative and sequenced for the presentation.

For example, if the concept you wish to teach is "square" the essential attributes are: a two-dimensional enclosed shape having four connected straight lines, each side of equal length, and each side perpendicular.

Plan to have the students consider questions such as the following: What are the essential attributes? Is the design inside the figure an essential attribute? Is the size of the figure an essential attribute?

The order in which you present positive and negative examples can play an important role in determining how hard or easy it will be for your students to identify a particular concept. If you want your students to identify the concept, "mammal;" i.e., warm-blooded animals that bear their young live, have fur-covered bodies, and live largely on land, you would be ill-advised to use the whale and the duck-billed platypus as your first examples since these two mammals live largely or completely in water, and one of them has little or no fur while the other lays eggs. In general, remember to start with the simplest, most straightforward examples, and introduce exceptions and fine points later on in the sequence.

Possible Positive examples are:

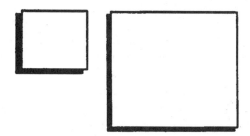

Possible negative examples are:

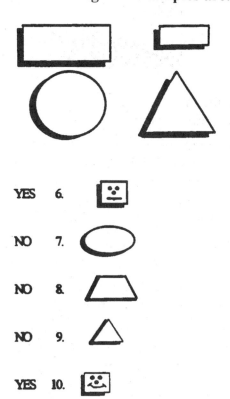

You may choose to sequence the examples as such:

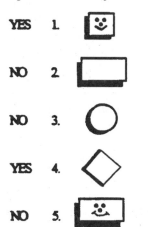

Putting the Concept Attainment Strategy to Work in Your Classroom

In your lesson, you need to present the labeled examples, serving as a recorder keeping track of student hypotheses or concepts and of the attributes as they are identified. You will also want to supply additional examples as needed, and prompt or cue students when necessary to stimulate the process.

Developing a concept is a complex thinking process involving numerous cognitive operations. What you want to avoid is a guessing game where the goal is to be the first student to come up with the correct name. You want instead to build a collaborative atmosphere in which the students realize that they are all working together to develop a common definition. In your opening directions, describe the goal as a group description rather than as a guessing game. Present several examples and non-examples before asking your students to respond. Ask your students to jot down the answer to the question, "What do you observe?" before allowing them to share their ideas. Be sure to record students' ideas on the board or an easel so that students can see them.

For many students who have little experience with the process of developing a concept, prompting or cueing questions are needed, for example:

1. Describe the characteristics of the positive and negative examples.

2. Compare the characteristics shared by positive examples. How are they similar? Contrast the characteristics of positive examples and negative examples. How do they differ?

3. How can you differentiate the positive examples from the negative examples?

4. How would you group the positive examples? Based on what characteristics?

5. Assume that you have never seen the concept before. Now combine all that you know about it and share that information with us.

The role of your students in the lesson is to observe the examples, to compare and contrast attributes, to generate guesses or hypotheses about the essential attributes or concepts, to test the hypotheses, and to define the concept according to the essential attributes identified.

How to Evaluate the Concept Attainment Strategy

To evaluate the lessons based on the Concept Attainment Strategy, you need to help students analyze the thought processes by which the concept was attained. Some students will focus on the concept rather than the specific attributes. Some will test the concepts or attributes one at a time while others employ multiple approaches and hypotheses. Some will approach the task sequentially and logically while others process the data randomly and intuitively. Recognizing a student's preferred method of conceptualizing will provide you and the student with the insights into that student's cognitive style.

Have all students attained the concept? Students need to be able to describe their thoughts about how they arrived at the concept. They should be able to identify additional examples as YES or NO, and then to generate their own examples to verify their hypothesis. They should be encouraged to evaluate the assets and liabilities of the process they used.

Summary

When to use it:
When you want students to figure out for themselves the essential attributes of a new concept or enrich and clarify their thinking on a previously acquired concept.

How to use it:
1. Select the concept to be studied and identify essential attributes or characteristics;

2. Select and organize material into positive and negative examples;

3. Sequence and present examples for students to compare and contrast;

4. Record attributes and hypotheses as they are generated by students;

5. Acknowledge and reinforce the sequence of responses by indicating if the example is a "yes" or "no;"

6. Present additional examples as they are needed; and

7. Have students describe essential attributes of the concept and test their understanding by discriminating among additional examples and developing their own examples.

How to evaluate it:

1. Have the students learned the essential characteristics of the concept?

2. Can they now distinguish the concept from other concepts?

3. Can they generate their own examples?

Things to remember:

1. Make sure you have enough examples and non-examples;

2. Make sure that all positive examples have the essential characteristics and non-examples possess none or only some of the essential characteristics; and

3. Make sure that students describe the essential attributes when identifying or discussing the concept.

Sample Lesson 1: Mathematics—A Prime Example

Dr. Mattine wanted to introduce her sixth grade students to the idea of prime numbers through the use of concept attainments.

Objectives:

Dr. Mattine's students will be able to identify numbers as prime or not prime, and will be able to express a conceptual definition of a prime number.

Anticipatory Set:

Dr. Mattine said to her students: "I have an idea that is important to our work. I would like us to work together as a group to build up a description of this idea so that we can use it correctly when we need it. Here's how I would like us to work—I'll give you positive examples of the idea, and we'll call these YES ideas; I'll give you negative examples of the idea, and we'll call these NO ideas. I want you all to observe the examples carefully and really think

about them. Let's see if we can use these examples to help us describe my idea."

Procedures:

Dr. Mattine divided the board into two narrow columns and one wide column. She labeled the two narrow columns YES and NO. She labeled the wide column DESCRIPTIONS. Then she listed the first several examples:

YES	NO
3	4
5	6
7	8

She waited: then she asked the students to write down three ideas that occurred to them as they studied the examples. Groans. Robert said, "I know the answer already. Why do I need three? Chorus of agreement.

Dr. Mattine explained that she wasn't sure there was enough evidence yet and that they should try to get at least one other possibility in case they were wrong. After waiting a few minutes or more, she asked Robert to say what his idea was. Robert said, "Odd number, They're all odd." Dr. Mattine asked for a description, and recorded it in the Descriptions column: "All odd. Even numbers are no."

"Now," said Dr. Mattine, "Here is 9, which is a NO." Disbelief. "What did you just learn?"

"Our idea is wrong," said Robert. "If 9 is a NO, and 9 is odd, then YES can't be all of the odd numbers. Maybe some odd numbers belong, but not all of them. Why is 9 a NO?"

"Good question, Robert," said Dr. Mattine. "Let's look at the lists and see if we can figure out why 9 is a NO and not a YES."

As students proposed ideas, Dr. Mattine wrote them in the Descriptions column without passing judgment. If the students were in agreement that a previously suggested idea was not correct, she insisted that they provide evidence from the list and then crossed it out, but she did not erase it. When student ideas faltered, she offered additional examples:

11 is a YES; 13 is a YES; 12 is a NO; 14 is a NO; 15 is a NO.

Finally… "What is a 2?" Dr. Mattine asked the students. "How many of you think it is a YES? How many of you think it is a NO? The 2 is a YES. Why?"

As the lesson continued, Dr. Mattine encouraged her students to observe the characteristics of the numbers in each list. "What do you notice about these numbers? What do you know about them? She encouraged them to brainstorm ideas with their neighbors.

Finally, one of the students tentatively offered, "I don't think there is anything that will go into any of the YES numbers, but you can divide all of the NO numbers." Dr. Mattine wrote that description on the board, and then asked the students to check the evidence. Everyone was agreed that the description was accurate until another student said, "What about 1? Every number can be divided by 1. Dr. Mattine suggested that the students list the numbers in the YES column and the NO column, and write their factors next to each to check this idea. There was great excitement as the students began to see a pattern: all of the numbers in the YES column had exactly two factors, 1 and the number itself, the numbers in the NO column had those same factors, but they had additional factors as well.

Dr. Mattine announced that the class had correctly identified the idea, and asked them to suggest a definition for the YES column. The agreed-upon definition read: Our idea is a number that can be divided by exactly two factors, one and itself. At this point, Dr. Mattine told the class that these numbers are called PRIMES, and asked that they find the four primes between 15 and 30 for homework.

Sample Lesson II:
First Grade—The Four Seasons

Mrs. Simpson wanted her first graders to understand the concept of the four seasons.

Objectives:
Mrs. Simpson's first graders will be able to use the characteristics of the four seasons (holidays, weather, growing cycle, seasonal activities, etc.) to define the concepts of fall, winter, spring, and summer.

Anticipatory Hook:
Mrs. Simpson told the children that they would learn to play a new game today, one that used cards. She showed them the stack of cards in her hand. "We have time to play a few times," she said.

Procedures:
Mrs. Simpson enlarged, cut out, and pasted the cards from the accompanying work sheet on oaktag. Then she arranged them in sequence. She chose to start working on the concept of winter, so the cards she planned to use as YES in the first round were 2, 3, 4, 6, 8, 10, 12. All of the other cards were to be used as non-examples in the first round.

Mrs. Simpson had the children sit in a semi-circle around her easel. When she had shown the children a card, she fastened it to the easel in the appropriate column. First she showed the following cards:

YES	NO
2	1
3	5
4	7

She read each card aloud and asked one of her students to describe it. Then she asked if anyone could think of a rule that she was following when she put some cards in the YES column and some in the NO column. "Why should some cards go in the YES column? What makes those cards YES?" She recorded their ideas on the easel, and continued to place the cards, one at a time, pausing after each card to encourage the children to share their ideas.

When the children were able to give the YES cards the name, "winter" and to describe some of the characteristics of winter, Mrs. Simpson showed the remaining cards and had the children tell her whether to put the cards in YES or NO.

Mrs. Simpson repeated the YES or NO game:

1. with the summer cards: 14, 16, 18, 20, 22.

2. with the fall cards: 1, 5, 7, 9, 11, 23.

3. with the spring cards: 13, 15, 17, 19, 21, 24.

When the children had played the four rounds and had defined the four seasons in terms of their holidays, weather, growing cycle, seasonal activities, etc., Mrs. Simpson told them that she would place the cards in the learning center so that they could play at organizing them.

Sample Lesson II: Seasons

1. Harvesting the crops
2. Making a snowman
3. Birds flying south
4. Icicles on a window
5. The temperature starting to drop
6. Merry Christmas/Happy Chanukah
7. We start school
8. It's cold outside
9. We play football
10. Bears hibernating
11. The leaves turning brown
12. The field is bare
13. Planting seeds in the field
14. It is July the 4th
15. The temperature starting to go up
16. We get a suntan
17. There are buds on the trees
18. We go swimming
19. Happy Easter
20. It's hot ou
21. Birds flying back home (North)
22. Watching plants grow
23. It's hallowe'en
24.

READING FOR MEANING STRATEGY

The Reading for Meaning Strategy is used when you want your students to interpret what they read and to find the main idea. The Reading for Meaning Strategy requires that students become problem solvers in reading. Problem-solving, as with any good detective work, means identifying and analyzing difficult passages, forming hypotheses, and sharing ideas with others.

The Strategy at Work

Ms. Ramsey wanted here third graders to learn to use the Reading for Meaning Strategy to read an adaptation of "The Mouse at the Seashore" from Arnold Lobel's Fables. Her objective was to help her third graders recognize cause and effect in this story.

First Ms. Ramsey prepared several Mastery statements which paraphrased the literal meaning of the fable. Then she prepared a somewhat longer set of statements in the Understanding style which focused on the causes for the mouse's happiness at the end of the story. She also prepared several Self-Expressive and Interpersonal statements.

Ms. Ramsey distributed the Mastery statements to her class. After the students had read the literal statements, she made sure that they understood what they were to find and put a check next to statements that said about the same thing as the sentences in the story. She distributed the story for the children to read independently.

THE MOUSE AT THE SEASHORE

Before you read the story, read the statements below.

A Mastery statement is a sentence that is trying to say what other sentences in the story say.

MASTERY SENTENCES WANTED
__ 1. The mouse thought he ought to go to the ocean.
__ 2. His parents said the trip would be much too dangerous.
__ 3. By the time he reached the seashore, he was pretty badly beaten up.
__ 4. The mouse felt that seeing the ocean was worth the trip.

Now read the story, "The Mouse at the Seashore." Any time you come to a sentence that says the same thing as one of the MASTERY STATEMENTS, place a check mark next to the MASTERY STATEMENT.

A mouse told his mother and father that he was going on a trip to the seashore.
"We are very alarmed!" they cried. "The world is full of terrors. You must not go!"
"I have made my decision," said the Mouse firmly.
"I have never seen the ocean and it is high time that I did. Nothing can make me change my mind."
"Then we cannot stop you," said Mother and Father Mouse, "but do be careful!" The next day, in the first light of dawn, the Mouse began his journey. Even before the morning had ended, the Mouse came to know trouble and fear. A Cat jumped out from behind a tree.
"I will eat you for lunch," he said.
It was a narrow escape for the Mouse. He ran for his life, but he left a part of his tail in the mouth of the Cat. By afternoon the Mouse had been attacked by birds and dogs. He had lost his way several times. He was bruised and bloodied. He was tired and frightened. At evening the Mouse slowly climbed the last hill and saw the seashore spreading out before him. He watched the waves rolling onto the beach, one after another. All the colors of the sunset filled the sky.

"How beautiful!" cried the Mouse. "I wish that Mother and Father were here to see this with me."
The moon and the stars began to appear over the ocean. The Mouse sat silently on top of the hill. He was overwhelmed by a feeling of deep peace and contentment.

When the children finished reading the story, Ms. Ramsey organized them into small groups to discuss their answers. She asked them to find out how many had the same answer, or to try to decide on one right answer by checking the story if they disagreed on an answer. She told them that they could not change an answer unless they could find proof in the story. As they worked with each other, she circulated, making notes on the statements that seemed to be difficult.

After the students had shared and worked together on the Mastery statements, Ms. Ramsey called the class together, she used the Circle of Knowledge Strategy to discuss the Mastery statements which seemed to pose difficulties for the students. She then repeated the process with the Understanding, Self-Expressive, and Interpersonal statements.

UNDERSTANDING STATEMENTS

An Understanding Statement tries to say what a lot of the story is about.

Sometimes in stories it is important to know why things happen. At the end of this story the mouse feels happy and contented. I wonder why?

Read the list of events below and write a "C" next to those events that you think helped cause the mouse to feel happy at the end.

___ 1. The mouse's parents did not want him to make the trip.
___ 2. The mouse wanted to see the ocean.
___ 3. He was attacked by some dogs and birds. A cat bit off part of his tail.
___ 4. He got lost more than once.
___ 5. He felt tired and hurt.
___ 6. The sunset was colorful.
___ 7. The waves rolled up on the beach.
___ 8. The stars and the moon came out to shine.

Remember… Be ready to tell your group why you thought a particular event helped him feel happy.

SELF-EXPRESSIVE STATEMENTS

Self-Expressive statements try to say what the whole story means.

"The mouse at the seashore" is a fable. Fables are stories that use animals to teach us how to behave in order to be happy. Fables have morals. These sentences say clearly what the story is trying to teach.

Read through the list of moral statements below and put a check mark next to those that you feel fit with the story.

___ 1. Always obey your mother and father.
___ 2. One must do what one feels is right.
___ 3. When the end is good, even a hard trip is okay.
___ 4. A little adventure is a wonderful thing.
___ 5. Other

Be ready to explain how your moral statements fit the story.

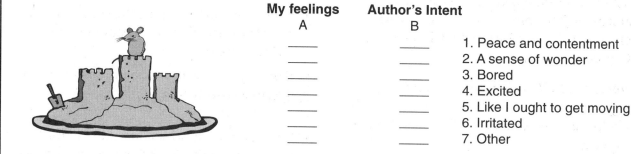

INTERPERSONAL STATEMENTS

Interpersonal statements try to say how the story felt.

Directions: Often authors want us to feel a certain way when we finish reading their stories. Sometimes we feel that way and sometimes we feel different. Think back over the story. Think about what the author said and what you felt. Then, in column A put a check mark next to those feelings you experienced. Put another check in column B if you think the author wanted you to feel that way. Be ready to talk about your responses.

My feelings A	Author's Intent B	
_____	_____	1. Peace and contentment
_____	_____	2. A sense of wonder
_____	_____	3. Bored
_____	_____	4. Excited
_____	_____	5. Like I ought to get moving
_____	_____	6. Irritated
_____	_____	7. Other

The Reading for Meaning Strategy

The Reading for Meaning Strategy is used to help students interpret what they read and to find the main idea. Most of us have been reading so well for so long that we have forgotten just how difficult the act of understanding can be. The Reading for Meaning Strategy asks students to identify what makes a particular passage difficult, and to use that information to show them how to work through the difficulty.

The strategy identified four kinds of difficulties:

- Mastery difficulties, in which the learner may have a hard time understanding what a passage says on a literal level;

- Understanding difficulties, in which the learner may have trouble seeing the important ideas or central themes in a passage;

- Self-Expressive difficulties, in which the learner may have a hard time applying what has been read to previously learned content, or to their own life; and

- Interpersonal difficulties, in which the learner has trouble handling feelings evoked by some passages, i.e., reading certain material elicits uncomfortable feelings which obstruct the learning and reading process.

In the Reading for Meaning Strategy, the teacher selects a passage which contains recurring difficulties students are likely to meet. The teacher reviews the reading passage to determine the essential information the students will need in order to be able to identify the main idea of the passage. The teacher then converts these points into Mastery (or literal) statements. These statements paraphrase sentences from the text rather than state them word-for-word.

The teacher then focuses on the Understanding issues of the passage. What are these issues? The teacher prepares three to six Understanding (or interpretive) statements. These statements require the making of inferences, and reflect the main idea and the purpose, keeping in mind that a text may have more than one main idea or purpose. One or two of these statements should be easy to eliminate, and at least three should lead to discussion and interpretation. These statements will help to focus student reading and discussion. If desired, the teacher may extend the reading to all four styles by preparing statements for Self-Expressive and Interpersonal investigations.

In this strategy, students review the Mastery statements before reading the text. As they read the text, they check off those statements which, in their opinion, restate the sentences in the text.

This procedure helps students focus on what is important in the passage and creates the need for "inner speech" during the reading process. Students are responsible for citing evidence in the passage to support their choices. Learners then meet in small groups to share their observations and to explore and resolve their differences They are then called back together to discuss those statements that provoked disagreement. This process is repeated with Understanding (and, perhaps, Self-Expressive and Interpersonal) statements.

The goals of the Reading for Meaning Strategy are:

1. To help students read and understand difficult passages;

2. To help students develop clear explanations of what they have read; and

3. To help students cite evidence from their reading.

The steps of the Reading for Meaning Strategy are:

1. Hand out Mastery statements developed from the text, and ask students to review them;

2. Hand out copies of a text, and ask students to check off any statements which say what is found in the text;

3. Have students meet in small groups to share observations and resolve differences of opinion;

4. Circulate to see which statements are causing difficulty;

5. Lead a whole class discussion about these difficult statements; and

6. Repeat this sequence of activities with Understanding, Self-Expressive, and Interpersonal statements.

How to Plan Lessons Using the Reading for Meaning Strategy

Reading for Meaning identifies four kinds of difficulties:

- Mastery, in which the student must understand the literal or factual content of the passage;

- Understanding, in which the student must be able to articulate important ideas or major themes;

- Self-Expressive, in which the student must describe how the reading applies to their own life; and

- Interpersonal, in which the student must identify and talk about feelings experienced when reading the passage or story.

In the Reading for Meaning Strategy, your first task is to select a passage from the text you have chosen which contains the difficulty students are most likely to confront in the remainder of the chapter, unit, or story. The type of difficulty will vary with the type of text you are using; a poetry anthology, short story, or novel will pose different requirements for the reader than will a social studies or science text.

Have you chosen a passage from the text that might be difficult for your students? What makes this passage difficult? What are the important facts in this passage? Review the reading passage and determine the important points the students will need to know in order to identify the main idea of the passage. Underline the statements you will paraphrase. Circle specific words you will change. What difficulties will these changes cause? Convert these points into three to six Mastery (or literal) statements answering the questions: who? what? when? where? Make sure that these are statements, not questions, and that you have written them so that the statements are paraphrases of sentences from the text rather than word-for-word repetitions.

Next focus on the Understanding issues in the text. Generate a list of ideas contained in the text. Prepare three to six Understanding statements from this list. These statements should require students to interpret the text, use inference, and recognize main ideas. Prepare one or two statements which are easy to eliminate, and at least three that can be discussed and interpreted. There may be more than one purpose or main idea in the text. These statements should bring out central concepts and themes to help focus student reading and discussion.

If you want to extend the reading to all four styles, prepare statements for Self-Expression and Interpersonal exploration as well. Indeed, for some types of reading, you may wish to focus attention on creative and personal responses. For Self-Expression, generate a list of what this information means beyond the text itself. What are some applications? Ask students to respond to statements that generate predictions, list alternative responses, provide a new ending, or develop a metaphor. For Interpersonal involvement, generate a list of the feelings the author revealed or evoked in the text.

Double check the statements you have written to make sure they are in the correct category, and prepare copies. You will ask students to read the Mastery statements before they read the passage. This set of statements should be on a separate sheet of paper.

You will need to form groups for discussion after students have responded to the list of Mastery statements. How will you form these groups? Will you use the same groups for discussion of Understanding, Self-Expressive, and Interpersonal statements?

When you have devised your groupings and thought about your classroom arrangement for small group discussion, consider how you will explain the Reading for Meaning Strategy to your students. How will you introduce the strategy to them?

Putting the Reading for Meaning Strategy to Work in Your Classroom

After your introduction to the Reading for Meaning Strategy, show your students the Mastery statements. Give them time to read these statements and to think about them before reading the text. Asking students to do this forces them to begin to think about what the possible content of the text is before they actually read it. These statements serve as grist for the reading mill.

Explain to your students that, as they read the text, they should check off those statements which in their opinion restate sentences in the text. This process helps them to focus on what is important in the passage, and creates a need for inner speech during the reading. Be sure that your students know they must be prepared to cite passages or sentences in the text which support their choices.

Have the students meet in small groups to share their observations. Encourage them to resolve their differences by finding proof in the text. Your emphasis here is on encouraging students to find evidence and build arguments to defend their positions. Circulate. Observe the student discussions. Note which statements are causing the most trouble. Make sure students in their small groups are surveyed so points of discrepancy can be discussed.

Now call the students back together in a large group to discuss those statements that provoked disagreement. Use the Circle of Knowledge Strategy to lead the discussion. In your discussion, use Q-Space: use Questioning techniques to help students think in depth when responding; provide sufficient silence and waiting time; probe student answers for further explanation; be non-judgmental of their answers; have students clarify their thinking by asking "Do you mean…?"; have students elaborate upon an idea by saying, "Can you tell me more?" It is possible for you to end the Reading for Meaning Strategy here if your major concern is on the literal level.

If you are concerned about expanding your students' ability to find central concepts and themes, distribute the Understanding statements you have developed. Remember that these statements should mirror larger ideas or feelings that may cause difficulty. Students independently reread the text, and once again, check those statements which are, in their opinion, supported either by the text or by their experience in reading the text. They meet as before in small groups to discuss, debate, and find evidence to defend their positions, and then in a large group to explore statements that provoked disagreement. This phase may be repeated for Self-Expression and Interpersonal involvement.

How to Evaluate the Reading for Meaning Strategy

Evaluation focuses on two aspects—one is how well students are able to use evidence in the text to support their choices, and the second is how they went about interpreting issues. What did they learn about themselves as readers? Have they learned anything about how to go about finding main ideas and evidence to support them? Ask your students to summarize the issues discussed, the arguments presented, and how people formulated their responses. Ask yourself whether the discussion focused on providing evidence and sharing how interpretations were made. Make notes for yourself regarding what students share and display about their own reading style and manner of comprehension. Plan in future work to focus on areas where your students had the most difficulty comprehending.

Summary

When to use it:
When you want students to interpret a text and use evidence from the text to support their claims.

How to use it:
1. Select the reading passage;
2. Prepare the Mastery (literal) statements about the story's content;
3. Prepare separate Understanding (finding the main idea), Self-Expressive (applications) or Interpersonal (feeling) statements;
4. Have students read Mastery statements first, and then the selected passage;
5. Have them check off the Mastery statements that they believe are in the text and identify where they are located in the passage;
6. Place students in small groups to discuss the items they have checked and to see if they can come to consensus;
7. Ask students to record different opinions— their own and others;
8. Survey class and determine items with greatest amount of disagreement. Use Circle of Knowledge strategy to discuss different positions;
9. Distribute Understanding, Self-Expressive, and Interpersonal statements. Have the students reread the text, and check off those statements which they believe are supported by the text;
10. In their small groups, let students discuss their decisions and try to arrive at consensus; and
11. Repeat survey of class and use of Circle of Knowledge strategy to discuss different positions.

How to evaluate it:
1. Can the students find evidence in the text to support their claims?
2. Are students able to hear and understand other points of view?

Things to remember:
1. Encourage students to support their decisions with evidence from the text; and
2. Use Mastery statements and one other type of statement. It is not necessary to go through all four types.

Sample Lesson I:
English—Across Five Aprils

Mr. Sheehan wanted his seventh graders to use the Reading for Meaning Strategy to increase their depth of understanding in the novel *Across Five Aprils* by Irene Hunt (1954).

Objectives:

Mr. Sheehan wanted his students to gain a deeper understanding of the text by interpreting Mastery, Understanding, Self-Expressive and Interpersonal statements.

Anticipatory Set:

Mr. Sheehan used the Inductive Learning Strategy to help students group the following words taken from the text: soldier, "the right thing," quite, blanket, grub, hero, quilt, Jethro, cousin, lay awake, antagonized, hopeless, sympathy, advice, problem, reassuring, hungry, searching, hunted, freezing, Lincoln, death, frightened, Civil War, shielding.

On the basis of their groupings, Mr. Sheehan had his students develop three predictions about the text they were about to read.

Procedures:

Mr. Sheehan had prepared a brief synopsis of the novel and copied an excerpt to be used with the Reading for Meaning Strategy. He had prepared six Mastery statements which paraphrased the literal meaning of the text.

Mr. Sheehan distributed the Mastery statements and asked his students to read them. He then distributed the excerpt, which was also to be read independently. When the students completed the Mastery assignment, Mr. Sheehan organized small groups to discuss responses. He circulated during the small group work, making notes on difficulties. He then used the Circle of Knowledge Strategy with the whole class to discuss the literal meaning of the text.

Mr. Sheehan repeated this procedure for the Understanding statements.

Mastery Statements

Directions: Before reading the Introduction and excerpt from "Across Five Aprils" read the six statements below. Next, read the story. Then, each time you come across one of the statements below that says the same thing as a sentence in the story, place a check mark next to that sentence.

Story Statements

1. _____ Jethro's first reaction, when seeing Eb, was one of gladness.

2. _____ Jethro's first reply to Eb was, "What is it you want of me?"

3. _____ Eb believes that he has more of a chance of surviving in battle than in being a deserter?

4. _____ Jethro sympathized with Eb's position because Jethro did not know what it would be like to be in a battle.

5. _____ Jethro realized that it was Eb calling him, and not really a wild turkey.

6. _____ Eb ignored Jethro's outstretched hand because he was scared.

Introduction to "Across Five Aprils"

In April, 1861, Jethro Creighton, the central character in the story, is nine years old, Jethro lives with his family on a farm in Jasper Country, Illinois, just north of the Kentucky border. The Civil War breaks out while his cousin Wilsey Graham, from Kentucky, is visiting. The dinner conversation clearly indicates the division of loyalties among those peoples living on both sides of the Mason-Dixon line.

While most of the Creightons favor the north, Jethro's older brother Bill joins the Confederate army. Bill views the war as a Southern farmer being pitted against the industrial wealth of the Northeast. Jethro's older brother, Tom, and his cousin Eb, who had lived with the family for many years, enlisted in the Union Army. Because his brothers have left for war, and his father suffers from a heart attack, Jethro must take responsibility for running the farm. Jethro follows the progress of the war across five

Aprils through newspapers, and from letters from his brothers and his teacher, Shad Yale. Early in the Spring of 1863, with the Union Army experiencing terrible moral problems, many Union troops have deserted. Jethro discovers his cousin Eb may be one of them.

Across Five Aprils: An Excerpt

There was an early spring that year. By the first of March the weather was warm, and the higher fields were dry enough for plowing. Jethro carried a rifle with him when he went down to John's place to work. The field he plowed that day was bordered on the East by dense woods, and Jethro was conscious that each time he approached the woods side of the field, the sharp, harsh call of a wild turkey would sound out with a strange kind of insistence—almost as if the stupid bird demanded that he stop and listen.

He walked slowly and carefully, pausing now to listen. The calls stopped for awhile, and he was half convinced that they had come from a wild turkey. He made no move for a few minutes, and then the calls began again, softer now and more certainly coming from the throat of a man. Jethro stood quite still. "Hello," he called finally, "What is it you want of me?"

"Put yore gun down, Jeth; I ain't aimin' to hurt ye. I didn't dast take the chance of Eb Turner hearin me call to ye. "Who is it?" Jethro asked again. "Come out and let me see your face." The skeleton of a Union soldier came out from among the trees. The sunken cheeks were covered with thin fuzz; the hair was lank and matted. Then Jethro realized who it was. It was Eb. For a few seconds Jethro forgot the Federal Registrars and could only remember Eb, the boy who had been close to Tom, and who would have more vivid stories to tell than any newspaper. He said, "Eb, it's good to see you," but Eb ignored his outstretched hand.

Eb said, "Yore ma and pa will be scairt for themselves and ashamed of me." Jethro could only stare at his cousin. Eb went on, "Desertin' ain't a purty word to you, is it? All at once I knowed I couldn't stand it no longer, and I jest up and left." Jethro asked him if he could just come up to the house and visit and get cleaned up, but he said he couldn't. It would get them into trouble and they probably wouldn't want to see the likes of him again. Jethro asked why he came and he replied in anger, "Because I couldn't help myself."

Jethro asked Eb how he managed to eat and he told how he lived off the land, shooting rabbits and squirrels. He ended by saying that nothing was good these days like they used to be. Jethro's insides twisted in sympathy. Eb said, "I'm allus hungry. Ye git used to it after a while. Eb ate some grub that Nancy had fixed for Jethro with an appetite like a hungry animal's.

"At least you got a chance in battle this way. I got none. I'll either freeze or starve or be ketched. There's no place on this earth fer me to go. A soldier don't have to feel ashamed," Eb said. To Jethro the situation appeared hopeless. He was frightened for the despairing man, for himself, and for his family. The pounding of his heart made his voice shake. Trying to sound reassuring he said he would get some quilts and grub, and that they would think of what could be done when Eb felt stronger.

The law loomed big in his mind; loyalty to his brother and all those men who had fought; how could loyalty to them be true if one harbored a man who said, "I quit"? On the other hand, how could one send his cousin to his death? How did he know what he would be like if he were sick and scared and hopeless? Maybe Eb had been a hero in battle over those two years. Sure, deep down Jethro wanted Eb to get out to leave him feeling free, but no, he wouldn't be free if Eb moved on. He wouldn't forget someone who was sick and living off the land like a wild, hunted animal.

Understanding Statements

Directions: An "Understanding" statement tells what the story is about. At the beginning of the novel Jethro is nine years old and clearly a child. As a result of his brother's going to war and his father's heart attack, Jethro is expected to do more than is normally expected of a nine year old. He matured quickly under these expectations.

Read the statements below and place a check mark next to those statements that you believe demonstrate Jethro's maturity. Which of the seven statements do you believe are the most significant?

1. ____ Jethro asked Eb if he could just come up to the house and visit and get cleaned up.

2. ____ Jethro was frightened for the despairing man, for himself, and for his family.

3. ____ Jethro tried to sound reassuring and said he would go get some quilts and grub, and that they would think of what could be done when Eb felt stronger.

4. ____ The law loomed large in Jethro's mind; loyalty to his brother and all those men who fought. How could he be loyal to them if he harbored a man who said, "I quit"? On the other hand, how could he send his cousin to his death?

5. ____ How could he, Jethro, know about how it felt to be sick, scared and hopeless?

6. ____ Deep down Jethro wanted Eb to leave him feeling free, but no, he wouldn't be free if Eb moved. He couldn't forget someone who was sick, and living off the land like a wild, hunted animal.

7. ____ But Mr. Lincoln looked at problems from all sides. That morning, as he plowed, Jethro decided to send him a letter.

Sample Lesson II: Mathematics— Interpreting Math Information

Ms. Yadin regularly uses collaborative learning groups for problem solving. She uses the Reading for Meaning Strategy within these groups to increase her students' ability to interpret and solve word problems.

Objectives:

Ms. Yadin wants her students to improve their comprehension skills in solving math word problems.

Procedures:

As part of her collaborative learning assignments, Ms. Yadin prepares two or three word problems within the Reading for Meaning Strategy. She preceded each word problem with several Mastery statements. After the students read the Mastery statements independently, they read the problem and check off the statements that say the same thing as the problem. The small groups discuss their responses, resolve their differences, and then repeat the activity with Understanding and Self-Expressive statements. Ms. Yadin ends her collaborative learning lessons with a Circle of Knowledge discussion of the small group work.

Problem #1

Directions: First read the five statements below. Then read the problem. Place a check mark next to the statements that say the same thing as the problem.

Section A

1. ____ John is selling a brand new set of golf clubs.

2. ____ The yard sale is expected to be a great success.

3. ____ The bicycle is only six months old.

4. ____ The golf clubs will be selling for $70.00, and the bicycle for $35.00.

5. ____ John wants to sell items for more than the original price.

Section B

The problem: John Simpson is preparing for a yard sale. He wants to sell his six month old golf clubs for 2.5 times the original price of $70.00, and his bicycle for 2.8 times the original price of $35.00. What is the selling price of the two items?

Section C

Read the statements below and place a check mark next to the correct statements.

1. ____ More information is needed to solve the problem.

2. ____ Multiply to solve the problem.

3. ____ More than one operation is necessary to get the answers.

4. ____ Solving the problems takes multiplication and subtraction.

5. ____ The most efficient way to solve the problem is by multiplying and adding.

Problem 2

Directions: Before reading the problem read the statements below. Then read the problem. Any time you come to a sentence that says the same thing as the problem place a check mark next to it.

Section A

1. ____ Mr. Smith had more five dollar bills than one dollar bills.

2. ____ The register contained $327.00.

3. ____ The register contained more $20.00 bills than $5.00 dollar bills.

4. ____ Mr. Smith had a very busy day at the store.

5. ____ The register was checked at the end of the day.

Section B

The problem: Mr. Smith checked his cash register at the end of the day. He found that he had seven fewer $5 dollar bills than $1 dollar bills, and no larger bills. In all he had $327.00. Find the number of $5.00 bills and $1.00 dollar bills.

Section C

Read the statements below and place a check mark next to what is to be found according to the problem.

1. ____ The total register receipts for the day.

2. ____ The number of twenty and ten dollar bills.

3. ____ How Mr. Smith can improve his sales.

4. ____ The number of one dollar bills.

5. ____ The number of five dollar bills.

Section D

Which of the following statements are correct?

Place a check mark next to the correct statement.

1. ____ To get the answer you must do more than one operation.

2. ____ You can solve the problem simply by adding.

3. ____ Subtraction may be used in solving the problem.

4. ____ To solve the problem all four operations will be used.

5. ____ Be sure to add together five, one, eleven, ten, three, and twenty to get the answer.

Problem 3

Directions: Before reading the problem read the statements below. Now read the problem. Any time you come to a sentence that says the same thing as the problem place a check mark next to it.

Section A

1. ____ Each family paid a total of $3.24 a week for newspapers and magazines.

2. ____ Some of the 30,000 families took no magazines.

3. ____ Magazines cost the average family more than newspapers.

4. ____ The city mentioned in the problem is New York.

5. ____ Most families like to read newspapers and magazines.

Section B

The problem: In an Eastern city there are 30,000 families which buy both newspapers and magazines. Each family spends an average of $1.25 per week on newspapers and $1.99 per week on magazines. How much money is spent in a year by all the 30,000 families for newspapers and magazines?

Section C

Read the statements below and place a check mark next to what is to be found in the problem.

1. _____ The number of magazines bought each year.

2. _____ The average amount spent for newspapers in a week.

3. _____ The Eastern city with a population of 30,000 families.

4. _____ The cost per year for magazines and newspapers paid by 30,000 families.

5. _____ How much 30,000 families spend each year for newspapers and magazines.

6. _____ How much 30,000 families spend on newspapers and magazines each week.

Section D

Which of the following statements are correct?

Place a check mark next to each correct statement.

1. _____ To get the answer you must first add, then multiply.

2. _____ First multiply, then divide to get the answer.

3. _____ The quickest way to do the problem is by adding.

4. _____ To get the answer you must multiply by the number 7.

5. _____ To get the answer you must multiply by the number 52.

Answers

Problem #1 A—5; C—5, 7; D—2, 3, 5, 6.

Problem #2 A—2, 5; C—4, 5; D—1, 3, 4.

Problem #3 A—1, 3; C—4, 5; D—1, 5

INQUIRY STRATEGY

In the Inquiry Strategy, the teacher presents students with a discrepant event. A "discrepant event" is a statement that appears untrue or implausible, but upon examination has a rational explanation. Students collect data through observation and experimentation, and by asking "yes" and "no" questions. Students formulate explanations or theories to explain the phenomenon under consideration.

The Strategy at Work

Mr. Cudjoe is leading his sixth grade class into a study of prehistoric man as evidenced by archaeological remains. After presenting an introductory lecture on prehistoric man, he asked his students to examine an archaeological problem situation:

"At many prehistoric sites around the world archaeologists have found skulls with holes in the crown. The bone around the upper crown is smooth and rounded. How might these holes have been made? For what reason(s) were they made? What can we conclude from the fact that the holes were smooth and rounded? What does this tell us about prehistoric people?"

Mr. Cudjoe suggested that his students begin by brainstorming what they knew about each of the three important ideas in the skull mystery: prehistoric beliefs, the holes, and the skulls. He explained that he would serve as the students' eyes, ears, nose, etc., and that they could ask him any question which could be answered by a "YES" or "NO" and which did not require him to explain why the holes existed. For example, "Were the holes bigger than the size of a quarter? Yes, no, or sometimes?" was a good question; but "Were they made for a religious purpose?" was not, even though it could be answered "YES" or "NO," because it would require him to verify their hypothesis. He explained that if they believed the holes had something to do with a religious ceremony, then they would need to think of specific questions they could ask to test and verify that hypothesis which could be answered "YES" or "NO." For example, "Did the people who made the holes dance before they made them? Did they chant, etc.?" "Was there a famine or natural disaster—a flood or hurricane before the holes were made?" Better yet, "If I was the Shaman of the tribe, would I be the one to make the holes?"

Explanations:

Mr. Cudjoe asked his students to examine the data, then to develop three lists of everything they knew about prehistoric people, holes, and skulls. After they had generated their lists, they were then asked to come up with three hypotheses that might explain the phenomenon.

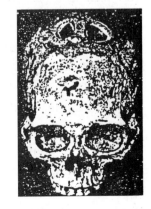

The Inquiry Strategy

Inquiry is a fundamental and natural process in learning. Inquiry occurs whenever individuals are confronted with events or situations that create a discrepancy between what they perceive and what they know and understand. Long before children begin formal education, they engage in the inquiry process.

In the Inquiry Strategy, the process of data gathering, analysis, and experimentation is under the control of the learners. Students become inquirers when faced with some situation that challenges their idea of the universe or that creates a dissonance between what they perceive and what they know or understand to be true.

The Inquiry Strategy is designed to move students from a traditional, intuitive, and concrete process to a more decentralized, analytical, and abstract one.

The goals of the Inquiry Strategy are:
1. To help students become more autonomous learners;

2. To encourage students to question why things happen as they do; and

3. To help students develop the intellectual discipline necessary to search out data, process it, and apply logic to it.

The steps in the Inquiry Strategy are:
1. Provide a climate suitable for inquiry, one marked by freedom, responsiveness, and focus;

2. Select and demonstrate a discrepant event, or design a situation in which students will encounter the problem;

3. Guide the inquiry process through which students collect, verify, and experiment with data in the following ways: use the language of inquiry, identify invalidated points, and ensure that students phrase questions so that they can only be answered "yes" or "no";

4. Press students to make clear statements and support generalizations;

5. Encourage students to test hypotheses;

6. Press students to formulate rules or explanations; and

7. Analyze the inquiry process.

How to Plan Lessons Using the Inquiry Strategy
To plan a lesson using the Inquiry Strategy, first construct or formulate a discrepant event. A discrepant event for young students could build on their innate curiosity about natural phenomena. If you show children the apparatus below, they will ask you many questions similar to the following:

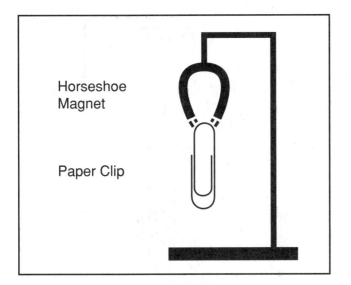

Horseshoe Magnet

Paper Clip

What keeps the paper clip up?

Will it fall if we poke it?

Would it stand up if the string were metal?

What is between the clip and the magnet?

What would happen if we put paper or cardboard between the paper clip and the magnet?

Will a bar magnet work?

A simple puzzle, riddle, optical illusion, or magic trick may be used to create a puzzling situation for older students. Consider the following riddles:

1. The First Man: A perfectly preserved man was found in a block of ice. The scientist who discovered the body proclaimed him to be Adam, the first man. All subsequent scientists examining the body agreed. Why?

2. The Headlights: Two headlights came directly at the child in the middle of the road. It was too late for him to move. His parents scolded him when he got home. Why did he survive?

After constructing the problem situation, the next step is to identify the factual information needed to support the inquiry. You also need to determine a theory or explanation that accounts for the discrepant event, and consider alternative theories or explanations for the problem.

Identify the objectives you wish to address. How will these objectives be met? How will data be collected, organized, and analyzed?

There are two types of data gathering: verification and experimentation. Verification is the process of gathering data pertinent to a single event. Verification questions help students to determine facts about the objects, events, conditions, or properties involved in the problem. A verification question might be, "Is the metal object on the stand a magnet?" Experimentation questions introduce new elements into the situation to see if the event might happen differently. Experimentation questions help students to discriminate between essential and non-essential variables or test a causal relationship. An experimentation question might be, "If the paper clip were made out of plastic, would the effect be similar?" Let's try it and see.

It must be emphasized that the focus of your role in the Inquiry Strategy is to create a climate that promotes investigation. This generally means adopting a less directive instructional role, as well as the attitude that knowledge is tentative. When you are considering data collection, decide whether you will need to set up an area in the room where experimental equipment or kits, idea books, or resources books and materials can be stored and used. Will students explore their questions about the discrepant event independently, on their own time schedule and at their own rate? Will you provide all students or small groups of students with a set of equipment and/or resource materials for their exclusive use? Will the inquiry take place during a lesson period? Do you want to use a whole group format for questioning, with individual students proposing, and some or all students investigating?

Answers to riddles:

1. The body has no belly button.

2. The headlights belonged to two motorcycles.

Putting the Inquiry Strategy to Work in Your Classroom

To start your students working on a lesson using the Inquiry Strategy, you need to explain the inquiry process, present the discrepant event, referee the inquiry procedures, respond to students' inquiry probes, help beginning inquirers establish a focus, and facilitate discussion of the problem situation among the students.

To facilitate a climate that promotes inquiry suggests the following rules are helpful in guiding the inquiry session:

1. Require the students to phrase questions in such a way that they can be answered yes or no;

2. Allow a student, once called on, to ask as many questions as he wishes before yielding the floor;

3. Refuse to answer yes or no to questions which are really statements or theories, or to questions that attempt to obtain your approval for a theory;

4. Allow students to test any theory at any time;

5. Help students feel free to confer with one another any time there is a need; and

6. Enable inquirers to work with experimental equipment, experimental kits, idea books, resource books, and materials at any time they desire.

The most important skill for you as a teacher to practice is that of helping students to inquire, rather than to do, or even lead, the inquiring. If students ask you a question that cannot be answered by a yes or a no, ask them to rephrase the question. If you cannot answer yes or no to a particular question, feel completely comfortable saying "I don't know." Introduce new information or additional resources related to the problem. Ask focusing questions to keep the inquiry on track. Point out when statements lacking validation are made; i.e., "We haven't yet established that the liquid is water." Use, and encourage students to use the language of inquiry, labeling questions as verifying or experimenting, testing hypotheses, or constructing theories.

Encourage your students to gather data through the use of experimentation questions. Help them to see that the purpose of their experimentation questions is to isolate relevant variables and to test for causal relationships. Encourage them to formulate rules or principles that explain the discrepant event.

How to Evaluate the Inquiry Strategy

As part of evaluating the Inquiry Strategy, provide feedback—corrective, descriptive, and intuitive—to students as they move through the process. Use corrective feedback to guide students to recognize the limitations of their own logic or assumptions. Require that students think logically and be able to support their theories or generalizations. Use descriptive feedback to define, acknowledge, and reinforce students' thinking. Neither approve nor disapprove students' theories. Use intuitive feedback to expand students' thinking about alternative explanations and possible questions to ask.

Involve students in the evaluation phase. Lead them in analyzing the strategy used in the inquiry and in determining the effectiveness of their questioning techniques. Remember that the focus of the analysis should help students to become more relaxed in their questioning, and should lead them to follow a general sequence of questioning; i.e., establishing facts, determining relevance, building concepts or explanations, and determining relationships.

Summary

When to use it:

When you want to make students more autonomous learners, to help them question why things happen as they do, and to encourage them to develop the intellectual discipline necessary to search out data, process it, and apply logic to it.

How to use it:

1. Provide a climate suitable for inquiry, one marked by freedom, responsiveness, and focus;

2. Select and demonstrate a discrepant event, or design a situation in which students will encounter the problem;

3. Guide the inquiry process through which students collect, verify, and experiment with data in the following ways: use the language of inquiry, identify statements lacking validation, and ensure that students phrase questions so that they can only be answered "yes" or "no;"

4. Press students to make clear statements and support generalizations;

5. Encourage students to test hypotheses;

6. Press students to formulate rules or explanations; and

7. Analyze the inquiry process.

How to evaluate it:

1. Do students phrase questions so that they can be answered "yes" or "no"? Can students rephrase invalid questions?

2. Do students demonstrate the ability to think logically?

3. Can students support theories or generalizations?

4. Are students developing the ability to recognize the limitations of their own logic and assumptions?

Things to remember:

1. Use corrective feedback (yes or no) in answering students' inquiries;

2. Use descriptive feedback to define, acknowledge, and reinforce students and thinking;

3. Use intuitive feedback to expand students' thinking about alternative explanations, and possible questions to ask;

4. Allow students to test any theory at any time; and

5. Enable inquirers to work with experiments, kits, idea books, or resource books whenever they wish.

Sample Lesson I: Prey and Predator Relationships

Objectives:

To use the Inquiry Strategy to determine why a town's action with an expected result (eliminating wolves, which killed deer, expected to increase the deer population) turned out to have the opposite result (the deer population actually decreased).

Anticipatory Set:

A number of years ago people in a rather large, isolated area witnessed a wolf pack devour two small deer from a herd and were horrified. As a result, they began a campaign to eliminate the wolves from the area. Prior to the elimination of the wolves in this area, deer were quite numerous, and their population fluctuated slightly. In most cases like this when the predator is eliminated, the prey population increases, then decreases, as the balance of nature takes over. To the surprise and dismay of many hunters in the area, the years following the elimination of the wolves showed a marked decrease in the population of the deer.

What caused the decrease in the deer population?

Procedures:

The key concepts in this inquiry are prey/predator, the balance of nature, wolves, and deer.

1. Begin by generating what you know about prey, predator, wolves, deer, and the balance of nature.

2. Generate two or three tentative hypotheses which might explain why the deer population decreased following the destruction of their natural predator, wolves.

3. In groups of four or five—generate five yes or no questions to ask to pursue one of your hypotheses.

4. Each group will be allowed five questions during each round. Rounds will continue until correct conclusions are drawn. Generate additional questions in case many rounds are needed.

5. What caused the decrease in the deer population following the elimination of wolves which are the deer's natural predator? Support your conclusions.

Sample Lesson II: Looks are Deceiving!

Objectives:

A hands-on experience with getting unexpected results, using two beakers with a clear mystery liquid and studying its affect on ice cubes dropped into them.

Anticipatory Set:

Inquiries often occur when we expect to see one thing but see something else. If you drop an ice cube into two beakers of clear liquid, what would you expect the ice cubes to do? Let's observe what happens.

Procedures:

1. Draw a picture of what happened to the ice cube in beakers A and B.

2. Let's begin by exploring what you know about the key concepts in this inquiry: liquids, ice cubes, and beakers. What else would we need to explore?

3. Generate two or three hypotheses that might explain the phenomenon.

4. In groups, generate five yes or no questions to pursue one of your hypotheses—the questions must seek information that can be observed. Record your observations.

5. What additional questions do you have?

6. Based on your inquiry and what you have heard from others, how can you best explain what happened in the beakers?

Sample Lesson III: Tragic Heroes

Objectives:

To analyze the basic characteristics of a tragic hero, to compare them with 20th century examples of American tragedies, and to speculate why the heroes of American tragedies don't fit the classical definition of a tragic hero.

Anticipatory Set:

Has the definition of tragic hero been changed since it was developed centuries ago? How do tragic heroes—if there are any left by the classical definition—affect our lives in 20th century America?

Procedures:

Examine the first four cases. Two are examples of tragic heroes and two are not. Compare the similarities between the two "Yes" examples and examine how they are different from the two "No" examples. Based on your analysis, develop a preliminary definition of a tragic hero.

Case 1—Hamlet, Prince of Denmark: The hero of this famous play by Shakespeare is a sensitive and subtle thinker, but his ability to see all sides of an issue makes it almost impossible for him to take decisive action. When his father's ghost appears and demands that he be avenged, Hamlet's inability to act stirs up a host of resentments and plots against him. Near the end, Hamlet discovers the value of actions and dies heroically, finally avenging his father and cleansing Denmark of evil. Yes.

Case 2—Frank Yanko: Frank sells used cars in Southern New Hampshire. He is successful, makes a fair amount of money, and seems happy much of the time. He is a good father and a supportive and faithful husband. No.

Case 3—MacBeth: The Thane of Cawdor is a great soldier and a brave man, but the central figure of this Shakespearean play is also a secretly ambitious man. When the king visits the castle, MacBeth kills him and takes control of the country. MacBeth's violent attempts to conceal his guilt and consolidate his power provoke more and more opposition. In the end these forces overwhelm him. Before his death, however, he attains new insight into himself and dies bravely, his former nobility and courage restored. Yes.

Case 4—Ronald Reagan: A sports reporter from a small Midwestern town becomes a Hollywood screen actor achieving wealth and fame. He is elected head of the Screen Actors'

Guild, and becomes an effective politician and a "great communicator." He runs for president, wins, and becomes the most popular president of the last 20 years. No.

Based on the previous four examples, write down your preliminary definition of a tragic hero.

Now read cases five through eight. Based on these additional examples, refine your definition.

Case 5—Oedipus: The king of Thebes, and the hero of two plays by Sophocles, he rules Thebes effectively but arrogantly. He is overly sure of his ability to use his power to solve any problems that might confront his city. When a plague strikes Thebes, he swiftly mobilizes all of the city to discover the culprit whose offense has induced the gods to send this plague on the populace. His arrogance sets loose a chain of events that eventually force Oedipus to realize that he is the cause of the plague, and that his arrogance has blinded him to his own faults. In the end he literally blinds himself and leaves the city. The plague ends and Oedipus, in exile, finally becomes wise and dies honorably. Yes.

Case 6—Superman: Clark Kent, Superman, is the hero of a long-running series of comic books, more than a dozen movies, and a successful TV series. He came to Earth from another planet (Krypton) as an infant and was raised in obscurity on a farm in a tiny Midwestern town called Smallville. Early on it became obvious that he had superhuman powers. He was able to fly, "leap tall buildings in a single bound," see through objects, and bend steel bars with his hands. He embodied all of the human virtues, and his only weaknesses were physical; i.e., he could not see through lead and kryptonite could kill him. No.

Case 7—Rocky: A little-known boxer is chosen to fight the heavyweight champion of the world. Seeing this as his last chance to prove himself, Rocky prepares for the upcoming fight by showing great discipline, energy, and nerve. He forces the champ to a draw, and in later fights, disposes of several cruel and vicious contenders who want to deprive him of his title. No.

Case 8—King Lear: King Lear, the subject of another Shakespearean play, has demanded of his three daughters that they tell him how much they love him. Based upon how he feels about their declarations of love he will divide his kingdom. The third and youngest daughter, who loves him the most, will not participate and is exiled. The game ends disastrously with the kingdom being divided between the two remaining daughters. War breaks out; Lear loses all his power and goes mad. Near the end of the play, he finally sees the nature of true love and dies humbly, his kingdom reunited under new and wiser leaders. Yes.

Now compare the characteristics of your definition with the two descriptions that follow, Emily (Case 9) and Willy Loman (Case 10). How are they the same as your definition? How do they differ?

Case 9—Emily: A normal girl from a small New Hampshire town is the most important character in Thornton Wilder's "Our Town." She lives her whole life in obscurity, marries the boy next door, and dies suddenly in childbirth.

Case 10—Willy Loman: A salesman is the central subject of Arthur Miller's "Death of a Salesman." Willy is driven by a powerful ambition—to be somebody. His yearning twists and distorts the lives of his two sons, alienating one and driving the other into relentless hypocrisy. In the end Willy kills himself by driving into oncoming traffic, his mind haunted by delusions.

Based on your analysis, are Emily and Willy tragic heroes or not? Explain.

Both Emily and Willy are considered 20th century American tragic heroes.

How did the American drama change the concept of a tragic hero? Why was such a change necessary in the American culture of the mid-20th century?

THE MYSTERY STRATEGY

The Mystery Strategy plays on people's natural affinity for mysteries. Presenting content to be studied as a mystery immediately suggests to students that they have an active role to play in the lesson. The strategy involves presenting the mystery, providing the students with clues, testing hypotheses, and evaluating the investigations.

The Strategy at Work

Mr. Yanderschnich told his ninth grade class they were going to study the mystery of why the early colonies founded in what is today America—such as the one in Jamestown, Virginia—survived despite a disproportionately high death rate in the first 20 years. He had the students break down into groups—"Historical Study Teams," he called them—to determine why this happened. To get them started, Mr. Yanderschnich gave his students some preliminary clues about the possible cause of the death rate. The clues involved soldiers deserting, murder and greed, poor housing, a lack of livestock for food, the often futile attempts to grow tobacco, continuously harsh laws punishing those who did not successfully farm corn, low wages/slavery, unsanitary working conditions, and frequent attacks by local Indians.

Based on the recording and close examination of these clues, and with Mr. Yanderschnich's guidance and direction, the students were able to decide in a fair amount of time the real reasons for the high death rate in Jamestown colony: the disease and poor conditions which were brought from Europe coupled with the lack of funds, disorganized and corrupt government, and unpreparedness for the tough winters of the new world.

The Mystery Strategy

As we said earlier, the Mystery Strategy involves students finding answers based on clues. The problems themselves can be in the form of a question to be answered, a riddle to be solved, unusual phenomena to be explained, or a secret to be revealed. For example:

- Why do top-loading washing machines require more detergent than front-loading machines?
- I am less than a score, more than a decade, divisible by three, and a little odd. What am I?
- How can relative humidity be under 100 percent when it is raining?
- Who really invented the cotton gin?

In the Mystery Strategy the event is presented as a mystery. The evidence is presented as clues, in oral, written, or visual form. The clues can be given at once, or a few at a time to make a lesson easier (like the Jamestown Death Rate mystery) or more difficult (like some of the sample lessons we will present shortly). Remember that clues provide information, not explanation.

The explanation is made by the students after careful examination of the clues and the continuous forming, testing, and refining of possible hypotheses. Throughout the process, students are also continuously involved in evaluation by reflection on how they analyzed and interpreted information, conclusions that were drawn, inferences that were made, and the logic of the final explanation or solution to the mystery.

The goals of the Mystery Strategy are:
1. To learn to gather, organize, and process information;
2. To learn to formulate and test hypotheses;
3. To learn to think creatively and analytically to solve problems; and
4. To learn to develop, defend, and present solutions to problems.

The steps in the Mystery Strategy are:
1. Determine what is to be taught;
2. Determine how easy or difficult the lesson should be;
3. Present the clues accordingly;
4. Gather and record students' hypotheses;
5. Evaluate the hypotheses; and
6. Summarize what was learned.

How to Plan Lessons Using the Mystery Strategy

First, identify a question, riddle, situation, or secret to be explained/resolved. When planning a Mystery lesson, you should begin by generating a list of questions that will puzzle students and engage their curiosity. Focus on questions that scholars in the field might actually ask. Rather than have your students read about how the Colonial Militia defeated the British troops in America, you can ask your students to explore the mystery of how the "rag-tag militia with little, if any, training and leadership" could have defeated the most well-trained army and navy in the world. Appropriate mystery questions are in the form of "Yes" or "No" with the addition of the more important question, "But, WHY?"

Second, develop a clear idea of the solutions that you would like your students to generate, and gather the necessary clues. Identify the big ideas and important details students will need to know to solve the mystery. You need to be clear about the possible explanations you hope to generate. Be sure to provide enough clues to help the students reach the intended overall generalizations (but not so many where the answers come too easily).

Third, decide how students will work to solve the mystery. Decide what roles they will play. You can have them work independently, in small groups, or as a whole class. If you choose to have them work in small groups, you might want to distribute the clues evenly among the group members: this maximizes participation and minimizes the possibility of any one student dominating the discussion. Or, to avoid the same trap, you could have each team identify a particular role for each of its members. Students can act as readers, recorders, questioners/critiquers, processors, proofreaders, etc.

Fourth, determine how you will present the clues. They can be written on strips of paper, placed into envelopes, and handed to a team all at once. If students are unfamiliar with the strategy or if they have difficulty organizing

large amounts of information, you can distribute the clues gradually, from vague to specific. Alternatively, you can set up the clues at different stations around the classroom.

Fifth, design a worksheet on which students can record information, group related clues, create hypotheses, and develop logical and coherent solutions. Of course, you can have students do these steps in their notebooks or on scrap paper.

Sixth, select a format of the presentation of students' conclusions. The explanations can be oral, written, or audio/visual. This decision should be made according to student preferences and time constraints.

Seventh, decide what assessment criteria to use to evaluate performance. Consider the content, processes, and product. It is a good idea to share a blank evaluation form with the students before beginning the lesson, so there are no doubts about what is expected from them.

Finally, design a set of questions you will use to encourage student self-reflection. Ask questions like: What happened in the activity?, What things did you do well/enjoy?, What would you like to do differently next time?, etc.

Putting the Mystery Strategy to Work in Your Classroom

Begin your lecture by telling students that a mystery will be solved today—to instill a sense of excitement. Other strategies may not seem as exciting to young, curious minds. For anticipation, ask them to think of times when they had to solve an intriguing question, much in the same fashion as you would with an Inquiry lesson. Point out to the students, however, that unlike previous Inquiry lessons, they will solve this lesson by their own innate reasoning abilities, not by simply probing specific and leading questions. Tell them to think of themselves as detectives.

As we have discussed, the rate, order, and difficulty level of presenting the clues is of utmost importance to the Mystery lesson.

The rate of distribution determines how much work the students are given at once. The order determines if the lesson will be easy or difficult. The level of the clues per se can modify the previous factors. Of course, the organization of the students—individual work, several small groups, or one large team; as well as the subdivision of the groups themselves into specific roles—all can have a great influence on the outcome of the lesson.

Once the lesson is over (and the mystery is solved), discuss with the students what they felt were the high and low points of the lesson. What did they like/dislike; what would they like to see changed about it? Most importantly, what do they feel they have learned from it? What have you, as a teacher, learned from the lesson? What would you change next time?

Much of the content we expect students to master can be presented in the form of a mystery that is interesting and engaging. Let's experience the Mystery Strategy by completing a few sample lessons.

Summary:

When to use it:
When you want students to solve a problem/mystery by probing and by examining given clues and insights.

How to use it:
- Encounter the problem;
- Strange phenomena;
- Secret that intrigues;
- Question that puzzles;
- Riddle to be solved;
- Examine and interpret the clues;
- Organize clues;
- Establish patterns;
- Seek cause/effect relationships;
- Make inferences;
- Draw conclusions;
- Establish an explanation;
- Form hypotheses;

- Test hypotheses;
- Select and refine hypotheses; and
- Support hypotheses.

How to evaluate the investigation:
- Reflect on the process;
- Determine effectiveness of the investigation; and
- Evaluate hypotheses.

Things to remember:
- Varying the rate/difficulty of the clues affects the outcome of the lesson;
- Consider whether there will be individual or group work when designing the lesson; and
- For a greater challenge to gifted students, use a time limit for solving the mystery.

Sample Lesson I: The Dinosaur Mystery

Objectives:
To solve the mystery of why the dinosaurs suddenly died after dominating life on Earth for 140 million years.

Anticipatory Set:
Dinosaurs were among the most successful life forms ever to exist on our planet. They dominated life for 140 million years. They thrived on all of the continents and in every sort of climate. Suddenly, millions of years ago, the dinosaurs disappeared. By the end of the Cretaceous period (70 million years ago) all of the dinosaurs were gone. They had become extinct. What happened?

Procedures:
Start by reading through all the clues. Cut them apart; lay them in front of you. Then, organize them into groups by putting related clues together. Label each group. Review the clues and record any important information or observations you have made. Review your observations and form at least three tentative hypotheses as to why the dinosaurs became extinct. Record them in the appropriate place on your "Detective's Notes." Test each of your hypotheses based on your information. Like

all good detectives, support your hypotheses regarding the disappearance of the dinosaurs. Be prepared to share with the class.

The clues:

- Cycads need high temperatures day and night to survive.

- Mammals survived the changes that killed the dinosaurs.

- Iridium-rich clay has been found in Italy and Montana.

- Large reptiles like alligators do not live much further north than Southern Georgia.

- Asteroid orbits sometimes shift.

- Whatever happened 65 million years ago affected the whole world; every continent and the air and sea as well.

- Certain types of plankton (microscopic plant and animal life) disappeared from the sea at the end of the Cretaceous period.

- Many species of dinosaurs were especially protective of their eggs.

- Flowering plants evolved gradually through slow growth and change beginning about 100 million years ago.

- Alkaloids (nitrogen-containing substances) in certain concentrations are poisonous to some animals.

- While flowering plants evolved, dinosaurs increased in population and in number of species.

- Some mammals eat eggs.

- Iridium is quite common in objects from space such as meteors and asteroids.

- Some scientists believe dinosaurs disappeared in less than one million years.

- In 1969, scientists found a skeleton of a lystrodaurus in Antarctica.

- In the late 1970s scientists discovered a thin layer of clay that had been laid down during the end of the Cretaceous period. The clay was rich in a mineral called iridium.

- Cycads declined rapidly during the late Cretaceous period.

- Asteroids can be several hundred miles across.

- Some flowering plants contain alkaloids.

- Iridium is very rare on Earth.

- Modern plankton populations become smaller when the temperature of the sea suddenly drops.

- Asteroids can travel at 100,000 kilometers per hour.

- Chickens under stress lay eggs with thinner shells than chickens not under stress.

- When an asteroid hits a planet it throws massive amounts of dust into the atmosphere.

- Dust reflects sunlight.

- In 1815, Mount Tambora, a volcano in Indonesia, erupted turning billions of tons of rock into dust, which was hurled into the atmosphere.

- In 1816, there was snow in New York during the month of June.

- Many of the plant and animal species on the Earth became extinct.

- Dinosaur eggs became thinner toward the end of the Cretaceous period.

- Even a nine-kilometer asteroid can carry the energy of 100 trillion tons of dynamite.

- Throughout the Cretaceous period, plankton populations became much smaller.

- In 1972, an eight-meter asteroid (1,000 tons) missed the Earth by only 58 kilometers (about 36 miles).

- Fossilized plants from the early age of dinosaurs were mostly tropical.

- Evergreen plants replaced tropical plants in the later years of the age of dinosaurs.

- Small reptiles are found today as far north as Canada.

- Birds survived the changes that killed the dinosaurs.

- A principal food for plant-eating dinosaurs was cycads (large tropical plants).

Sample Lesson II: The Autobiography of Bertrand Russell

Objectives:
To figure out the intended order and possible meanings of the clippings of Bertrand Russell's essay on passions.

Anticipatory Set:
What comes to mind when you hear the word *passion*?

What color do you see?

What food do you taste?

What music do you hear?

Take a moment to think about your own life. What things or ideas are you passionate about? How do these passions influence your life?

Procedures:
The mystery: A recent discovery was made of a Bertrand Russell essay on his three passions. Unfortunately, the essay parts were not put together. Your challenge is to figure out how the parts are connected. Complete the essay and prepare a written defense of your position.

The parts of Russell's essay:
- Echoes of cries of pain reverberate in my heart.

- I long to alleviate the evil, but I cannot, and I too suffer.

- And I have tried to apprehend the Pythagorean power by which number holds sway above the flux.

- I have sought it, next, because it relieves loneliness—that terrible loneliness in which one shivering consciousness looks over the rim of the world into the cold unfathomable lifeless abyss.

- I have sought love, first, because it brings ecstasy—ecstasy so great that I would often have sacrificed all the rest of life for a few hours of this joy.

- I have wished to know why the stars shine.

- A little of this, but not much, I have achieved.

- This is what I sought, and though it might seem too good for human life, this is what— at last—I have found.

- I have wished to understand the hearts of men.

- Love and knowledge, so far as they were possible, led upward toward the heavens.

- This has been my life.

- Three passions, simple but overwhelmingly strong, have governed my life: the longing for love, the search for knowledge, and the unbearable pity of the suffering of mankind.

- I have sought it, finally, because in the union of love I have seen, in a mystic miniature, the prefiguring vision of the heaven that saints and poets have imagined.

- I have found it worth living, and would gladly live it again if the chance were offered me.

- With equal passion I have sought knowledge.

- These passions, like great winds, have blown me hither and thither, in a wayward course, over a deep ocean of anguish, reaching to the very verge of despair.

- But always pity brought me back to Earth.

- Children in famine, victims tortured by oppressors, helpless old people a hated burden to their sons, and the whole world of loneliness, poverty, and pain make a mockery of what human life should be.

Compare your arrangement with Russell's organization. Think about how your organization is different. Can you justify your work?

Now analyze the structure of the essay— beginning, middle, end. Write an essay about your passions and how they influence your life.

Sample Lesson III:
A Trigonometry Mystery

Objectives:
To solve a trigonometry-based mystery
to determine a practical question.

A TRIG MYSTERY

When the sun's angle of elevation is 57°, a building casts a shadow 21 feet long. How tall is the building?

The flag pole next to the building is 28 feet tall. How long is the shadow cast by the flag pole?

The clues:

1.

2.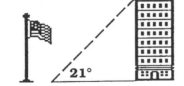

3. TAN 57° = 1.5399

4.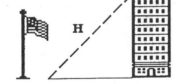

5.

6. SIN 21° = .3584

7.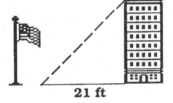

8. SIN 57° = .8387

9. COS 21° = .9336

10.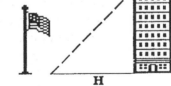

11.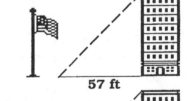

12. COS 57° = .5446

13.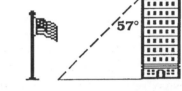

14.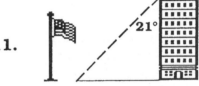

15.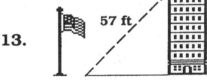

16. TAN 21° = .3839

17.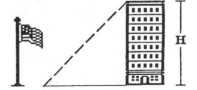

by James Holt, McIntosh County Academy, Darien, Georgia

Sample Lesson IV:
European History— The Black Plague

Mr. Feinberg decided to use the Mystery Strategy to help his students understand the process historians employ to establish facts, determine relevance, build explanations, and determine relationships in historical events.

Objectives:

Mr. Feinberg wanted his students to learn to use effective questioning techniques, and to develop the ability to search out data, process it, and apply logic to it while, at the same time, learning about what caused the Black Plague, why it spread so rapidly, and why it ended.

Anticipatory Set:

To introduce his students to the yes or no questioning technique, and to give them an opportunity to practice it, Mr. Feinberg explained the requirements for such questions, and then played a game he called "Careers."

For the game, Mr. Feinberg wrote the following careers on the board: director, producer, art director, film editor, screenplay writer, set designer, casting person, and cinematographer. He then said "Consider these careers. I have one of them in mind. Try to determine which one it is by asking questions to collect evidence. When you think you have sufficient evidence, make hypotheses and come to a conclusion. Be aware, however, that I will NOT tell you if your hypotheses or conclusions are correct. I will ONLY answer yes or no to questions of fact. YOU will have to decide which conclusion or conclusions are best supported by the evidence. An example of a yes or no question is: Does a person in the career you have in mind work with actors?"

As the game proceeded, Mr. Feinberg took time to discuss the questions posed, explaining which ones were hypotheses or conclusions phrased as questions, and therefore disallowed. He wrote good questions on the board to reinforce his students' understanding of the requirements. His board list included:

- Does such a person do the job throughout the entire making of the film?
- Does this person usually work on the set?
- Does this person appear in the credits of film advertisements?
- Does this person learn the job at a college or university?
- Are there more men than women doing this job?
- Does this person require special equipment in performing the job?

Mr. Feinberg knew the answers to most of the questions his students asked. For a few questions, however, his response was, "I don't know." He pointed out that he would certainly not know all of the answers to their questions, and that they might have to search out answers for any questions they deemed vital to developing a conclusion.

Procedures:

At the game's end, Mr. Feinberg introduced the Black Plague inquiry. He explained that students could choose to work independently, in pairs, or as small groups of no more than four students. He suggested that students confer whenever they felt it would be helpful, and that proposed conclusions be posted on easel paper, together with supporting evidence, so that everyone would have access to a wide range of ideas. He announced that he would begin the lesson on the following day with a yes or no question period, and suggested that his students come prepared with questions.

Mr. Feinberg then distributed an introductory statement on the Black Plague, a worksheet containing three main questions, several focus questions, and a resource packet.

BLACK PLAGUE INQUIRY

In the Dark Ages, not many people traveled. One thing that did travel, however, was disease. The "Black Death" was one such disease. The "Black Death", (or plague) was the worst killer of the Middle Ages.

People who caught the plague broke out in swellings which turned into boils and black spots. Nearly all victims died within a few days.

The plague arrived in Europe in the middle of the l4th Century. It first spread to Italy around 1345, prompting the Italian writer Boccacio to write "It started in the East, either through the influence of heavenly bodies, or because of God's just anger with our wicked deeds, was sent as a punishment to mortal men, and in a few years killed an innumerable quantity of people. Ceaselessly passing from place to place, it extended its miserable length over the west. Against this plague, all human wisdom and foresight were in vain. No doctor's advice, no medicine could overcome or alleviate the disease." (*The Decameron*, 1348)

The plague hit England in May 1348. The first town to suffer was Melcombe Regis, a coastal town near Portsmouth. The information was obtained by looking at parish records and registers which told about burials, and the causes of death for individuals in the town.

By August, the plague had reached London. It continued to spread through the winter and reached the northern parts of England by early 1349. Finally, it began to die out, and only a few cases in Scotland were ever reported.

By the time the plague ended in 1349, between half and two-thirds of the population of England was dead. It was to them what a nuclear war would be to us today. The number of people affected was enormous.

The plague came back again and again until the l8th century. In the outbreak of 1665, the progress of the plague in England stayed mainly in London and in the south of England, but the effects were the same.

Directions:
Read the overview of the Black Plague. Then, examine the source material in your envelope. Based on this evidence and on other things you know, see if you can solve the mystery.

What caused the plague? Why did it spread so rapidly? Why did it end?
Here are some questions to consider in your investigation:
Why was there no evidence of the plague before 1345?
Why did it begin in Italy?
What did people think caused the plague?

BLACK DEATH SOURCE MATERIAL

Source 1—Filth lying in the streets

To the Lord Mayor of London

An order to cause the human excreta and other filth lying in the streets and lanes in the city and its suburbs to be removed with all speed. Also to cause the city and suburbs to be kept clean, as it used to be in the time of previous mayors. This is so that no greater cause of death may arise from such smells. The King has learned that the city and suburbs are full with the filth from out of the houses by day and night that the air is infected and the city poisoned. This is a danger to men, especially the contagious sickness which increases daily. (*Letter from King Edward III*, 1349)

Source 2—Avoid stinks

The pestilence come from three things. Sometimes from the ground below, at others from the atmosphere above and sometimes from both together as we see a privy next to a bedroom, or anything else that corrupt the air. Sometimes it comes from dead carrion or the corruption of stagnant waters in ditches.

The plague sores are contagious because the humours of the body are infected and so the reek of such sores is poisonous and corrupts the air. In time of plague people should not crowd together because some man may be infected. All four stinks are to be avoided, the stable, stinking fields or streets, dead carrion, and most of all stinking waters. Therefore keep your house so that infected air cannot enter into it. Let your house be clean and make a clear fire of flaming wood. Fumigate it with herbs. (*Bishop Aarhus, "A Good Little Book against the Pestilence,"* London, 1485)

Source 3 (right)

The quarantine station at Naples in the 18th century from J. Howard *"An account of the Principal Lazarettos in Europe"*, Warrington, 1789. *Quarantine* comes from an Italian word meaning 40 days. People who might carry plague had to wait here for 40 days before being allowed into the city. The system was widely used in Europe in the 18th Century.

Source 4—(below) Scene from a broadsheet about the plague, published in London, 1666.

Source 5—Cleansing the city

In the city of Florence in the beginning of the year 1348 the sad effects of the pestilence began. This happened in spite of all that human forethought could think to avoid it, such as the cleansing of the city from many impurities, the refusal of entrance to all sick fold and humble prayers addressed to God. Any that touched the clothes of the sick or anything else that had been touched or used by them seemed to catch the disease.

Source 6—Orders by the Lord Mayor of London, 1665

Examiners: The examiners if they find any person sick of the Infection, to give order to the Constable that the House is to be shut up.

Searchers: Women searchers of every parish to be of honest reputation. These to make search and true report whether the person do die of the Infection, or of what other diseases. No searcher to keep a shop or be employed as a laundress.

Shutting up of the sick: As soon as any man shall be found to be sick of the Plague, he shall the same night be shut up in the same house and the house shall be shut up for a month.

None to be removed: None to be moved out of the house where he falls sick into any other house in the City, except to the Pest-House.

Burial of the dead: Burial to be always before sun-rising or after sun-setting, no neighbors and friends to be allowed to go with the corpse to Church or to enter the house.

Houses to be marked: Every house visited by the Plague to be marked with a red cross of a foot long, and with these word, "Lord have Mercy upon us."

Houses to be watched: The Constable to see every house shut up and attended with watchmen, who are to get food for the people at their own expense if they can afford it, at the public expense if they cannot.

Streets to be kept clean: Every householder to keep the street clean before his door all the week long. The sweeping and filth of houses to be daily carried away by the rakers. No hogs, dog, cats, pigeons, or rabbits to be kept within any part of the city, or swine stray in the streets. Dogs to be killed by the dog-killers.

When Mr. Feinberg's students had developed a number of proposals and supporting evidence, he used the Circle of Knowledge Strategy to lead a discussion focused on the three main questions: What caused the plague? Why did it spread so rapidly? Why did it end? At the end of the discussion, he conducted a cognitive review of the Inquiry Strategy, based on the questions: What have we discovered? How have we discovered it? What do we still need to know? In this way, Mr. Feinberg encouraged his students to reflect on the inquiry process, and to examine the strengths and limitations of their work in establishing facts and building explanations.

At the end of the lesson, Mr. Feinberg distributed copies of the following explanation of the Black Plague:

BLACK PLAGUE: EXPLANATION

The Black Plague was the worst killer in the Middle Ages. The plague was spread by fleas, which lived on black rats. The disease often caused large black lumps or spots on a person's body.

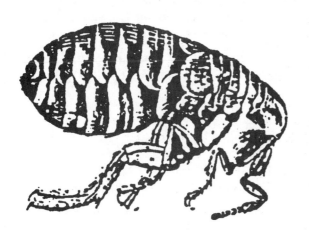

The black rats lived in China. In about AD 1200, explorers from Europe discovered China. They called it Cathay.

When the ships docked in China, the rats were attracted on board by the spices and food in the cargo holds. The ships sailed for Europe with the rats on board. These rats had fleas. The fleas lived on the rat's blood. The blood contained the plague germs.

When ships docked after leaving China, the rats often got off the ships to find more food. They would go into the town. They could actually live in the walls of the houses, which were made of wood, straw, and animal dung. The fleas were fussy whose blood they lived on, but if the rats died from the plague infection, the fleas would jump off the rats and onto the people.

The ships carrying the plague left China in about 1345-6. The first place that the plague spread to was Italy. The plague reached England by 1348. It had been brought ashore by sailors. The rats also came ashore and the fleas were able to affect many more people.

In those days, people knew nothing about germs. They had no microscopes. Since they couldn't see germs, they didn't know that germs existed. They didn't know that germs love filth.

The people in the Middle Ages were very dirty. They lived in houses that were more like huts. They shared these homes with animals. They had no toilets. They had no water supply except the stream or well. The conditions that the people lived in made them easy targets for the disease.

WHAT?

WHY?

HOW?

INTERPRETATION OF DATA STRATEGY

The Interpretation of Data Strategy, based on the work of Hilda Taba, is designed to help students identify and explain the dimensions of data collected, determine relationships, make inferences about cause and effect, and formulate generalizations to be applied in future learning.

The Strategy at Work

Mrs. Justice teaches a unit on flight as part of her fifth grade science curriculum. She wanted her fifth graders to collect information, to relate points to one another to determine cause and effect, and to determine implications and formulate generalizations. As an introduction to the unit, she developed a learning center on aerodynamics in which she placed a number of resource books on the making of paper airplanes, some computer-generated models to be cut out and assembled, and paper of various types for constructing original models.

Directions for Mrs. Justice's aerodynamics center were posted, and copies were distributed to each student. The directions were as follows:

1. Construct one or more paper airplanes.

2. Work with other students to fly your airplanes, measure, and record the distance flown.

3. Group the planes according to those that flew the farthest, average and least distances.

4. Examine the groups, talk to each other, and write a paragraph, answering each of the following questions:

   What do you notice?

   How are the groups the same?

   How are the groups different?

   Look at the planes in each group. How are the planes in each group the same, and how are they different?

5. What do you think are some of the causes for one group of planes to glide further than another?

6. How are some planes superior to others?

   Why? Give specific reasons.

7. For each reason, try to explain the cause and effect the design has on the flight.

8. From what your group has discussed, what would you conclude about designing airplanes for the purpose of gliding? What made you conclude that?

9. From what your group has decided about paper airplanes, their design and ability to glide, what could you say generally about aeronautical principles of flight? Why would you say these things?

10. Choose one of the airplanes from the group which flew the least distance. Based on what you have learned, how would you improve the aircraft's performance?

    Can you modify the design to make the airplane fly farther?

When her students were engaged in learning center tasks, Mrs. Justice made herself available to those students who were at work in the aerodynamics center. As students worked, she prompted them with eliciting questions such as: What did you notice? Why did that happen? What do you think caused that? What does this mean? What picture does this create in your mind? What would you conclude? She reminded them to record not only their findings on flight distances, but also their thinking on aircraft design.

After all of her students had sufficient time to work on the aerodynamics project, Mrs. Justice used the Circle of Knowledge Strategy to lead a discussion in which her students shared their findings and developed criteria for evaluating their own generalizations.

The Interpretation of Data Strategy

The Interpretation of Data Strategy focuses on the development of students' ability to interpret data, infer cause and effect, and produce generalizations.

As in the Inductive Learning Strategy, the teacher uses focusing questions to initiate the Interpretation of Data Strategy. Focusing questions are designed to stimulate students to:

1. Select specific data they have studied or observed in a story, a film, an experiment, or a research project;

2. Look for cause and effect relationships among the data and support their statements or inferences by giving evidence or explanations;

3. Extend and support inferences they have made; and

4. Arrive at conclusions and generalizations from the explanations they have made.

As in the Inductive Learning Strategy teachers can organize thinking over three areas: overt behavior, covert mental operations, and focusing questions.

In general I would say...

If A > B and B > C, then...

From what I observe...

I conclude that...

OVERT BEHAVIORAL OBJECTIVES	COVERT THINKING OBJECTIVES	FOCUSING QUESTIONS (GENERAL)
Enumerating data	Recall data from prior knowledge or intake experience. Differentiate relevant from irrelevant data.	What did you see? Find? Notice? What do you recall? What difference did you notice?
Inferring cause and effect	Infer cause and effect; identify evidence or reasoning to support inferences.	What do you think are some of the causes of ____? What are some effects? Why do you think ____ caused ____?
Inferring prior causes and subsequent effects	Infer causes and/or effects or previously supported causes or effects; identify evidence or reasoning to support inferences.	What do you think have been some of the causes (or some of the results) of ____? What do you think has happened as a result of ____?
Formulating conclusions	Synthesize inferences to form conclusions; identify evidence or reasoning to support conclusions.	From what we have said, what would you conclude about ____? From our discussions, what made you decide that?
Formulating generalizations	Generalize to other similar situations; identify reasoning or evidence.	What could you say generally about ____? Why would you say that?

In summary, the steps in the Interpretation of Data Strategy are:

1. Enumerate relevant data;

2. Infer cause and effect;

3. Infer prior causes and subsequent effects;

4. Formulate conclusions; and

5. Formulate generalizations.

How to Plan Lessons Using the Interpretation of Data Strategy

During the planning phase, you need to select the content to be addressed, determine what data is needed and what materials will be used as references, and decide how the data will be gathered and organized. Materials need not be limited to textbooks; other possible resources include films, filmstrips, overhead transparencies, demonstrations or experiments, magazines, interviews with people, etc. Data may be gathered by individuals working independently, by small groups of students, or by the class working and sharing together.

Plan for the discussion which needs to take place prior to presenting the data. Develop focusing questions for each step in the process, and consider possible responses students might give as well as support procedures that might be needed. Decide how to present focusing questions for each step; i.e., a worksheet, a set of sequenced cards, a list of questions posted on newsprint, a teacher-led discussion, etc.

Careful planning is needed to make this strategy work successfully but be sure that your plan does not dictate the number of possible relationships students will make during the process. Do not restrict students' discussions and explorations to only those elements you have determined in advance. Use your plan as a starting point which allows students to explore any number of possible relationships among the data and to reach as many conclusions as are warranted.

The lesson which follows, "The Box and the Jar: A Comparison of Containers," demonstrates a sample plan for using the comparison of containers to lead students to explore the effects of differences in materials, size, shape, and design or the purposes for which the containers are used. Note that while this plan enumerates focus questions for each step, classroom management issues are not addressed. Would you use this lesson with a whole class? How could it be make appropriate for use in a learning center? What changes would you make to allow small groups to go through each step?

Putting the Interpretation of Data Strategy to Work in Your Classroom

You are the initiator for each step in the process of interpreting data. You ask or arrange to present the focusing questions, record or verify student responses (when necessary), prompt or cue students to facilitate discussion, and help students to follow a sequence of activities which you have determined in advance.

You want to lead your students through each step in the Interpretation of Data Strategy, from collecting data to drawing conclusions. Examine the steps and initiating questions in the lesson which follows. Notice how the questioning leads students through each step in sequence.

You want your students to examine the data and identify points of information. You want them to look for cause and effect relationships among the data and to support their inferences by giving evidence or explanation. You want them to extend and support prior causes and/or subsequent effects or inferences they have made. Finally, you want them to arrive at conclusions and generalizations from the explanations.

How to Evaluate the Interpretation of Data Strategy

Evaluation takes place during and after student performance. Monitor students' abilities to perform necessary operations in order to complete each step in the process. If students have not developed the necessary inference skills, it is unlikely that significant generalizations will be formulated.

While students are working with the Interpretation of Data Strategy, you should provide them with descriptive and intuitive feedback on both the role and the tasks to be accomplished. Use descriptive feedback to acknowledge and reinforce student responses, and intuitive feedback to expand the number of alternative responses students develop in each step of the process.

Help students to evaluate their own responses by asking them to justify their reasoning. Self-correction or modification is important to the process. Use value feedback to encourage the entire group.

When students finish, you should lead them in a discussion of the thinking abilities they used to complete the process. Additionally, help students to formulate criteria for evaluating their own generalizations.

It is important to define the term generalization as well as to distinguish it from the term concept. Both concepts and generalizations are end products of a process of differentiation. They result from judgments applicable to a whole class of events which are often based on experience with a limited number of members of that same class. They differ in the fact that the concept label is represented by a single word, while the generalization is represented by a sentence distinguishing a relationship among concepts.

Both generalizations and concepts exist in a hierarchy of abstractions and degrees of inclusiveness. Each hierarchy is both widely ranging and intertwined with the other because, just as a series of concepts can makeup a generalization, a highly abstract concept can only be understood or arrived at through a series of generalizations.

In working with your students to formulate criteria for examining generalizations, you need to look at the issue of inclusiveness. Inclusiveness relates to the students' ability to generalize across a broad spectrum of possible meanings. The most effective generalizations are those which have the greatest depth of meaning. Based on this rationale, a response to the question, "What kind of people are those you read about in the story," would more appropriately be, "They were people who were concerned about physical fitness," rather than one which says, "They worked out every day." Inclusiveness means to generalize upward to the most comprehensive idea.

Another useful criterion for examining generalizations with your students is tentativeness. Generalizations by nature are derived from a sample of a total population. Generalizations should not be seen as absolute truth since there is usually more information on a particular topic than can ever be known by the person generalizing about it. Generalizations that include some kind of limitation should be rated higher than generalizations that do not. Encourage your students to avoid words like all, always, never, every, and instead use terms such as many, some, often, and seldom.

Generalizations should provide important distinctions while avoiding vagueness. Another criterion, therefore, is the use of qualifying elements which describe the limits of a particular generalization. A statement such as "When… then…" includes a qualifying element.

Another criterion is applicability. Generalizations should yield hypotheses or predictions about other similar situations.

Accuracy and precision are other criteria to include. Statements should be supported by evidence.

It is essential that you provide your students with many opportunities to form generalizations about the important elements in what they read, hear, and see. By providing your students with criteria for examining their generalizations, you will assist your students to learn to think conceptually. Encourage your students to focus on one criterion at a time. Tentativeness or inclusiveness is a good place to begin.

Summary

When to use it:
When you want students to develop the ability to interpret data, infer causes and effects, and produce generalizations.

How to use it:
1. Enumerate relevant data;
2. Infer cause and effect;
3. Infer prior causes and subsequent effects;
4. Formulate conclusions; and
5. Formulate generalizations.

How to evaluate it:
1. Use descriptive feedback to acknowledge and reinforce student responses;
2. Use intuitive feedback to expand the number of alternative responses in each step of the process; and
3. Help students to formulate and apply criteria for evaluating their own generalizations.

Things to remember:
1. Plan for the discussion which needs to take place prior to presenting the data;
2. Plan focusing questions for each step in the process, and consider possible responses students might give;
3. Do not restrict students' exploration of possible relationships among the data; and
4. Be aware of students' developmental level, and the effect on students' ability to use the generalizing process.

Sample Lesson I:
The Box and the Jar—
A Comparison of Containers

Purpose:

To draw warranted conclusions about the effects of differences in design, material employed, and purpose for which the containers can be used.

Process:

To make and support cause and effect inferences, to draw conclusions, and to generalize from specific inferences.

A. Data Collection:

What are some ways in which these containers are alike and different?

B. Causes and Effects:

- Cause: What do you think are some of the reasons jar lids screw on and off, and box lids usually lift on and off?

- Cause: Why do you think jars are made of glass and boxes made of paper? (cardboard)

- Cause: Items that are wet have water in them. What does this have to do with which type of container you would use to hold wet items?

- Effect: Why do you think jar lids screw on and off whereas box lids just fit over the edge?

- Effect: Why might things spill out of a box more easily?

- Effect: What are some things that might happen because a jar is glass and a box paper?

- Cause: What is the purpose or advantage of a jar being made of glass?

- Cause: If a picture on a box was different from its contents, would that make a difference?

- Cause: What did the makers have in mind when they invented jars and boxes?

- Effect: Jars break more easily than boxes. What do people do because of this?

- Effect: Glass jars are often dangerous when broken. What inferences can you make for the use of jars with small children?

- Effect: What happens when wet items are put in paper boxes?

C. Conclusions:

Thinking back to all that has been said about glass jars, what would you say about glass jars with screw-on lids? What happens because a box is cardboard paper and has a loose lid? Have students speculate why earlier peoples made greater use of jars than they did boxes.

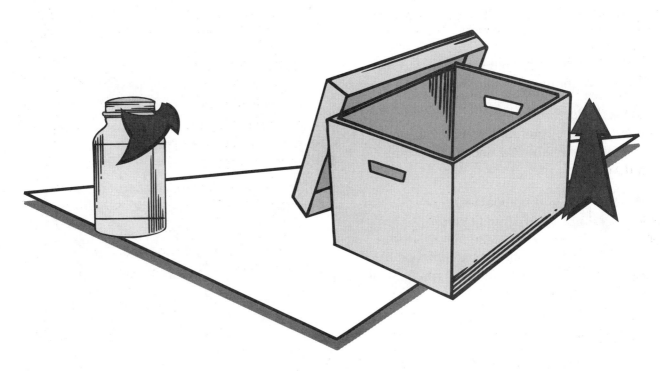

D. Generalizations and Support:

What would you say happens because the jar and the box are different in so many ways? Explain why you believe earlier peoples made greater use of jars than they did boxes.

COMPARISON OF CONTAINERS		LEVEL: EARLY ELEMENTARY
Possible Immediate and Prior Causes	Possible Responses Possible Data	Possible Immediate and Subsequent Effects
JAR	DIFFERENCES	BOX
Easier to hold—fits into hand—Jar: round Would not leak—holds wet things, liquids— has water in it Know what you are getting—can see inside— glass to make		Square—stacks—takes up less room Has shoes—dry items—wet things leak through inside Made of paper (cardboard)—cheaper, easier —disposable: i.e., don't need to keep shoes inside

Has lid that screws on:
  Items stay fresher—items do not dry out
  Keeps things longer—does not spill
  Hard to unscrew:
    Need help to open it
    Safety: keep small children out
		Lid fits on edges—easy to open—shoes spill out—wouldn't break

Dangerous: use with caution—Breaks when dropped—brittle		Bends easily—Loses shape easily—wears out: needs to be discarded

Sample lesson II: Animal Adaptation

Purpose:

To draw conclusions based on evidence to support how animals adapt to their environment.

A. Data Collection:

Have students carefully examine the picture of the fantastic animals. Propose the following questions:

- What do you notice about them?

- How are they similar/different?

Consider their anatomy, apparent mode of movement, and any other features you think are important to their way of living.

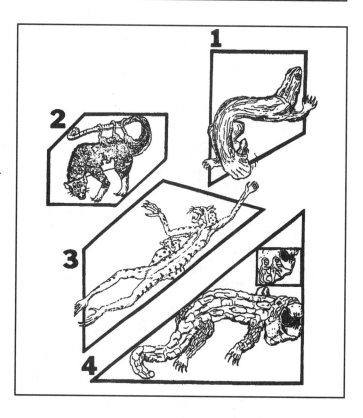

B. Causes and Effects:

Ask students what they think are some possible causes or reasons for the differences in physiology of these animals. Have them consider how these differences would affect the ways in which they gather food, hunt, care for their young, and defend themselves.

Ask students to hypothesize about these animals. If they are animals of the future, why do you suppose they evolved in certain ways to be different from their immediate predecessors?

C. Conclussions:

Finally, have students form conclusions and generate action by asking them to think back to all that has been said about these futuristic animals. Ask for any generalizations they consider to be true about how the animals change and adapt to their environment.

APPLICATION OF PRINCIPLES STRATEGY

The Application of Principles Strategy is designed to help students apply generalizations, explain new phenomena, or predict consequences from conditions which have been established.

The Strategy at Work

For a sixth grade science unit on the food chain, Ms. Burns used an adaptation of a lesson on prey and predators developed by Carl Carozza. To introduce the topic, she used an Inductive Learning Worksheet:

Directions: Look at the chart of animals below. What do some of these animals have in common? How could you group them? What might the name or label for each group be?

After giving her students time to collaborate in small groups, she discussed how each animal might be described.

Then, moving into the Interpretation of Data Strategy, Ms. Burns asked her students to work together to identify features, traits, or characteristics about each animal which might categorize them or have an effect on how they behave, live, and survive. Under her guidance, the students investigated comparisons and contrasts, and patterns they saw among animals or groups of animals. They considered the question: How could these animals relate to each other? How does this affect the overall scheme of things in nature?

When her students had developed generalizations regarding the relationships between predators and prey, Ms. Burns gave them the following Interpretation of Data worksheet to consider:

PREY AND PREDATOR CYCLE

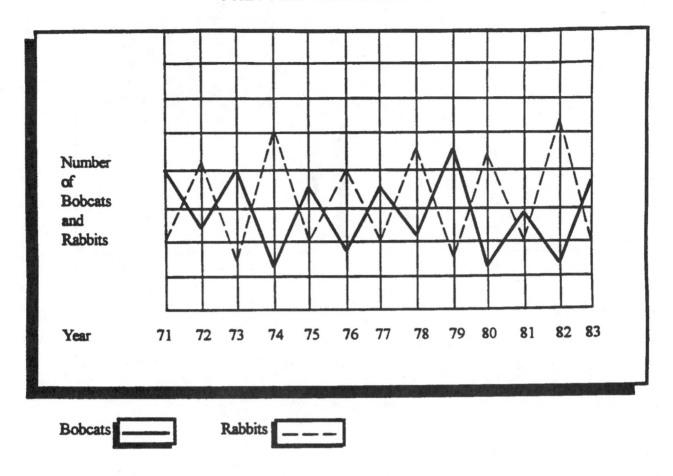

Bobcats [———]　　Rabbits [– – –]

Directions:

1. Look at the Prey and Predator chart. What can you say about it?

2. a. What do you notice about the number of bobcats?

   b. What do you notice about the number of rabbits?

   c. In what year were there the most bobcats?

   d. In what year were there the most rabbits?

3. What pattern(s) do you see emerging from the information on this chart?

4. Can you identify and explore possible causes and effects of this trend or pattern?

After discussing the patterns, relationships, and generalizations developed, Ms. Burns asked her students to consider the following Application of Principles question:

What do you think would happen to the predator and prey cycle if engineers discovered that a large amount of oil lay underground in the area where the bobcats and rabbits live?

This question required Ms. Burns' students to analyze the nature of the problem and retrieve relevant facts, principles, and generalizations from their previous work on predators and prey. It also required them to use support material Ms. Burns had provided to determine how the presence of a large amount of a natural resource such as oil might change the context of the situation.

Ms. Burns' students worked together to predict the consequences of the oil discovery, and to explain and support their predictions. They used factual knowledge and principles of logic to verify their predictions, and considered their feasibility.

The Application of Principles Strategy

The Application of Principles Strategy is designed to improve students' thinking abilities, and to emphasize the application of generalizations, principles, and facts derived by students from the Inductive Learning and Interpretation of Data Strategies.

These three strategies—Inductive Learning, Interpretation of Data, and Application of Principles—are seen as sequential steps in expanding students' capacities to handle information, develop new concepts, develop new ways of applying established principles, and apply established principles in new situations.

The goals of the Application of Principles Strategy are:

1. To help students predict consequences, explain unfamiliar phenomena, and hypothesize;

2. To help students explain and/or support predictions and hypotheses; and

3. To help students verify predictions.

Again, as in both Inductive Learning and Interpretation of Data Strategies, the teacher can organize student thinking over three areas: overt behaviors, covert mental operations, and focusing questions.

The steps in the Application of Principles Strategy are to:

1. Present an organized body of information based on prerequisite activities;

2. Identify and describe the facts, principles, and/or generalizations with which the students are to work;

3. Look for patterns;

4. Present a problem which involves changing something;

5. Predict consequences of the change;

6. Explain or support predictions or hypotheses; and

7. Verify the predictions or hypotheses.

How to Plan Lessons Using the Application of Principles Strategy

Your first step in planning an Application of Principles Strategy lesson is to consider the prerequisite activities that have taken place and to identify the facts, principles, and/or generalizations with which you want your students to work. The next step is to design a problem and to plan for the necessary initiating or focusing questions. The problem you pose should create a new content in which your students will apply previous knowledge to generate possible hypotheses.

OVERT BEHAVIORAL OBJECTIVES	COVERT THINKING OBJECTIVES	FOCUSING QUESTIONS (GENERAL)
Predicting consequences, explaining unfamiliar phenomena and hypothesizing	Analyze the nature of the problem or situation; retrieve relevant knowledge.	What would happen if...?
Explaining and/or supporting predictions and hypotheses	Determine the causal links leading to prediction or hypothesis.	Why do you think this would happen?
Verifying the prediction	Use logical principals or factual knowledge to determine necessary and efficient conditions.	What would it take for ____ to be generally true or probably true?

Consider ways to present a review of the facts, principles, and/or generalizations elicited through previous activities. The information should be presented in an organized way, perhaps through a visual organizer, a matrix, or a flow chart. Choose your format, and organize the body of information to be presented. Develop questions which will lead your students to describe the data and look for patterns and relationships.

How will you pose the problem you have designed? What possible predictions or hypotheses might your students develop? What kind of support material might you provide to make the lesson more effective? Consider also the way in which you want your students to address the problem or issue; i.e., through independent work, in small groups, or in a large group. How will predictions and hypotheses, together with supporting evidence, be gathered, organized, recorded, and shared?

Putting the Application of Principles Strategy to Work in Your Classroom

Present the organized body of information from prior activities through a visual organizer, matrix, flow chart, or other device. Ask focusing questions which lead your students to describe the data and to find patterns and relationships.

Have your students review the previously developed hypotheses and generalizations.

At this point, your students are ready to contemplate the problem or issue you have designed. How will the change you propose create a fresh context for students to think about? For example, in a social studies lesson, if you wanted your students to apply the generalization that particular geographical features affect the manner, rate, and type of development in an area, you might ask: What are some possible consequence for the development of the United States if rivers flowed west to east instead of north to south? Such a question produces an unusual construct within which to apply previous thinking to develop new predictions or hypotheses.

Once the problem has been stated, identify resources that are available for your students to use in their inquiry. Bring up pertinent facts when necessary. Set guidelines for recording and sharing responses, and help students to verify their predictions.

Your students need to address the problem, predict the consequences, think divergently, and consider what is possible. As a result of this activity, they will be ready to formulate hypotheses about the problem. Once they have formulated hypotheses, they must acquire evidence to support their ideas and determine their feasibility. Their last step is to verify their predictions by designing experiments or demonstrations which illustrate their hypotheses and how they apply.

How to Evaluate the Application of Principles Strategy

Focus on the content and process of the strategy when evaluating it. The content evaluation attends to the students' ability to use previously acquired knowledge to address a new situation. What concepts or generalizations did the students apply? What evidence did they use to support their hypotheses? How able were they to design their own activity, demonstration, or experiment in order to verify their hypotheses? How effective was the activity? What conclusions were indicated by the results?

As is generally the case, it is important that students be actively involved in the evaluation process. You need to serve as a facilitator to assist your students in establishing their own criteria for evaluating their performance.

Summary

When to use it:

When you want students to develop the ability to predict consequences, explain and support predictions, and verify predictions.

How to use it:

1. Present an organized body of information based on prerequisite activities;

2. Identify and describe the facts, principles, and/or generalizations with which the students are to work;

3. Look for patterns;

4. Present a problem which involves changing something;

5. Predict consequences of the change;

6. Explain or support predictions or hypotheses; and

7. Verify the predictions or hypotheses.

How to evaluate it:

1. Were students able to use previously acquired knowledge to address a new situation?

2. Were students able to support their hypotheses? How feasible were their hypotheses?

3. Were students able to design their own activity, demonstration, or experiment to verify their hypotheses?

Things to remember:

1. Present previously elicited facts, principles, and generalizations as an organized body of knowledge;

2. Plan focusing questions for each step in the process, and consider possible responses students might give; and

3. Do not restrict students' exploration of possible predictions and hypotheses, but encourage them to use logical principles or factual knowledge to determine necessary and adequate conditions for their ideas.

Sample Lesson I: Theme—What's Behind a Name?

I. Inductive Learning
A. Listing:

Pretend you founded a new town or city in a brand new place where no settlement had ever been before. What would be the name you would choose?

B. Grouping:

List choices on the board.

Do any of these names you have chosen go together in any way?

Why do you think so?

C. Labeling

What can we call these different groups? (descriptive, possessive, commemorative, euphemistic)

II. Interpreting Data

A. Identifying Points:

Display a map of the United States. The circles on this map all have the same name. Some are cities, some are towns or counties, and some are the names of physical features. Make a guess about what the name is, (hypothesizing). Inform students since it is almost impossible to guess that the name is Buffalo.

What do you notice about where the names are found?

Why is this so? Why are so many places named Buffalo?

Can you think of other names that may have once been descriptive but no longer are?

B. Making Generalizations:

What are some of the things we can conclude after our discussion about places and names? Work in small groups; then share with the entire class.

C. Making Inferences:

What can you say about names of places which don't seem to mean much to us now?

Why do you think people give names to places?

D. Making Generalizations:

Do places have names that absolutely belong to them and have always been used?

Do you think that some day New York might have a different name?

What are some of the names New York used to be called?

III. Application of Principles

A. Predicting Consequences:

Suppose that suddenly the government passed a law that overnight all places named had to commemorate important national events or honor national heroes or presidents. What would happen?

B. Explaining the Prediction:

Ask the students to explain and verify predictions.

What would happen if places didn't have names at all?

C. Verifying the Prediction:

Can anybody tell us how to get from your house to school without using any names at all? Try this in your small groups. Is there any other kind of experiment we could perform to verify the fact that a lack of names would make things difficult?

4

CHAPTER FOUR

Self-Expressive Strategies

OVERVIEW OF THE SELF-EXPRESSIVE STRATEGIES (NF)

In the Self-Expressive Strategies the emphasis is on the acquisition of knowledge and skills through creative and divergent thinking, aesthetic/artistic expression, clarification of values, and analysis of moral dilemmas. In this position the teacher provides students with challenges or dilemmas for which they are to generate solutions. Teaching behavior focuses on promoting student curiosity, insight, imagination, and metaphorical thinking. Self-Expressive Strategies emphasize originality, flexibility, the ability to see old things in new ways and new things in different ways. The teacher's role seeks to expand students' thinking rather than direct it. The self-expressive environment values creativity and ingenuity.

The teaching strategies described include Divergent Thinking, Metaphorical Teaching, Inductive Learning, and Dilemma Decision Making.

In the *Divergent Thinking Strategy*, students engage in flexible and creative thinking in response to the teacher's evocative questions. The purpose is to break the students' mind-sets or rigid response patterns so that they can discover new possibilities for previously unseen relationships. This strategy values the student's ability to be fluent in enumerating new ideas and images. The teacher's role is to be flexible in generating alternatives and originality in coming up with new and different ideas, to challenge students to go beyond their initial responses, and to encourage risk-taking by providing intuitive feedback and minimizing the temptation to give out the correct answers or value judgements. This strategy references the work of J. P. Guilford (1967).

In the *Inductive Learning Strategy*, students use specific situations, objects, and ideas to arrive at generalizations, principles, or rules. In this process, students observe phenomena, compare and contrast attributes, and group things together to form a general statement that is applicable to a class or group of objects or situations. This strategy, developed by Hilda Taba, enhances thinking ability requiring students to generate and group data, and to formulate their own concepts. The role of the teacher is to determine the concept to be addressed, and to plan for ways to present or elicit the data.

In the *Dilemma Decision Making Strategy*, students engage in identifying, clarifying and selecting alternative solutions to moral dilemmas. The purpose of the strategy is to assist students in recognizing the various positions that can be taken when looking at moral issues. Based on the long term research of Lawrence Kohlberg (1973) and Carol Gilligan (1982), students are introduced to the stages of moral development represented in Kohlberg's justice/rights orientation to moral choice and the qualities which mark the care/responsibility orientation to moral choice described by Gilligan. Through the process of considering hypothetical and real-life dilemmas, students come to appreciate the issue of choice in making moral decisions. The role of the teacher is to select the moral dilemma to be resolved, plan an effective presentation of the dilemma, facilitate discussion and conduct an analytic review of the problem-solving process.

DIVERGENT THINKING STRATEGY

The Divergent Thinking Strategy is designed to help students explore problems in fresh and unconventional ways. The teacher asks an evocative question to stimulate students to engage in fluent, flexible, and creative thinking. Student responses are original, divergent, and elaborative.

The Strategy at Work

Mr. Samuels' eighth grade pre-algebra section is about to review the basic concept of numbers. To introduce the concept that the number symbols we write and see are not numbers but names for numbers, Mr. Samuels has asked his class to consider the question: "How many ways can you make '10'?" His students have taken three minutes to write down as many ways to make ten as they can, and now he has asked them to share their ideas so that he can make a class list.

The first responses included "8 + 2," "1 + 9," "20 x $\frac{1}{2}$," "60 - 50," and so on. Mr. Samuels then asked his students to share their lists with a neighbor to come up with new and different ways. As a result, one student says "Ten—I mean the word." Another says "Dix;" another, "Zed;" another, "Diece." Still other students come up with the Roman numeral "X;" then "XX - X;" "5 + 2 + 3;" "(4 x 2) + 2;" and "Four squared take away six." Mr. Samuals continues to push his students to come up with new and different ways when Joey calls out excitedly, "I have one, I have one." He sits up very straight, with a smug expression, and holds both hands—palms and fingers outstretched—straight up in the air. At first the students are confused, but then the class bursts into laughter—then Amy says, "Look! Ten fingers!"

The Divergent Thinking Strategy

The Divergent Thinking Strategy is designed to help students explore problems in fresh and unconventional ways, and to encourage them to engage in fluent, flexible, elaborate and original thinking. The goal is to move from the usual to the unusual. Rather than settling for one immediate or "correct" response, students search for a variety of solutions, patterns, and insights to a given problem.

The goals of the Divergent Thinking Strategy are:

1. To help students explore problems in fresh and unconventional ways;

2. To help students view a problem in a variety of contexts;

3. To help students realize that there is not always one correct solution to a given problem;

4. To help students engage in fluent thinking; i.e., in brainstorming, or producing different ideas or categories which reflect changes in meaning, interpretation, use, understanding, or direction of thinking;

5. To help students engage in original thinking, i.e., in producing unusual, imaginative, or clever responses, which may be novel, either for the individuals who have them, or for the group;

6. To help students engage in elaborate thinking; i.e., in expanding upon previous original ideas; and

7. To demonstrate increased creative expression through fluent, flexible, elaborate, and original thinking.

The steps in the Divergent Thinking Strategy are to:

1. Present to students an evocative question;

2. Encourage students to engage in divergent thinking;

3. Withhold or minimize the use of corrective feedback so as not to inhibit the flow of ideas; and

4. Evaluate the quality of thinking with students by helping them to look for evidence in their responses of fluency, flexibility, originality, complexity, and elaboration.

How to Plan Lessons Using the Divergent Thinking Strategy

You want to consider using the Divergent Thinking Strategy with your students whenever you want them to develop a wide range of possibilities; free, fluid expression of ideas; predictions; exploration; fanciful or aesthetically pleasing options. The emphasis is on encouraging students to find multiple patterns or solutions for a particular problem.

Divergent Thinking may be used for all subject areas and topics. You need to select the content to be addressed, and design an evocative question. You might ask students to think of all the possible things that could have happened to Goldilocks and the Three Bears if they hadn't been afraid of each other, or to imagine the consequences for United States history had the Dred Scott case been decided in favor of the plaintiff; or you might ask students to demonstrate how they might convey sadness to an audience; or you might ask students to see how many ways they can form closed figures using square units and still obtain perimeters of 36 units. The first four tasks are examples of evocative questions which have internally verifiable answers. The students' answers to these four questions are based on individual attitudes, values and perceptions; and, while some might be more feasible than others, as far as divergent expression is concerned, they are all correct. The last task, on the other hand, is an example of an evocative question having multiple responses which can be verified externally; each response can be compared with the criteria closed figure, made of square units, perimeter of 36 units to determine whether the answer is correct.

In this strategy, you cannot plan for the number of appropriate responses, nor can you determine the quality of acceptable responses prior to the lesson. You want to create a climate in which free and spontaneous responses are accepted by all. To this end, consider the mode of expression—speaking, writing, movement—which you will use, and the support equipment or materials which may be needed to enhance the active search for solutions.

Putting the Divergent Thinking Strategy to Work in Your Classroom

When you are ready to implement the Divergent Thinking Strategy in your classroom for the first time, you need to set the scene by explaining what divergent thinking is to generate many different respones to a question, and by emphasizing the need for students to break with traditional mind-sets. By breaking the mind-set, we mean to break stereotypic

patterns of thinking. Students need to know that they will think and feel differently when they are engaged in divergent thinking, and that all responses are valuable, no one response more than any other.

An introductory activity to allow students to experience the process of breaking a mind-set is often helpful. You may wish to ask your students to work in small groups or with a partner to decide how to draw three straight lines which will connect all four dots and form a closed figure:

Students initially assume that the lines must be drawn within the perimeter established by the four dots; most people look at the positions of the dots and "see" a square. However, this assumption makes it impossible to solve the problem. Students must set this assumption aside and experiment with other shapes in order to find a solution. For example:

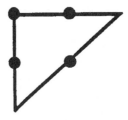

Can your students come up with any other ways to solve this problem? Are their responses truly different from one another, or are they variations within the same category of response?

While this activity demonstrates the need to break the traditional mind-set, you may also wish to encourage your students to experience and discuss the process of generating multiple solutions to a problem. Give each of your students a Cheerio and ask them to list as many uses as they can think of for it. Stimulate your students to think in new and different ways by accepting all ideas, and by asking, "Who has another idea" or "Who is thinking about this in a different way?" Devise ways to ask the students to go on further, or to think of alternative responses; for example, "What if you were the same size as the Cheerio? What kinds of uses do you think you would find?"

In the Divergent Thinking Strategy, your students are involved in making quality decisions based on their ability to generate novel and unusual responses. Quality depends on previous experience with the problem, ability to think divergently, and the intent and intensity exhibited in generating multiple solutions. Quality is often linked to quantity. The greater the number of ideas produced, the greater the number of high quality ideas.

As you work with your students, consider whether they produce more and better ideas working alone or working in groups. Some researchers contend that the response of one peer stimulates another and allows for greater elaboration of ideas. Osborne reports that about a third of the ideas produced in group brainstorming sessions are of the "hitchhiking" type. Taylor (1960), however, found a larger number of non-repeated ideas produced by individuals working alone than by those working in groups. You may want to try a combination of approaches, giving students some time to formulate and jot down their own responses, and then encouraging them to brainstorm with the group.

In the Divergent Thinking Strategy, you need to look for ways to provide students with intuitive feedback which will continue to stimulate student thinking. Intuitive feedback may sound like this: "Is that a possibility? Does anyone have another idea to offer? Can we think about this differently? Is there another approach? What if so and so happened? What if we turn this upside down?" Each response should encourage the students to go further, to continue to search for new ideas and alternative responses. Minimize the use of corrective or value feedback which generally can be verified externally; i.e., if all possible responses can be determined to be correct or incorrect, it is important for you to assist students in making their own corrective decisions.

How to Evaluate the Divergent Thinking Strategy

In the evaluation phase, students should engage in verifying their solutions whenever appropriate. They should determine fluency by counting the number of ideas generated. They should group their responses to assess flexibility and elaboration, and to identify responses which are original either to themselves or to the group.

Summary

When to use it:
When you want your students to explore a situation in new and different ways.

How to use it:
1. Prepare "evocative" questions or activities for students to think about divergently;

2. Encourage students to think fluently, flexibly, and originally, urge them to elaborate on their ideas; and

3. Record and verify student responses when necessary.

How to evaluate it:
1. Are students able to think:

   fluently—count the number of ideas;

   flexibly—group similar ideas, and count the number of different ideas;

   originally—note unique ideas;

   elaborately—count number of ideas built off other ideas; and

2. Are the students able to break from "stereotypic" ideas?

Things to remember:
1. Corrective and value feedback on the part of either the teacher or other students may inhibit the flow of ideas; intuitive or possibility feedback stimulates the flow of ideas;

2. Students need to go beyond the obvious, to break their "mind-set." Create cognitive dissonance or mental strain by asking for another new and different idea, or by suggesting a fresh perspective;

3. The quantity of ideas often breeds quality; and

4. Original responses may be novel for the individual responding, or for the group as a whole.

Sample Lesson I: Mathematics—Why do we measure?

Ms. Ansima planned to provide her third grade students with an opportunity to develop a conceptual understanding of measurement through the use of flexible and creative thinking.

Objectives:

Ms. Ansima wanted her students to use divergent thinking to explore the reasons for measurement, and, through this process, to develop a conceptual understanding of measurement.

Anticipatory Set:

Since her students had not used divergent thinking before, Ms. Ansima told them that they would be examining some ordinary ideas, but that they would be asked to look at those ideas from a different perspective. She explained that often there is more than one way of looking at something, and that she wanted them to explore ideas about a topic in a creative and original way.

As an example of the value of changing perspective, Ms. Ansima read *Amelia* by Peggy Parish, and had her students list the humorous interpretations of "dressing" the chicken and "trimming" the steak that Amelia Bedelia used.

Next, Ms. Ansima told her students that they would be working in groups on a project to find as many possible answers, humorous or serious, ordinary or original, as they could to a basic question, and that any answer that "worked" would count.

Procedures:

Ms. Ansima divided the class into groups of four students, and provided each group with a large piece of butcher paper on which to record their work. She told them that the topic for the day was MEASURING, and the question they needed to consider was WHY

DO WE? She told them that they would have exactly five minutes to write down as many different answers to this question as they could. She asked them to close their eyes and think for a minute about the question, "Why do we measure?", while she set her timer. After giving the students a brief period to prepare, she announced that the students were to begin.

Ms. Ansima was delighted to see how quickly the groups went to work, and how well they stayed on task. Only John's group had a brief argument about who would do the writing, but it was settled before she could intervene when Ricardo pointed out that they were wasting time. Annal's group decided that each person should write his or her own ideas on a section of the butcher paper as soon as they were shared to make sure they were really different, but all of the other groups chose a secretary.

When the five-minute limit was up, all of the students begged for more time. After promising to give them another try Ms. Ansima asked the groups to share their results, and she recorded all of their answers on a master list without evaluative comment or feedback.

WHY DO WE MEASURE?

to buy shoes	to tell how far
to win a broad jump	to say how much
to make a new dress	to put butter in a recipe
to share a soda	to tell what size
to see what you weigh	to see how tall you are
to see how old you are	etc.

Then she pointed out that some of the answers might suggest some other possibilities, and that some students might have additional ideas that were different from those already recorded. She allowed the groups to meet for an additional five minutes to explore new ideas.

After recording the additional answers on the master list, Ms. Ansima suggested that the students see how many different groups or patterns could be found by organizing the answers in some way. As students worked to make groups, they noticed that some items on their list, such as "to put butter in a recipe," could belong to more than one group, e.g., "Measuring to cook," and "measuring the weight." Students also saw additions that could be made: "Measuring age" suggested additional items related to measuring time, using clock and calendar.

When the solutions had been classified in different ways, Ms. Ansima asked the students to think of a way to represent the answers to the question, "why do we measure?", in an art project such as a poster or collage.

Sample Lesson II: USA in 100 years

Mr. Walsh decided to use the Divergent Thinking Strategy in his ninth-grade social studies class to begin a lesson on the fall of ancient Rome.

Anticipatory Set:

He began the lesson by asking his students which country they thought was the most powerful in the world. Everyone in the class said it was America. He then said, "Suppose this was 100 years from now and I asked the same question to my class and no one in the room said the USA as a possible answer. What would have had to happen during the past 100 years for this to be so?

Procedures:

Mr. Walsh told his students to write down two different ideas; then, he told them to use the "Give one, get one" technique to generate new ideas. He reminded his students that in "Give one, get one" each student met with another student to exchange new ideas. If they had the same ideas, they had to brainstorm together to get a new idea. Then they went off to work with a new partner. The goal was to generate as many new and different ideas as they could in five minutes.

After five minutes, the students met in groups of four to share the ideas they had collected. They listed how many different ideas they had about why the United States was no longer considered the world's most powerful country. Mr. Walsh then collected the classes' ideas on

the board. He was impressed with their thinking. He pointed out that they were to begin a unit on the fall of ancient Rome and that this activity had already generated the reasons for Rome's fall before they even began their research.

Sample Lesson III: Frog and Toad

Miss Lopez used the Divergent Thinking Strategy to help her students generate a potential solution to a problem Frog and Toad were having in a book they were reading by Arnold Lobel.

Anticipatory Set:

The lesson began by asking students to think about a time they had a problem with a friend and what they did to solve it. She explained that Divergent Thinking was a good technique for generating ideas when you had a problem to be solved.

Procedures:

The students were presented with a problem Frog and Toad were having. They had baked cookies. They tasted so good they couldn't stop eating them. They knew if they ate all the cookies they would get a bellyache and there would be none left for tomorrow. As hard as they tried, they couldn't stop eating the cookies. Then Miss Lopez asked her students to think divergently to come up with as many ideas as they could to help Frog and Toad. After they generated a long list, the class selected the one idea they thought would work best.

The solution they selected was to invite the rest of the animals to their house to have a party and serve the cookies. This way, all of the cookies would be eaten, but the other animals would reciprocate and would have parties of their own with other good foods. This would also prevent Frog and Toad from getting sick.

THE METAPHORICAL TEACHING STRATEGY

The Metaphorical Teaching Strategy is designed to engage students in metaphorical activity, stimulate their creativity, and to lead them to produce solutions reflecting new and different ways of thinking about a topic.

The Strategy at Work

Mr. Rothenhausler's Advanced Placement United States History classes have just finished studying the Civil War, and he has planned to repeat last year's successful review using the Metaphorical Teaching Strategy. His students arrive at third period to find that Mr. Rothenhausler has arranged to show a video.

When the class is settled and attendance taken, Mr. Rothenhausler explains that he will show the students a brief segment of a video, and that they are to observe as closely as possible. He tells them not to write during the video, that he will give them time to write about what they have seen immediately following the showing. He says "I know this is going to be primarily visual, but as you watch, try to bring all of your senses into play. Feel, hear, smell, and even taste what you are seeing."

The video Mr. Rothenhausler has selected explains how volcanoes are formed. The segment to which the video has been forwarded shows a volcanic eruption at night, the volcano spewing its insides. Lava flows showing brilliant red patches, trees on the mountain side bursting into flame. The section takes only a few minutes, but makes a dramatic statement. Following the video, Mr. Rothenhausler asks the class to write down what they have observed.

After three minutes, Mr. Rothenhausler asks his students to stop writing and to reread what they have written, underlining words and phrases that seem to capture the essence of the volcanic eruption they have just witnessed. When they have done so, he says, "Now… we have just finished studying a time of crisis in our nation, the Civil War. How was the Civil War like a volcano? Look at the time line we constructed to bring to mind the most important events of that period. Let's see what kinds of connections you can make between the events of the Civil War and the volcano you have just watched."

Last year Mr. Rothenhausler's two A.P. United States History classes ended this metaphoric exploration by producing a collage, poem, essay, or piece of artwork to display and share. Each artistic piece had to use specific information about the events of the Civil War to answer the question, "How was the Civil War like a volcano?" His favorite creative response to the question was an essay on the Battle of Gettysburg which built on the phrase another student had used in describing the volcano: terrifyingly beautiful. In the essay, the student evoked powerful images of honor, pride, patriotic duty, Lincoln's stirring words, the serenity of the rows on rows of crosses marking soldiers' graves, and contrasted them with equally powerful images of destruction, terror, death, families ripped apart, a nation at war with itself. Although this essay was especially compelling, Mr. Rothenhausler had been impressed with the thoughtfulness and vigor of all the artistic summaries his students had created to express their new insights. He plans to ask this year's students to do the same assignment using earthquakes as the metaphor.

The Metaphorical Teaching Strategy

In the Metaphorical Teaching Strategy, based on the pioneering work of W.J.J. Gordon (1961), students engage in a metaphoric journey using three different types of analogies: direct analogies, personal analogies, and compressed conflicts. The strategy is designed to help students make the strange familiar or the familiar strange. As with the Divergent Thinking Strategy, the role of the teacher is to pose evocative questions, to provide intuitive feedback, to encourage insightful responses, and to minimize judgements and evaluate responses.

A direct analogy is a simple comparison of two objects or concepts, such as "How is a novel like a river?" or "How is democracy like a diamond?" The function of a direct analogy is to help students detach from a topic in order to develop new insights about it. The direct analogy uses distance or strangeness between two ideas to foster creative exploration of topics often dealt with primarily through analytical thinking (NT).

A personal analogy requires that students involve themselves by personally identifying with the topic or object being examined. Students are asked to become part of the physical and emotional elements of the idea. Examples of personal analogies include, "How would it feel to be a rainbow without any color?" and "How would it feel to be the minus sign in a subtraction example?" Personal analogies allow students to use conceptual distance to expand personal involvement with the topic, and consequently, to increase creative thinking.

The compressed conflict analogy demands that students consider a topic or object by using two words that seem to be opposite or contradictory to each other. "How is silence soft and loud?" and "How is love joyful and painful?" and "How is water both a servant and a master?" are examples of compressed conflict analogies. Essential to the compressed conflict analogy is the ability to see a topic or object from two contrary frames of reference.

How is democracy like a diamond? Cheryl?...

It is like a diamond because it is valuable, and a product of long evolution.

I think it's because they are both imperfect.

The goals of the Metaphorical Teaching Strategy are:

1. To help students understand and experience the various psychological states necessary to creative thinking;

2. To draw students into the states of deferment, speculation, autonomy and innovation;

3. To use distance or strangeness between two ideas to foster creative exploration of a topic;

4. To use conceptual distance to increase personal involvement with a topic; and

5. To see a topic or object from two different frames of reference.

The steps in the Metaphorical Teaching Strategy are to:

1. Present to students a metaphorical question phrased as a direct analogy, personal analogy, or compressed conflict analogy;

2. Elicit from students ideas about the topic, problem, or idea addressed by the metaphorical question;

3. Analyze the direct analogy, personal analogy, or compressed conflict analogy;

4. Form original analogies about the topic; and

5. Continue to explore the topic.

Each of the metaphorical explorations— the direct analogy, the personal analogy, and the compressed conflict analogy—can be used separately or in combination. Metaphorical Teaching may function as a whole lesson, perhaps leading to a product, or as only a small part of a lesson, perhaps as an introduction or review of a topic. A lesson reviewing students' previous work on atoms may begin with the hook, "How is an atom like the wind?" A lesson explaining the layers of the Earth may end with students using a clear plastic straw to "drill" into a frosted, cream-filled cupcake, so that they may consider ways in which the Earth and the cupcake are alike. A lesson on earthquakes may be interrupted by asking students to imagine what it feels like to be a fault line just before an earthquake occurs. A unit on poetry may have students collecting and reflecting on favorite analogies; i.e. Robert Burn's "Oh,

my love is like a red, red, rose, that's newly sprung in June," or Lord Byron's "She was… the morning-star of memory," and writing parodies or making analogies of their own.

Just as the Write to Learn Strategy provides students with regular practice in thinking, so too does frequent use of the Metaphorical Teaching Strategy allow students to practice detaching from a topic, taking risks when generating ideas, searching for unconventional insights, and developing honest personal responses.

How to Plan Lessons Using the Metaphorical Teaching Strategy

You want to consider using Metaphorical Teaching with your students whenever you wish them to experience sufficient distance from a topic to engage in playful speculation leading to intuitive understanding. Through Metaphorical Teaching you help your students to see old problems, ideas, or products in a new, more creative light, and to make unfamiliar ideas more meaningful. The emphasis is on working with students to enable them to view the topic in an unconventional, rather than in a stereotypical, manner so that they may experience subtle, "aha," and in-depth understanding.

Deciding on a concept and the way in which a metaphorical question will be used in your lesson form the first steps in planning to use the Metaphorical Teaching Strategy. You need to choose a concept or topic which you would like students to investigate from a fresh viewpoint. Then consider whether you will use a metaphor to structure a whole lecture. Or, will it link prior lessons to the next? Will a metaphorical question lead to a review of previously learned information? Will it introduce a new idea?

If, for example, you want to introduce the concept of how the circulatory system works, and to provide information through a lecture format (New American Lecture Strategy), you might want to design your lesson around the metaphor of a toy train. In this case, your metaphorical question might be a direct analogy: "How is the circulatory system like a toy train?" Your visual organizer might support the metaphor through the use of artwork representing a set of toy trains and tracks. As you provide important facts about the parts of the circulatory system and the functions of each part, you want to plan ways in which students can extend the metaphor: train tracks and blood vessels; engine and heart; etc. In this situation, you are providing both the information on the new topic, and the direct analogy through which the information may be explored. The process may be extended by having the students invent their own direct analogies, or by using a personal or compressed conflict analogy to explore the topic from a different angle.

If you have already studied the immune system, you might want to use a metaphorical question to review previously presented information. Beginning a lesson with a brief consideration of the direct analogy, "How is the immune system like a platoon of soldiers," allows you to have students recall and recast what they have learned about the immune system, while you can efficiently assess their understanding of its functioning.

Once you have established the concept you want to teach, you need to formulate a direct analogy, personal analogy, or compressed conflict analogy with which to explore the concept. The goal here is to select an analogy which will create positive strain and elicit divergent thinking about the topic.

When your students are proficient at responding to metaphors of various types, you will want to have them create their own metaphors. When you use the strategy in this way, you will select a topic and plan a brief review of the various types of metaphors. The students, however, will offer the metaphors, and you will list them with their explanations. If the topic was democracy, for example, students might say, " Democracy is like a bird because in a democracy you are free to move," or "Democracy is like a tiger because you go after what you want and play the game of survival of the fittest." Students formulate and explain their own analogies.

Putting the Metaphorical Teaching Strategy to Work in Your Classroom

Begin by introducing a concept, problem, or task for students to explore divergently. Work with your students to create positive strain. Use the group process to facilitate creativity. Aim for fluency, flexibility, and originality. Use stretching activities and the metaphor you have created for the topic to provide examples of the analogy types you want your students to use. Use "intuitive feedback" such as "Who has another idea?" or "Close your eyes and imagine how this would look" to stimulate divergent answers. Minimize value feedback.

If you want your students to work at establishing direct analogies, define the term by telling the class that you want a simple comparison of two objects, concepts, procedures, or problems. Explain that you are looking for analogies that contrast the topic. Give examples of organic (living) and inorganic (non-living) connections to show how these types of analogies result in great strain. Elicit direct analogies, and have students explain how the topic is illustrated by the metaphor.

If you want your students to empathize with the idea, problem or task, you want them to be able to construct personal analogies. Again, define the term; explain that a personal identification with the object or idea may be expressed by a statement of how they would feel as the object or idea, how they would look, or how they would act. Move your students from descriptions of facts to identification of feelings, to an empathetic position combining the physical and emotional at a deeper level.

To have your students work with compressed conflict analogies, present two words that describe the same object or idea, but which are opposite or antagonistic to each other. Use these words to describe the object: "How is the sun both hot and cold?" Discuss and define the term, and encourage your students to create examples.

When you work with any of these metaphors, you may want to ask your students to use the metaphoric experience to express a new understanding of the topic through poetry, a collage, an essay, a picture, or a reaction statement in their Learning Logs.

How to Evaluate the Metaphorical Teaching Strategy

One way of evaluating the activities which result when the Metaphorical Teaching Strategy is used is to assess the quality of the metaphors as a measure of student creativity. When you look at the metaphors your students forge, consider both the level of involvement and the conceptual distance achieved. Look at final metaphors with an eye to determining how original or strained they are.

For direct analogies, the distance between the two topics or ideas is greater if the comparison is between organic (living) things and inorganic (non-living) things. The result is greater insight as a result of analyzing greater differences or polarities.

For personal analogies, assess the level of distance in terms of the student's identification with the object. A student who demonstrates kinesthetic involvement can get inside the living or non-living thing and show an understanding of its movements and actions. A student who demonstrates emotional involvement experiences a conscious loss of self while identifying with the feelings and understanding expressed through the analogy.

Students who are able to respond to or invent compressed conflict analogies in their most advanced form exhibit a poetic capacity. The quality of the compressed conflict analogies they devise can be judged by the surprise evoked by the contradictory statements describing the idea or object.

When you begin to discuss a topic with the intent of introducing a metaphoric activity, make particular note of the students' responses. Then compare these responses with those offered by your students after the metaphoric activity. Assess your students' fluency, flexibility, elaboration, and originality.

Summary

When to use it:

When you want students to think imaginatively about a previously learned topic or new topic through the use of metaphorical activity.

How to use it:

1. Describe the topic—list specific understandings;

2. Choose one or more of the following types of analogies:

   - Direct analogy—Describe and explore the direct analogy. "How is democracy like a diamond?"

   - Personal analogy—Form a personal analogy. Ask students to be the thing, to describe themselves emotionally and physically as the analogy. "What is a diamond like?" "What are its feelings?" Then compare their responses to the content being examined.

   - Compressed conflict analogy—Find a compressed conflict analogy—words which fight each other that might be used to describe the analogy. "How is a diamond delicate and tough?" Then compare it to democracy;

3. Separate analogy and content. Determine how they are different; and

4. Have students develop their own direct, personal, or compressed conflict analogies, and express their ideas through writing, art, or drama.

Things to remember:

1. Creativity can be enhanced by direct attempts to promote the creative process;

2. Imagination is a powerful tool for helping students to remember and understand new information;

3. Metaphorical activity attempts to give students experience in the following stages of the creative process (Gordon, 1961):

   • detachment

   • deferment

   • speculation

   • autonomy

   • intuition of rightness, or "aha" response; and

4. A direct analogy is a comparison of two objects or concepts: "How is a book like a river?" A personal analogy requires that students involve themselves personally by identifying with the object under analysis: "How does it feel to be a waterfall without color?" A compressed conflict analogy asks students to describe something using two words that seem to fight each other or are contradictory: "How is water soft and loud?"

Sample Lesson I:
Social Studies—The Kingdom of Kush (c. 800 B.C.—300 A.D.)

The information we have about the kingdom of Kush is fragmentary. While archaeologists are fairly certain about some information, there are major questions which remain to be answered. Consequently, it is helpful for students to have some sense of how archaeologists are able to infer from scant evidence, and how conflicting interpretations of data can exist. Dr. Griswold thinks it is possible to use this focus as a framework as her seventh graders study the kingdom of Kush.

Objectives:

In this lesson Dr. Griswold will ask her students to attempt to get information from an incomplete jigsaw puzzle to make predictions about what the completed puzzle might look like. Discussion of the process they employ will serve as a metaphor for the work of archaeologists who use bits and pieces of a civilization's artifacts to try to reconstruct the history of that civilization. In other words, how is the student's work to discover the whole jigsaw puzzle from examination of fragments of the puzzle like the work of archaeologists?

This activity is designed to encourage students to consider an underlying question:

How do we know what we think we know when we don't know very much?

Procedures:

Dr. Griswold has taken two 100-piece jigsaw puzzles, randomly separated each puzzle into sets of 25 pieces, and put sets into 8 unmarked envelopes.

She has also designed a work sheet to be filled out by the recorder for each group:

IT'S A PUZZLE

Prediction	Reason, Evidence, Support

Dr. Griswold divided the class into 8 groups, and gave each group one of the unmarked envelopes. Without telling the groups that their set was incomplete, she asked the groups to work together to put together their puzzle. She emphasized that the group's success will be determined NOT by their ability to complete the puzzle, but by their ability to correctly PREDICT what the completed puzzle would look like; for that reason, their record sheet was the most important part of the assignment.

Dr. Griswold took time to discuss the record sheet with the class. She had them notice that the recorder's sheet was divided into two columns: in one column, the recorder was to write any predictions that students in the group made; in the other, the recorder was to write the REASON or EVIDENCE or SUPPORT the students offered for their prediction. She made sure students understood that they MUST give reasons for their predictions and moreover, they could change their predictions or offer conflicting predictions, but they should not erase or cross out predictions they came to believe were inaccurate. While the groups worked, Dr. Griswold circulated, reminding the students that their success depended on their predictions, not on their ability to put the puzzle together.

After the students had worked for a time, Dr. Griswold had them discuss their puzzle predictions. A list of puzzle predictions was compiled. Then she asked the students to compare their predictions to the pictures on the puzzle box covers. How accurate were the predictions: Could the predictions be divided into groups: completely right, partly right, totally wrong? Did any group have a set of predictions that was totally wrong? What made it difficult to tell exactly what the finished puzzle would look like?

Continuing the discussion, Dr. Griswold and the students made a list of the REASONS or EVIDENCE students used for making their predictions. Then they grouped the evidence statements into categories of reasons: for example, some students used reasons that showed experience doing other jigsaw puzzles; others used reasons that showed they had made decisions about what the whole looks like when you can only see a part.

Finally, Dr. Griswold asked her students to make a list in their journals to answer the following question:

How is doing a jigsaw puzzle with missing pieces like the work of an archaeologist?

She listed and led a discussion of students' responses.

For homework, Dr. Griswold asked her students to make their own metaphor for the work of an archaeologist. She suggested that they try to see if they could think of a metaphor based on a personal experience. If they found their original metaphor pleasing or surprising, they would have the option of explaining it in prose writing or poetry, or representing it through art. They would then have the right to include this assignment as a first piece of "draft" work in their student portfolio for this unit.

Sample Lesson II: English—Wuthering Heights Character Analysis

Objectives:

In this lesson, Mr. Gurney wanted his students to develop a deeper understanding of the relationship between characters in a text. He also wanted his students to be able to think creatively and to express themselves metaphorically.

Procedures:

He began the lesson by having his class discuss what they knew about the relationship between Heathcliff and Kathy, the two main characters of the book. After a complete description, Mr. Gurney had his students form groups of four. He then took out a paper bag which had numerous objects inside of it; i.e., a can opener, scotch tape, staples, a clothes pin, an alarm clock, etc. He had each group select an object, describe it in detail, and then use it to describe the relationship between Heathcliff and Kathy in the story. Josh's group explained that the relationship was like an alarm clock going in circles; that it kept ticking and one day went off. Every time they tried to press the snooze button to put an end to the relationship, it went off again and could not be turned off. Each group shared their insights and Mr. Gurney listed them on the board. The class then found words from all that they had generated which could be used as compressed conflicts:

on/off

sensitive/strength

dramatic/boredom

passionate/pain

neverending/death

ringing/silence

The students selected one set of the compressed conflicts—ringing and silence—and generated a list of as many things as they could think of that could be described as "ringing silence." Some of the ideas were a bell without a clapper, a screaming yawn, and a stare of contempt. A bell without a clapper was selected as the most unusual. The students were then asked to freewrite for five minutes by "being" a bell without a clapper. Mr. Gurney asked his students to pretend that they were in fact the bell, and to try to get inside its heart and mind.

Mary explained that she would not feel "whole," that as much as she tried to ring out her cries would fall on deaf ears. Shawn said that he knew he was handicapped and would have to make up for it in other ways; that he needed to seek an alternative way to fulfill his mission in life.

Mr. Gurney then asked his students to read what they had written again, but this time to think of the bell as Heathcliff and Kathy's relationship. The students began to smile— they were surprised by what they had written and how it described the relationship.

Mr. Gurney ended the lesson by having his class write a one-page essay describing their new understanding of the relationship between Heathcliff and Kathy. The depth of writing and introspection was wonderful.

Sample Lesson III:
Social Studies—Martin Luther King

Objectives:
Miss Johnson wanted her students to develop a deeper understanding of struggle, in particular the struggle Dr. King was confronted with in changing the laws of the American South in the 1960s. Miss Johnson decided to use a direct analogy to help her students understand the concept of struggle.

Procedure:
She began her lesson by reading to her class a story about Dr. King and his non-violent approach to bringing about changes in the law. The class discussed some of the indignities blacks were faced with in the South, and that these indignities were a part of the law which needed to be changed.

She then had her students form small groups and gave them each a hand-held can opener with which to open a large can of peaches. At first Tom was not sure what the hand-held can opener was used for. Tanisha said she knew. Miss Johnson said to her class: "Your task is to use the can opener to open this can of peaches so you can enjoy what's inside."

Each group began to struggle with opening the can. How do you use a can opener? How do you attach it to the can? How would they turn the handle with their small fingers? How could they get enough pressure on the handle to make it turn?

After the students had experienced this struggle, Miss Johnson had them record all of their ideas about opening the can. She then asked, "How was this experience like the struggle Dr. King faced in changing the laws?" After exploring all of the connections, the students selected their own direct analogy to explain Dr. King's struggle.

INDUCTIVE LEARNING STRATEGY

In the Inductive Learning Strategy, students are engaged in grouping and labeling data in order to form original conceptual frameworks. As a result students are able to form generalizations, make predictions, or establish rules or principles. The strategy is one of three thinking strategies, developed by Hilda Taba, to promote conceptual development and inductive learning abilities.

The Strategy at Work

To introduce a series of readings on the Middle East, Mr. Tedeschi designed a lesson using the Inductive Learning Strategy. His aim was to have his ninth grade World Cultures students develop some hypotheses about the relationship between geographic location and cultural development prior to beginning their study. The groups would be investigated, and evidence from the readings would be collected by each group to verify their predictions.

After dividing his class into working groups of five, Mr. Tedeschi began his lesson by having the students use the wall map to find the geographic area known as the Middle East and having them list the modern countries which occupy the region. Then he distributed a copy of the "puzzle map" (shown on the next page) to each student.

Mr. Tedeschi led a brief whole class discussion in which he had the students describe the puzzle map and relate it to the geographic area they had just examined. He then asked the students to work in groups to sort the data on the puzzle map into sets. "Which of these do you think belong together? When you think you have a complete group, write a statement which tells why you placed these things together. You may use an item in more than one set if you wish," he said.

As his students worked to organize the data, Mr. Tedeschi moved from group to group, encouraging his students to make clear the relationships they noticed as they worked, and to develop a label for each set of items.

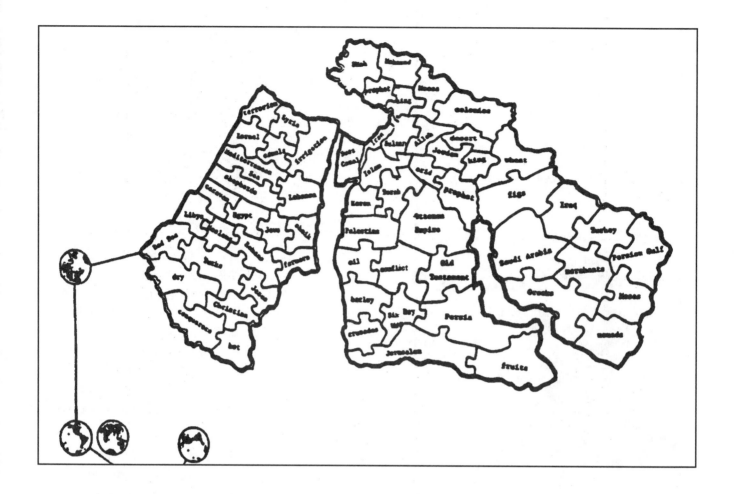

When the groups had had an opportunity to organize the items, Mr. Tedeschi led a whole class discussion which began with each group reporting its ideas for organizing and labeling the data. He next asked each group to develop and share with the class three statements about the Middle East which they believed to be true based on their organization of the data. Mr. Tedeschi collected and published these statements; he then required his students to list the statements in order from "most likely to be true" to "least likely to be true." At this point, the groups were ready to begin reading about the Middle East to gather evidence to verify or refute their hypotheses.

Inductive Learning Strategy

The Inductive Learning Strategy is based on a three-part process designed by Hilda Taba (1971) to improve students' thinking abilities.

In the Inductive Learning Strategy, students use what they have studied or observed to enumerate related items. They then group the information they have generated, and label and categorize it to form concepts. The strategy requires that students find and identify a variety of ways of grouping details which are similar to or related to each other, label the groups appropriately, and determine the inclusiveness of the groups by subsuming items using subgroups where possible. In both the Inductive Learning and Concept Attainment Strategies, students are asked to organize data to form a concept. In the Inductive Learning Strategy, however, either students or teachers may generate data, but students determine the concept. In the Concept Attainment Strategy, both concept and data are determined by the teacher.

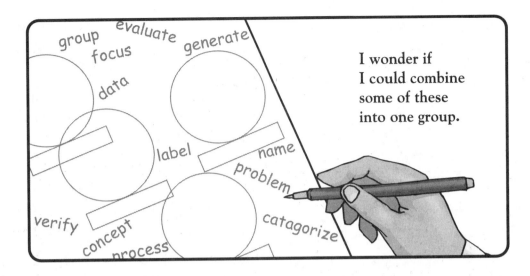

The goals of the Inductive Learning Strategy are:

1. To help students formulate concepts and generalizations;

2. To help students see relationships and patterns in what is taught;

3. To help students explain reasoning clearly; and

4. To help students learn to cite evidence.

When engaging in the Inductive Learning Strategy, students need to be flexible and fluent, to make associations, to respond spontaneously to focusing questions, to identify ways of grouping, to classify, to categorize, and to determine the relative inclusiveness of groups.

The teacher needs to organize student behaviors in terms of overt operations, covert mental operations, and the use of elicitation questions, as follows:

OVERT BEHAVIORAL OBJECTIVES	COVERT THINKING OBJECTIVES	FOCUSING QUESTIONS (GENERAL)
Generating data	Recall items from prior knowledge or intake experience. Differentiate relevant from irrelevant data.	What did you see? Hear? Read? What did you notice?
Grouping data	Notice relationships, search for common attributes.	Which of these do you think belong together? Why do you think A, B, and C go together?
Labeling groups	Synthesize common characteristics. Generate word or phrase. Compare, evaluate for appropriateness.	What would be a good name for this group? Why do you think ____ would be an appropriate label?
Subsuming items under other labels; labels under more inclusive labels	Notice hierarchies and relationships not noted before. Name or label the hierarchies or relationships noted.	Which of these items now under one label would also belong under another label? Why do you think ____ belongs under ____?
Suggesting different ways of grouping, labeling, and subsuming items based on other relationships	Notice different relationships or common characteristics from before: identify different relationships or characteristics from before.	Which of the items belong together for entirely different reasons? Etc. Why do you think ____, ____ and ____ belong together?

In summary, the steps in the Inductive Learning Strategy are:

1. Generate the data;

2. Record the data;

3. Organize the data into groups;

4. Use a label to describe each group;

5. Place additional items into categories; and

6. Subsume items and labels into larger groups.

How to Plan Lessons Using the Inductive Learning Strategy

During the planning phase you want to select the topic to be addressed, plan the necessary focusing questions for each step in the strategy, determine possible responses to each question, and plan any support procedures which might be needed. The students may be responsible for the generation of data to be grouped or labeled; if so, they must have the necessary prior knowledge and experience to do so. Consider whether you will provide data or plan an activity which will result in observations to be used as data, or whether your students will need to be involved in a series of lead-in activities in order to be able to generate data or information about a particular topic.

In addition, students will need to possess certain cognitive skills in order to be able to complete the overt tasks in the strategy. For example, the enumeration task requires recall, association, and divergent expression. The grouping task requires classifying and summarizing. The subsuming task requires regrouping, classifying, and categorizing. Your planning should take into account the differences in your students' abilities.

To plan your lesson, review each of the steps in the strategy. Who will generate the data, you or the students? If you plan to generate the data yourself, consider your objectives and select appropriate data. If the students will generate the data, do they need background information? If so, how will they obtain the information they need? What questions should you ask to facilitate the process of generating data?

Who will record the data generated? Will you work with the whole class and act as their recorder? Will you divide the students into small groups and have a recorder for each group? Will individuals generate their own data? Will there be sharing of data at this point, or will each small group or individual use its own data set?

How will the recording of data take place? Will data be recorded on the board, on easel or mural paper, or in individual learning logs? Would transcribing data onto index cards facilitate grouping of items? How will individual students, small groups, or the whole class record decisions about groups and levels? Would a worksheet be helpful?

Given the data you have generated yourself, or using a set of data similar to the one you believe will be generated by your students, consider the possible reasons for putting things together in groups. Think of possible labels, and develop additional reasons for grouping. Then try to organize your groups into more inclusive groups. Considering your groups and labels, what hypothesis can you make about the data as a whole? How is this information or pattern of thought related to the concept you want to develop? Does the lesson design lead toward the development of connections between and among essential elements of the concept you have chosen for your students to investigate?

As you reflect on the concept to be investigated, plan how the discussion will proceed, how the data will be collected and organized, and whether (or when) students will work individually, in small groups, or as a whole class.

Putting the Inductive Learning Strategy to Work in Your Classroom

Your role in implementing the Inductive Learning Strategy is to ask focusing or eliciting questions, to record and verify student responses, and to prompt or cue students when necessary to facilitate the discussion. During your lesson, it is important that you allow students to perform all the needed cognitive operations for themselves so that they will experience the complete process. It is essential that you accept students' responses and ask them to explain why they grouped the items in the particular way they did, and why they chose a particular label.

The role of your students is to discriminate among the data generated, to identify common properties by which the data may be grouped, and to label the grouped data. Your students are also required to subsume labels under more inclusive labels, and to suggest different ways of grouping, labeling, and subsuming items based on different relationships.

Your opening question is extremely important; it must be neither too broad nor too narrow. Too broad a question will result in such a wide range of responses as to be unwieldy for grouping purposes. Too narrow a question will yield responses which will be insufficiently diverse. You must rephrase the opening question in different ways if students have difficulty responding. Be aware of what is required from the opening question, so that you can determine whether or not the students are providing appropriate responses. Be ready to ask focusing questions when the process slows down or moves off target and to provide feedback to stimulate fluency and flexibility.

When recording student responses, be sure to let students volunteer. Calling on particular students to speak may be misinterpreted as your desire that they wait for your signal before volunteering. Spontaneity is enhanced by letting students respond when they are ready. Secure wide participation by using the kindling technique described in the Write to Learn Strategy.

Determine how much time to spend in the listing phase. While not necessary to compile an extensive data set, it is important to continue until enough items have been generated to allow the grouping task to take place.

A problem in recording may occur if you judge a student's response as inappropriate too quickly. First record the response and then ask,

without implying any judgment, that the student explain how this specific item relates to the topic. Frequently teachers are surprised to discover how a particular response does, in fact, relate to the topic. If the response does turn out to be inappropriate, allow the student to withdraw, modify, or replace it without penalty or comment.

Another difficulty you may face in recording is in knowing whether to write down exactly what the student has said, or to interpret the comment. It is best that students see that what they say has been recorded. However, you do not need to write every word; the intent must be accurately represented. Shorthand may be used.

Number or letter each item so that it can be easily referred to after all the responses have been recorded. Review the completed list and help the students to evaluate what has been written.

When your students are engaged in grouping items, be aware of their mental abilities. Six or seven year olds will not handle the grouping task with the same sophistication older children will exhibit. In fact, if you compare student responses to this strategy early in the year with responses in the spring, you will discover fundamental differences in ability. Increase your level of expectation as your students' abilities develop.

How to Evaluate the Inductive Learning Strategy

To evaluate the Inductive Learning Strategy, monitor the process and provide appropriate feedback. As students generate data, provide intuitive feedback to assist students to think fluently, flexibly, and with originality. Such feedback might sound like this: "That's a possibility. Who has another idea?" "How else might we group this information?" "Can you think about this in a new and different way?" Such responses stimulate the students' intuition, help to break their "mind-set," and encourage them to expand their conceptual thinking abilities.

During the regrouping and naming phase, where students need to verify and subsume responses, provide corrective feedback by asking students why they made the choices they did, and to give evidence to support their decisions. Students should be able, with this prompting, to examine their own conclusions and to make necessary adjustments.

Be aware of the different ways in which your students approach the grouping task. Look for techniques which will help students expand their grouping strategies. Students will often agree to put things into a particular group, while their reasons for grouping in this way will differ. Sometimes individual students, or even an entire class, will rely on one method of grouping more than another. Examining the strategies your students use for grouping may lead you to decide to foster more variety in grouping strategies. Compare your students' reasons for grouping with the following common classifications:

1. Is the reason for grouping RELATIONAL? Does it rely on the same location, same time, same function?

2. Is the reason for grouping DESCRIPTIVE? Does it rest on shape, appearance, color, texture, or material?

3. Is the reason for grouping CATEGORICAL or INFERENTIAL? Are the items grouped according to an abstract quality shared by the whole group; i.e., rain, cloud, and fog because they have to do with weather?

4. Is the reason for grouping MIXED? Does it use some combination of the above?

Evaluate the way in which students group information. Decide how to introduce them to other ways of grouping the data, and encourage them to experiment with these ways. Measure any changes in grouping styles, and assess how individual students or a class is working cognitively.

Invite your students to join you in evaluating their work. Encourage them to examine the criteria established for grouping and subsuming, and to verify responses according to those criteria. Discuss with them the process they used to group data, and aid them to assess their ability to think fluently and flexibly throughout the process.

Through this self-examination students will discover that all items and events have varied characteristics which allow them to be grouped in many ways. In the course of grouping and labeling items, verifying responses, and exploring their own methods and strategies, the students' suggestions and questions will reveal how sharply they perceive these relationships.

Summary

When to use it:
When you want students to make connections between and among essential elements of an idea and generate conclusions, hypotheses, questions, or hierarchical structures.

How to use it:
1. Provide or have students generate data relevant to a particular question or problem;

2. Ask students to group data according to common attributes;

3. Have students label groups with a word or phrase;

4. Ask students to subsume items under other labels or under more inclusive categories;

5. Have students suggest different ways of grouping, labeling, and subsuming items based on other relationships; and

6. Have students synthesize by forming hypotheses, drawing conclusions, raising questions, or formulating conceptual hierarchies.

How to evaluate it:
1. Are students able to group data?

2. Are students able to group data in different ways?

3. Are students able to synthesize labels for groups?

4. Are students able to identify hierarchies and relationships previously noted?

5. Are students able to generate conclusions, hypotheses and questions to be answered?

Things to remember:
1. Provide students with opportunities to practice grouping and labeling before using the strategy;

2. Design focusing questions for each step of the process;

3. Number or letter data so that it can be identified; and

4. Put data on cards or strips of paper to make it easier to manipulate.

Sample Lesson I:
Reading—Making Predictions about the Main Idea

Objective:

To use the Inductive Learning Strategy to predict the main idea about a story.

Procedure:

In Mr. Quinlan's third grade, the students use vocabulary from a story they are about to read to form predictions about the main idea. For a short story or novel to be studied by the class as a whole, Mr. Quinlan often uses the Inductive Learning Strategy as a teacher-directed lesson, but, as in this instance, when the students are to be assigned to read a short piece on their own, Mr. Quinlan prepared a work sheet based on the strategy. For the story, *Spiders and Diamonds*, the work sheet looked like this:

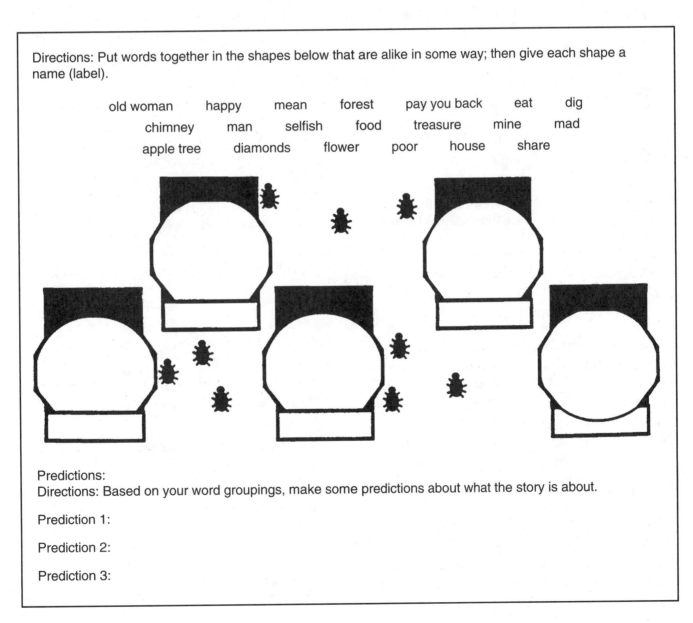

Directions: Put words together in the shapes below that are alike in some way; then give each shape a name (label).

old woman	happy	mean	forest	pay you back	eat	dig
chimney	man	selfish	food	treasure	mine	mad
apple tree	diamonds	flower	poor	house	share

Predictions:
Directions: Based on your word groupings, make some predictions about what the story is about.

Prediction 1:

Prediction 2:

Prediction 3:

Throughout your lesson, provide your students with patient encouragement to verbalize their thinking. One seven-year old, organizing rocks into sets, explained that he was grouping them "by age." When asked how he decided which rocks belonged in which age group, he replied, "You know, big rocks and little rocks." You can never be sure why students group things as they do unless they reveal their thought processes. Ask "why" questions in different ways: "How did you happen to put these together?" or "Tell me something about this group…"

In labeling and subsuming tasks, students attempt to establish a hierarchy of information. Encourage your students to find a group into which all of a class of items can fit. For example, trees, flowers, bushes and plants and birds, lions, humans, and snakes can be subsumed under the category "living things."

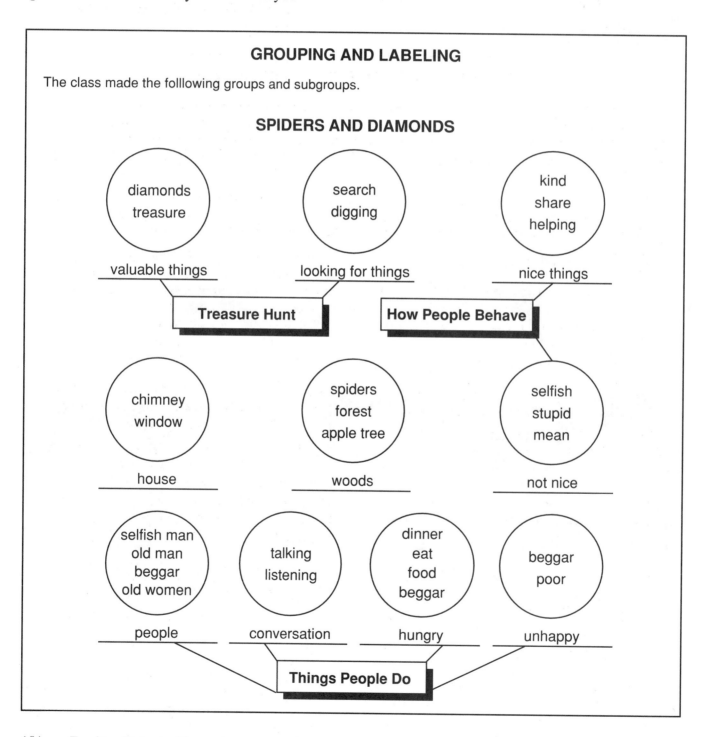

GROUPING AND LABELING

The class made the folllowing groups and subgroups.

SPIDERS AND DIAMONDS

diamonds
treasure

valuable things

search
digging

looking for things

kind
share
helping

nice things

Treasure Hunt

How People Behave

chimney
window

house

spiders
forest
apple tree

woods

selfish
stupid
mean

not nice

selfish man
old man
beggar
old women

people

talking
listening

conversation

dinner
eat
food
beggar

hungry

beggar
poor

unhappy

Things People Do

Hypothesis:

The students were asked to look at their groups and make predictions as to what going to happen in the story. After each student wrote down a few predictions, the teacher wrote some down on the chalkboard. Here are a few of the predictions:

1. A beggar digs for treasure.

2. A kind man searches for diamond treasure.

3. An old man and woman are begging for food.

4. A selfish man was mean to a beggar.

5. The people were digging in the woods for treasure.

6. The selfish man is stupid and mean to the beggar, old man, and old woman.

7. The selfish man listened to the old man and the beggar talk about treasure.

8. The old man found the treasure in the chimney of the house.

After having their curiosity stimulated by making predictions, the students were eager to hear the story.

THE STORY OF SPIDERS AND DIAMONDS

A kind old man and woman lived in a house by the forest. They were poor but very happy. A mean, selfish man lived nearby. He had many possessions. One day, a beggar came to the mean man's house and asked for food. The mean man asked why he should have to share his food. He laughed and threw the beggar out of his house. The beggar then went to the house of the poor people. They invited him to stay for dinner, and let him eat as much as he wanted to.

After dinner, the beggar told the poor people that he wanted to pay them back for being so kind. He told them they could find treasure by digging under the apple tree in the forest. The wife said it was too late in the evening to go digging. They decided to go to sleep and search for the treasure in the morning.

The selfish old man had been standing outside the old couple's window listening to their conversation. When he heard about the treasure, he ran to the forest as fast as he could. He found the apple tree and started to dig. All he found was a jar of spiders. He thought that the kind people were very stupid for helping the beggar when there was no treasure. He was very angry. So, when he reached the old couple's house, he threw the jar of spiders down the chimney. When the jar hit the ground it broke, and the spiders turned into diamonds!

Looking back, we can see that a number of the students' predictions were right on target. After reading the story, the teacher asked her students to determine which of the predictions were the best, and why they thought so.

Sample Lesson II: Reading—Word Analysis: The Short "I" Sound

Miss Praeger uses the Inductive Learning Strategy frequently with her first graders as a way of reinforcing sight vocabulary as well as to help her students develop their conceptual systems. She makes packets of words, one word to a card, often with a picture or clue on the reverse. Since she usually breaks her class into five working groups, she duplicates each packet in a different color marker—red, blue, green, purple, and brown—for easy sorting. Thus far, her students have worked with packets having to do with their study of their town and the buildings, locations, activities, and people in it. Since her first graders enjoy the "groups game" so much, she has planned to use the Inductive Learning Strategy to introduce and reinforce the short "i" vowel sound.

From their sight vocabulary, Miss Praeger has selected the following words:

FISH IN HIS IT WIND TRIP

IF SIT WIN THIS DISH MISS SIP

Because this activity involves seeing and analyzing word parts, she has decided to sit with each of her groups in turn while the others work at learning centers. She displays all of the cards on the floor in the learning circle so that the group with which she is working can see all of them at once, and begins by having the children read all of the words. "I want you to notice how these words are written," she says, "and we will play the 'groups game' while we study the letters in these words and how these words sound." Jamie immediately raises his hand and simultaneously says, "I have a group. I see a group, Miss P.!" Jamie's group consists of the words that begin with "i" in, it, is, if. Miss Praeger moves these cards together and has the children read the words aloud. When they have verified this group, she records the group on the easel with its rule: all begin with "i."

Miss Praeger continues to work with the group while they identify the following groups:

Has "I" inside

sit	win	trip
sip	his	wind
this	fish	dish
miss		

Has "IS" inside

is
his

End in "Z" sound

is
his

Has "IN" inside

in
win
wind

Other groups suggested and recorded included words beginning with "s", words with an "s" sound, words with three letters, rhyming words.

When the groups had been recorded, Miss Praeger asked the children to look at one group—"has 'i' inside"—to see if they could add any word. Sue said, "hit," John said, "little," and Ramon said, "ride." Where Miss Praeger had previously written the suggested words down as soon as they were given, she appeared to hesitate at "ride", but made no comment. Sammy promptly said, "Ride doesn't sound right." Ramon stuck out his lip and said firmly, "It follows the rule. It has 'i' inside." After some discussion, it was decided to put "ride" on the list for the rule "has 'i' inside," and to make two

new groups, one for words with "i" inside where "i" sounds like "i" in "fish" and "in" (Miss Praeger told them that this "i" was known as "short 'i',") and another for words with "i" inside where "i" sounds like the "i" in "ride" and "side" (Miss Praeger told them that this "i" was know as "long 'i'").

The children continued to put new words into the groups they had made, and, as they did so, they noticed that some of the groups they had made could be combined under the new group, "has the sound of short 'i'." They put "has 'is' inside," "has 'in' inside," and "begins with 'i'" in this new category.

At the end of the lesson, Miss Praeger put the cards into a learning center so that the children could continue to explore ways of grouping these words.

Sample Lesson III: Colonial New England

Objective:
To use the Inductive Learning Strategy to consider life in colonial New England.

Anticipatory Set:
Imagine that you are in a time machine and have returned to the year 1750 to one of the original American colonies in New England. What would you expect to see? Make a list of these items.

Procedures:
Listed below are words you would hear spoken by the people of a Colonial town. Group any words that have some feature in common. Decide what the words in each group have in common and use this common characteristic as a label.

faith, oak, apprentice, axe, fall, pelt, baptize, freeman, pine, barrel, harvest, pray, bible, herdsman, Providence, beggar, hoe, saw, house, servant, congregation, horse, sin, community, leather, squash, conversion, cooper, tan, journeyman, corn, master, town meeting, devil, whipping, trap

Based on your groupings, draw three conclusions about life in the Colonial period. Look at each of your groups, think of three hypotheses about this period of time, and write them down. Next, read the following passage about Colonial times. Any time you find evidence to support or refute a hypothesis, record the line number and a key word on your chart.

"When people first began colonizing New England, they mirrored the Old World in their everyday life. They acted as if they were an extension of England. They thought, spoke, dressed, and retained the customs of Europe. The social structure, like Europe's, consisted of several classes. At the top was the "gentry" made up of wealthy merchants, planters, lawyers, and doctors. Under the gentry were the men who owned property but were not wealthy. They include farmers, shopkeepers, and craftsmen. The bottom level consisted of the poor, unskilled laborers who were generally slaves or contracted servants. The difference between the social structure in the colonies and in England was that it was much more flexible and allowed for members of a lower class to rise to a higher one, except for slaves.

England controlled the government of the colonies. Each one had a governor appointed by the king. The members of the legislative houses were either elected or appointed. Local governments were in charge of law enforcement, levying taxes, and road services. The death penalty was customary for crimes of armed robbery, counterfeiting, murder, and treason. Drunkenness, slander, swearing, theft, and breaking the Sabbath were considered minor offences. Punishment for these types of crimes included public whipping, public humiliation in the pillory or stocks, or the ducking stool.

The lifestyle of the New England colonies also developed from the old European ways. The households were large and generally included resident in-laws. All members of the family were the responsibility of the father, who made all the important decisions. The first houses were built similar to those in Europe, but were later changed to adapt to the local weather conditions around the fireplace. It provided heat and light essential for everyday living. Much of the style and design of one's home and lifestyle depended on one's individual wealth. The wealthy imported fine furniture from Europe, but most of the settlers had homemade items along with whatever they were able to bring from Europe. The homemade furniture was plain and sturdy. Blocks of wood, barrels, or benches served as chairs. They used oil lamps and candles for lighting. Tinder boxes, bed warmers, iron pots, and spinning wheels were generally considered necessities.

Clothing also varied according to wealth and occupation. The wealthy imported their clothes or had them tailored to resemble European styles. On farms, workingmen wore breeches and a long shirt made from linen woven by the women of the household. Male servants who worked in the field likely wore only breeches. In cold weather, the men wore a loose-fitting overcoat, leather leggings, mittens, and a wool cap. Women wore dresses, a petticoat, and a single undergarment called a "shift."

Most New Englanders had small farms located near villages or small towns. They raised cattle, hogs, sheep, chickens, fruit, and vegetables. They also hunted and fished for deer, clams, lobsters, squirrels, and other game in the local woods, rivers, and oceans. Corn became one of the basic foods in most households. Cornmeal was made into various ashcakes, hoecakes, and breads. Storing food for the winter was a problem as they had not developed canning or techniques for refrigeration. Meats were smoked, salted, and dried. They dug cellars to keep roots, fruit, and vegetables, but the usual winter diet consisted of bread and meat.

Religion strongly influenced the social and political life of the New England colonies. Most colonists came to the New World seeking religious freedom. Church officials did the work that governments do today. This included education, care of the poor, and record keeping for marriages, baptisms, and deaths. The churches were not just sites for worshipping. They were the places for community gatherings and town meetings. The rules of the church generally became the laws of the colony and were very strict. Many everyday activities like cooking, shaving, and other domestic activities were forbidden on Sunday. The colonists also believed in folklore as highlighted by the Salem witchcraft trials.

Eventually the New England colonies developed their own way of life as they adapted to the conditions in the New World. Men and women who had at one time seen themselves as an extension of England soon began to consider themselves Americans."

Resolved:

Capitol punishment ought to be abolished.

Let's debate this...

DILEMMA DECISION MAKING STRATEGY

The Dilemma Decision Making Strategy is designed to help students grow in their ability to make moral choices by proposing them with hypothetical or real-life moral dilemmas.

The Strategy at Work

To introduce his high school class to issues of moral reasoning, Mr. Smith is posing a moral dilemma for class discussion. The moral issue is as follows:

Carl's wife is desperately ill and will die without a certain prescription. The drug is available but costs twice the amount that Carl has in his wallet. He pleads with the druggist to allow him to pay off the balance in installments. The druggist, not knowing Carl, insists on full payment or no drug. Carl offers his watch as security but the druggist refuses saying he is a pharmacist, not a pawn broker. In desperation Carl grabs the drug and runs out of the store. The druggist calls the police. Carl is apprehended and is taken to jail, and then to court.

Students are now asked to play the roles of plaintiff (Carl), accuser (druggist), judge, a panel of 12 jurors, an attorney for the defense and an attorney for the prosecution. Class members not playing roles in the proceedings will serve as observers. The observers' roles are to determine 1) the moral state (a la Kohlberg) of Carl's actions; 2) if found guilty an appropriate sentence; or, if determined innocent a method for compensating the druggist, and 3) alternatives Carl might have tried other than theft.

The teacher serves as a facilitator/observer of the proceedings. The purpose of the trial is to make arguments for the higher morality; i.e., which behavior is the more highly principled, and why.

I am going to play the devil's advocate for just a moment. In sitting and observing the debate, I have a couple of questions...

The Dilemma Decision Making Strategy

The Dilemma Decision Making Strategy is designed to help students make moral choices and to understand the paths that others follow in making moral choices. The strategy uses the approaches and philosophy of Lawrence Kohlberg (1973) and Carol Gilligan (1982).

In Kohlberg's approach, modified by Gilligan to reflect gender differences, students are confronted with hypothetical or real-life moral dilemmas. The students discuss or role-play the dilemma, and then draw from their own personal experiences to help solve the problem. In this interactive process students listen to one another's reasoning, argue, compare, and join their concerns for justice and equality, as described by Kohlberg's morality of rights, and/or their concerns for care and connection, and as represented in Gilligan's morality of responsibility, into a set of beliefs or moral standards that work for them. While there are no pronouncements of right or wrong on the part of the teacher, there is an obligation to assure a complete exploration of consequences, and to create a classroom atmosphere in which all voices and views can be heard and considered with respect. Moral development evolves as students experience and practice moral choices.

Kohlberg's Stages of Moral Development

Kohlberg, a Harvard professor, based his ideas of moral education on a definition of what he believed to be universal principles of justice independent of specific religious traditions. Moral education in the school, in his view, should be focused on a doctrine of justice which, in his opinion, guides all societies, and which reason indicates to be just. Kohlberg's theory of moral development addresses how the child's structure of thought changes and matures.

Kohlberg constructs six stages for the development of moral understanding:

1) The first stage addresses the need not to be punished; the person is obedient to avoid pain or displeasure. The child's motivation for obeying rules is a fear of getting caught.

2) At stage two in Kohlberg's theory, "right" action becomes that which satisfied the child's own needs. Human relationships are viewed in terms of reciprocity; "You scratch my back and I'll scratch yours." The individual is motivated by self-interest; "What's in it for me?"

Kohlberg's conventional level at stages three and four is associated with Piaget's "concrete operational" level of thinking (Rosen, 1977). These stages are often exhibited in late pre-adolescence. At this level maintaining the expectations, rules and standards of the family, group or nation, has value in its own right. There is a concern not only with conforming to the social order, but also with maintaining, justifying, and supporting this order.

3) At stage three, there is a good person orientation. Good behavior is that which helps others and gains approval.

4) At stage four, "concern for others" is expanded to a wider scale. Young people begin to acquire the concepts of society, law, and the individual's role within that larger social and legal system. Behavior is motivated by a sense of duty and obligation; morality is shaped by external expectations.

Not until stage five, the level of principled moral reasoning, do individuals stand apart from their social framework and make judgments about what is right and wrong. The recognition that particular laws or institutions need to be changed to protect the rights of individuals is characteristic of the post-conventional level of moral reasoning. The post-conventional stages, like Piaget's formal operations level of thinking, first appear in adolescence.

5) Stage five emphasizes a legalistic or contract orientation, generally with utilitarian overtones. Law is based on mutual concern and the welfare of citizens, rather than simply, as in stage four, on respect for authority. Laws which are not constitutional, which violate human rights, or which are not in the general interest, are judged invalid.

6) At stage six, moral principles have universal validity; law is derived from morality, not vice versa. Individuals demonstrate an internal commitment to principles of conscience, respect for the rights, life, and dignity of all persons. Principles or rules are abstract and ethical, rather than concrete. They are universal in nature, and emphasize the ideals of reciprocity, equality, human rights, and respect for the dignity of individual persons.

Over the last decade, Kohlberg and his associates have compared systems of moral reasoning in diverse cultures (Taiwan, England, Turkey, Yucatan, and the United States). They have experimented with various techniques to stimulate advances to higher developmental stages of moral reasoning. Their central findings are:

1. The stages of moral reasoning appear to be the same for all persons, regardless of social class or culture.

2. Stages can't be skipped, because one stage supports another.

3. Stage change is gradual because a new stage can't be instilled directly, but must be constructed out of many social experiences.

4. Stage and age can't be equated because some people move much faster through the stage sequence than others; some also get further. Only a relatively small percentage of American adults reach the fifth stage of principled morality.

5. Experiences that provide opportunities for what Kohlberg calls "role taking" (assuming the viewpoints of others, putting yourself in another's place), foster progress through the stages. Children who have many peer relationships, for example, tend to move to more advances stages of development than do children whose peer interactions are low. Within the family, children whose parents encourage them to express their views and to participate in family decisions generally reason at higher moral levels than children whose parents do not encourage or allow these behaviors.

Gilligan's Research on Moral Development in Women

Carol Gilligan, a colleague of Kohlberg's at Harvard, has been studying moral development with the aim of providing a clearer understanding of women's development, especially in terms of women's identity formation and their moral development in adolescence and adulthood. Following the work of Nancy Chodorow (1974) and others, Gilligan noted the masculine bias of developmental theorists, for example, Freud and Erikson, and reflected in the observations of Piaget. While these theorists all describe sex differences in personality formation, they adopt the male developmental pattern as the norm, and consider women's development as deviant. It has been suggested by some writers that, because masculine values prevail in our society, women often question whether their feelings are normal, and tend to defer to the judgment of others. Gilligan takes a different point of view, seeing women's concern for others as "inseparable from women's moral strength, an overriding concern with relationships and responsibilities"; "Sensitivity to the needs of others and the assumption of responsibility for taking care can lead women to attend to voices other than their own and to include in their judgment other points of view" (1982, pp. 16-17).

In responding critically to Kohlberg's research, Gilligan points out:

Research is currently being done following Gilligan's suggestion that theories of moral development be based on listening to the ways people talk about morality and about themselves, and how people define the conflicts they face and how they describe their real-life choices. Gilligan and her colleagues have referred to this investigation as "mapping the moral domain," a process which they expect to clarify the different voices of women and men.

D. Kay Johnston, Associate Professor of Education at Colgate and a Research Associate at Harvard, recently studied adolescents' solutions to the dilemmas presented in two of Aesop's fables. She was interested in seeing whether, in making moral choices, boys and girls differed in their predominant moral orientation—one focusing on justice and rights, the other on care and response. Moreover, she sought to test the premise that, regardless of the orientation spontaneously chosen, the respondents would be able to use the other orientation if asked if there was another way to look at their problem.

For her study, Johnston used a standard research design. She conducted in-school interviews with an equal number of boys and girls who were volunteers from sixth-grade classes (eleven-year olds) or from mixed levels of sophomore English classes (fifteen-year olds). After each fable was read, students were asked, "How would you solve it?" As the interview continued, students were asked, "Is there another way to solve the problem?" If the spontaneous solution relied on the logic of a morality of rights, using impartial rules based on obligation, for example, and the person being interviewed was unable to spontaneously switch orientations, the interviewer asked, "Is there a way to solve the dilemma so that all of the animals will be satisfied?" A spontaneous response orientation, for example, considered the welfare of all, was followed by the same request for another solution. If the person was unable to switch to a right orientation, the interviewer asked, "Is there a rule you could use to solve the problem?" Finally, each interviewed person was asked to choose a best solution from among those discussed during the interview.

Johnston found a pattern of girls using the care and response orientation and boys using the justice and rights orientation. However, all of the boys and girls were able to represent the two orientations in some way. Johnston concluded that "the gender difference does not reflect knowing or understanding only one orientation, but rather choosing and preferring one over the other as a solution to a moral dilemma" (1988, p. 60).

This example of current research suggests that Kohlberg's emphasis on a single problem-solving strategy, "justice reasoning," needs to be expanded to include strategies used in both moral orientations, justice and care.

The goals of the Dilemma Decision Making Strategy are:

1. To help students interpret a problem requiring moral choice;

2. To support students in taking a stand;

3. To help students identify, clarify, and share reasons for their choice;

4. To encourage students to listen actively to alternative positions and arguments;

5. To provide an opportunity to discuss and debate different views; and

6. To support students in reviewing their original positions so that they can confirm or modify them.

The steps in the Dilemma Decision Making Strategy are:

1. Design or select a dilemma to be discussed;

2. Present the dilemma;

3. Facilitate discussion through role-playing, playing the devil's advocate, paraphrasing, clarifying, encouraging role reversals, etc.; and

4. Conduct a cognitive review.

How to Plan Lessons Using the Dilemma Decision Making Strategy

In order to use the Dilemma Decision Making Strategy effectively, you need to work toward creating an environment that will encourage students to speak their minds, challenge the thinking of others, and be both open and sensitive to themselves and with others. Your arrangement of seats, the way you relate to the students, and the way you expect students to relate to one another contribute significantly to the establishment of an appropriate atmosphere conducive to moral dilemma discussions. Use the Circle Teaching Strategy—you and the students seated in a circle and participating as peers, everyone facing one another so that there is no leader and all can be heard. Make

sure that each student is given an opportunity to share thoughts and feelings. Allow students not to share if they so chose, but expect everyone to listen actively to the person who is sharing, and be careful to model active listening yourself. Never allow interruptions or put-downs; model supportive responses such as paraphrasing ("I think I hear you saying…" "I'm interested in knowing more about…" "Can you tell me how you arrived at that idea," "I'm not sure I'm clear on what you mean when you say…" "Can you give me an example?") Never allow participants to equate numerical superiority with a "winning" position. Be careful to link views with the individuals stating them; recalling in a non-judgmental way that Clare feels that such-and-such is the solution and that Robert prefers a different answer assures both Clare and Robert that their solutions have been heard and considered seriously, that their solutions are worth thinking about.

Where possible, consider forming smaller groups rather than trying to lead discussions with an entire class. A group size of eight to ten gives all students ample occasion to participate. When you plan for smaller groups which will work independently, be sure that students are first familiar with your expectations for their roles; review, model, and role-play responses to sharing which are designed to elicit clarifying statements and which show support for the individual's right to an opinion. Your role in working with smaller groups is to move from one group to another, sitting in for a few minutes to monitor the discussion, refocus attention on the specific problem to be solved, ask a challenging question, or play the devil's advocate.

Small groups which are working independently will be most effective if students are held accountable for a specific product; i.e., a list of their reasons pro and con about a particular solution, a strategy for changing other people's opinions, preparation for a mock trial, or legislative battle. Each small group must be held responsible to the entire class, or to you, for the work covered in the group.

Crucial to your planning is the development of a moral dilemma that challenges students. Especially pertinent to students through junior high schools will be issues over friendship, family, peers, and authority. High school teachers may choose to focus on dilemmas involving conflicts relating to law, legislative issues, or deeply held convictions which will stimulate controversy.

Dilemmas should be geared to the genuine interests and concerns of students pertinent to their own experience, or that of their peers. The more closely the dilemma corresponds to important business in students' lives, the more successful it will be in stimulating the kind of discussion likely to produce moral growth. Very young students respond especially well to real-life classroom issues concerning relationships, sharing, fairness, rules and procedures, and individual versus group rights.

Discussion of moral dilemmas can be used in many areas of the curriculum. Social studies, history, literature, and science offer controversy, opposing viewpoints, and differing interpretations as part of the content. The stimulus for a discussion of a moral dilemma may be an incident in a novel or play, an historical event, a newspaper editorial, or a magazine article. A particularly powerful stimulus for discussion is a brief segment from a good film or TV program.

Prepare questions which are truly open-ended. On the one hand, you must make sure that the dilemma involves judgment about what is right or wrong as contrasted with dilemmas of expedience, preference, or simple choice. On the other hand, the dilemma must be one about which thoughtful, fair-minded, and caring people may disagree. If you believe there is a right and wrong answer to the question, students will tend not to draw their own conclusions. Avoid the possibility that your class will become conditioned to playing the game of guessing what you want to hear. Only genuinely open-ended questions, and the

encouragement of differing opinions, will generate meaningful discussions.

Moral issues generally concern decisions regarding social customs, civil rights, life, truth, property, acceptance/rejection, sex, and authority. Such questions are more likely to stir thought and debate than are questions which call only for a relating of facts or reasons. Asking students to explain why a slave woman killed her baby is not a moral question; asking them to determine whether she should have killed her baby is. Your students need to have knowledge about the dilemma, and the main characteristics of the dilemma should be ones which deal with kinds of people and situations with which your students are familiar. Limit dilemmas at first to ones in which there is a clear choice between two different, but equally compelling alternatives; i.e., Should Harry Truman have used the atomic bomb? Later, you might try expanding the dilemma to include three or four characters whose points of view may differ; i.e., in a discussion about euthanasia, the doctor, the patient (conscious or comatose? of sound mind?), and immediate family members.

When your students are discussing moral choices from a justice/rights orientation, they will frequently use words such as should, must, justified, fair, lawful, and right. When they are discussing moral choices from a care/responsibility orientation, they will frequently use words such as care, understand, cooperate, hurt, be responsible for, and depend on. Remember that, although these orientations are gender-related, the relationship is not absolute; boys and girls spontaneously use both orientations to solve problems. Furthermore, your prompts will encourage students to consider the dilemma fully from both orientations before they choose their own best solution.

Include role-playing as a way of enriching the discussion of a moral dilemma, and of appreciating voices and viewpoints. Prepare briefing sheets for each of the roles students are to play. On each sheet, describe the role of the character in the scene, and be specific about the character's feelings. Then devise an observation form that tells students what to look for and gives them a place to write down their comments. Follow the role-playing with a time for students to write (see Write to Learn Strategy) a description of what they have observed; after they have shared their observations with one or two other students, ask them to define the dilemma to be solved. Then proceed with a discussion of the moral dilemma.

Putting the Dilemma Decision Making Strategy to Work in Your Classroom

Present the problem according to your plan—through a film segment, an article, an editorial, a role-playing, a poem or fragment of literature, or a description of a real-life dilemma. Have students review the important facts of the case and then describe their perceptions of the issues. Such questions are less threatening than asking students to share a personal judgment; more important, they give you the first sense of moral orientation—justice/rights for some students, care/responsibility for others—in the context of this particular problem and this particular group of students. Stimulate the discussion by asking divergent thinking questions such as, "What are some of the possible reasons for John's behavior?" and "What do you think his father thought about when he heard what had happened?" Continue in this manner to encourage interpretation of the dilemma and open exploration of the issue.

When the group seems ready, ask them what they would do in the dilemma and why. (This is another good place to use the Write to Learn Strategy since each student is able to make a private decision uninfluenced by "the crowd" and has a few minutes to gather together the reasons for this judgment.) As each student shares with the group, follow with several questions which encourage clarification, ask for evidence to support the position, and/or request that the student consider the problem from a different moral orientation. When you postpone calling on other students, you increase their desire to participate; you also signal the degree of seriousness with which you consider each student's offering. Encourage students to respond directly to each other's solutions: "I agree with Alec's solution, but I have different reasons," or "I disagree with Beth. Wouldn't John's father be breaking the law if he did that?"

Your role at this point is to stimulate the debate and to make sure that differing points of view are addressed. One approach, when there is no significant disagreement, is to pose additional conditions which change the terms of the dilemma; changing a problem from smoking cigarettes to smoking marijuana may dramatically affect some students' positions. Increase dissonance by asking students to argue for an opposite position, or ask students to switch moral orientations from care/responsibility reasoning to justice/rights reasoning or vice versa.

When students are engaged in justice/rights reasoning, stimulate their moral growth with arguments at a reasoning stage slightly higher than the one they are using. A student who argues that it is wrong to "rat" on a friend who is shoplifting might be presented with a stage four argument based on the need to uphold laws against stealing. This technique of confronting a lower stage of reasoning with a higher and, in Kohlberg's theory, more adequate stage is called "Plus one." This tactic forces students who are using the justice/rights orientation to consider opposing viewpoints argued at different stages, and helps to create the dialogue essential to moral development.

During the discussion, accept students' responses, suggestions, and feelings in a non-evaluative manner. Respond in such a way that students will be willing to explore various sides of the problem and the consequences of the suggested solutions, and recognize and contrast alternative points of view. Reflect, paraphrase, and summarize responses to increase students' awareness of their own views and feelings.

You are responsible for initiating the dilemma and guiding students through the activities within the strategy. Your students play a significant role in deciding the content to be discussed, and the positions to be taken. Your students are responsible for listening to other points of view, sharing their own ideas with the group, making choices from among the possible solutions to the dilemma, and identifying reasons for their decisions.

How to Evaluate the Dilemma Decision Making Strategy

The Dilemma Decision Making Strategy can be evaluated on a number of dimensions. What is the active participation of students in the discussion? Assess the amount of teacher talk versus student talk (you can do this yourself by using a tape recorder). Consider the amount and quality of the interaction among students— is it fluent? patient and accepting? supportive? rigorous? Determine the moral stages of students sharing a justice/rights orientation; are these students progressing from one stage to another? Consider the moral choices of students sharing a caring/responsibility orientation; do these students share their solutions comfortably? Are all of the students able to switch moral orientations to consider alternative solutions? Is there freedom of dissent as indicated by the variety of solutions, or does the group bow to peer pressure and speak with one voice?

As in the Circle Strategy, conduct a cognitive review of the different solutions and their supporting arguments. Ask students to relate the dilemma to real-life experiences and current problems. Ask them to reflect on whether their initial position has shifted or been reinforced. Ask the students to evaluate what they have done as a group by considering: What have we discovered in talking about this particular dilemma? How have we discovered it? What do we still need to know or do?

Summary

When to use it:

When you want students to grow in their ability to make moral choices when confronted with hypothetical or real-life moral dilemmas.

How to use it:

1. Design or select a dilemma to be discussed;

2. Present the dilemma;

3. Facilitate the discussion through role-playing, playing the devil's advocate, paraphrasing, clarifying, using role reversals, etc.; and

4. Conduct cognitive review.

How to evaluate it:

1. Are students active participants in the discussion?

2. Have students progressed in their ability to reason morally?

3. Are students willing and able to express different points of view?

4. Are students able to support their views with arguments?

5. Are students able to switch moral orientations from care/responsibility to justice/rights and vice-versa to add alternative solutions?

Things to remember:

1. According to Kohlberg's theory, moral development reflects universal principles of justice independent of religious tradition, and it proceeds in stages which can't be skipped;

2. Kohlberg's stages and age can't be equated because some people move faster through the stage sequence than others; only a relatively small percentage of American adults reach the fifth stage of principles morality;

3. Gilligan's research suggests that there are not one, but two distinct moral orientations, justice/rights and care/responsibility, that are linked to gender;

4. Moral development can be enhanced by confronting hypothetical or real-life moral dilemmas; the way a person reasons influences how he actually behaves in a situation requiring moral choice; and

5. Opportunities for "role-taking" foster progress in moral development.

Sample Lesson I:
Biology—Genetic Engineering

In Ms. Hailey's tenth grade biology class, the students have finished a unit on genetics. She has planned to have them consider the dilemma faced by scientists as their knowledge of genetics grows to encompass the ability to manipulate genetic combinations.

Objectives:

Ms. Hailey's students will be able to identify and describe the dilemma faced by geneticists as they develop the technology which will allow them to manipulate genetic material in such a way as to have an effect on society. They will be able to express their personal and moral choice, and will be able to explain and defend that choice.

Procedures:

Ms. Hailey presents her students with the following problem:

A group of scientists are working on a plan for a genetically structured society. They would like to use all of their biomedical engineering technology to produce a blueprint for a super-intelligent human being. This would eventually mean that there would be a number of superior people to lead society and manage higher-level operations in government.

It is time for a final funding vote to be taken so that the project planning can be completed. One of the scientists, Dr. Wright, clearly realized the advantages to implementing the plan, but also sees the liabilities.

Discussion Question:

How should Dr. Wright vote and why? Should she vote for the plan because it will mean the most capable leaders will be the decision-makers and benefit the world as a whole, or should she vote against the plan because of the questionable ethics involved?

Points to Ponder:

• Discuss the fate of people who may not be superior in this society;

• Discuss the ramifications of such a plan for family life, world politics, and religion;

• Discuss what would happen if the rules for the scheme were to change, who would change them?; and who would decide the criteria for superiority?;

• Discuss the implications of living in a more controlled society with less freedom; and

• Discuss the problems involved in identifying those who are to be labeled "superior."

Teacher's Notes:

This moral dilemma evokes responses from students on a series of important issues: integrity, loyalty, discrimination, freedom, and the technological advancement of society at an indeterminate social cost.

Responses according to Kohlberg's stages of justice/rights:

Possible Stage 1 responses might have Dr. Wright voting for the completion of the plan in order to appear to be subordinate.

Stage 2 might have the scientist thinking she should vote against the plan because someday the rules of the experimental society might change and she will be at a disadvantage.

Stage 3 might find Dr. Wright torn between wanting to keep harmony at her job and reaping the positive benefits of the plan, and worrying about what the plan would mean to the less superior people.

Stage 4 might see Dr. Wright thinking more about the global context of the plan and trying to weigh the pros and cons in a worldwide social context.

Responses in a moral orientation of care/responsibility as described by Gilligan:

Care/responsibility responses will focus on ways to solve the problem so that the needs of the people involved will be met in such a way that the least harm will be done, and relationships will be maintained. Responses in this orientation, for example, will certainly show an awareness of the precariousness of Dr. Wright's career position vis a vis her colleagues who stand to benefit from the funding decision and who will be hurt by her refusal to support it.

5

CHAPTER FIVE

Interpersonal Strategies

OVERVIEW OF THE INTERPERSONAL STRATEGIES

The Interpersonal Strategies focus on acquiring new knowledge and practicing vital skills through personal sharing, individual and social awareness, group-focused learning, and students' prior insight and knowledge. Unlike the Mastery Strategies, the primary information source is the students—guided by the teacher. The goals of the Sensing-Feeling Style and the Interpersonal Strategies are development of positive self-concept, increased communication skills, and more effective interpersonal skills. The content of the Interpersonal Strategies consists of both student interaction and teacher-determined subject-matter.

A notable aspect of these Interpersonal Strategies is their ability to reduce learner anxiety by making students aware of other students' needs, wants, and capabilities. These Interpersonal Strategies affirm the value of each student's experiences, personal thoughts, and feelings. These Interpersonal Strategies also use the student's need to learn in peer and interactive settings; they build on the constructive aspects of peer pressure. As such, these SF Strategies provide an environment that gives voice to praise, understanding, gratitude, empathy, and freedom of expression. These collaborative learning strategies emphasize the need to learn about oneself by learning about others.

All of the teaching strategies contain dimensions of the Sensing-Feeling Style; however, the Team Games Tournament Reciprocal/Learning Strategies are used to acquire mastery content and issues, while Role-Playing Strategies are used to decide conceptual understanding, each by using cooperative and interpersonal approaches.

The *Team Games Tournament Strategy (TGT)* came from the work of an ESEA Title III funded project at Johns Hopkins University. There, building on the ideas of many teachers over many years, the traditional tournament notion was converted into a collaborative and competitive team-learning situation. Team-learning and the interactive dimensions of TGT mark it as an Interpersonal Strategy. In TGT mastery content is practiced and learned in small supportive groupings.

The Team Games Tournament Strategy provides a team games setting for collaborative learning. Heterogeneous teams are formed, and these teams collaborate in drill and repetition to learn correct answers to specific questions selected by the teacher. During collaborative team practice sessions, students assume responsibility for their own learning, and support and assist their teammates' learning. In subsequent competition, they follow the rules of the tournament, score points for their team, and may share team and individual achievement through the writing and distribution of a team newsletter.

The *Jigsaw Strategy* is another cooperative learning technique designed to increase the students' sense of responsibility for their own learning by making them "experts" in one part of an instructional unit. Students work in collaborative learning teams, and prepare assigned topics to teach to their teammates. Team achievement is measured through competition. In the Jigsaw Strategy, students assume direct responsibility for their teammates' learning as well as their own. As in TGT, the teacher selects the content, provides the background material, teaches the procedures of the strategy, and acts as facilitator.

In the *Reciprocal Learning Strategy*, the emphasis is on a collaborative rather than an independent learning process. Students are taught how to help one another. The Reciprocal Learning Strategy may be categorized as a Sensing-Feeling strategy because, again, the primary information source is the student, and the primary process is an interactive one. In this strategy, students work together as peer partners, each functioning in turn as the "doer" and the "guide" in completing the task(s). The guide evaluates the doer's performance against specific criteria established by the teacher. In this strategy, responsibility for evaluating performance has been shifted to the students. The teacher's role is to model and teach cooperative skills, and to provide feedback to the guides to help them support and assist their partners.

These three cooperative teaching strategies— Team Games Tournament (TGT), Jigsaw, and Reciprocal Learning—permit teachers to develop their students' cooperative skills while simultaneously covering the curriculum. At the heart of each of these cooperative strategies is the idea of role. These three strategies succeed because they clearly describe the roles teachers and students play in cooperative learning. These roles are interdependent, easy to learn, and clearly focus on the acquisition, practice, or application of content knowledge.

The *Circle Strategy* has been adapted from the work of Unaldo Hill Palomares and Geraldine Bell. Like TGT, the Circle Strategy builds on the work of many teachers and group dynamics theorists over the years; however, the Circle Strategy is devoid of any elements of competition. In the Circle Strategy, students, with the teacher as a peer, involve themselves in journeys of self-discovery. By understanding and appreciating others, students learn more about themselves.

The *Role-Playing Strategy* is essentially a problem-solving activity in which students learn to assume other roles and identities. Dramatizing new situations and meeting varied constraints changes the way participants think about issues and conflicts. The specific Sensing-Feeling dimensions of the Role-Playing Strategy are the assumption of other roles, self-analysis in the roles, empathy toward the positions of others, and improved self-understanding as a result of walking in someone else's shoes.

I like TGT because of the team effort and spirit.

I enjoy TGT because I seem to get better and better.

I like TGT because I like tutoring and helping

Why do you like this strategy...?

TEAM GAMES TOURNAMENT STRATEGY

The Team Games Tournament Strategy (TGT) maximizes the benefits of learning through collaboration and competition. In TGT, students are placed in teams and engage in academic tournaments with students of equal achievement levels from other teams. Through team collaboration and competition, students simultaneously commit to memory the assigned material, help one another to master new material, and earn points for their teams.

The Strategy at Work

In Mr. Pillemer's ninth grade English class, students are studying different types of thought patterns represented in sentences and paragraphs: cause and effect, compare and contrast, sequence/time order, and simple listing.

Mr. Pillemer's class is organized into heterogeneous teams of five or six students, depending on class size. These teams work together to master skills, and then compete against each other in a Team Games Tournament. This week's tournament will require that students be able to recognize different thought patterns.

After a class discussion in which five types of thought patterns were presented and analyzed, and after Mr. Pillemer gave several practice examples for each type, the students met in their heterogeneously grouped teams to practice with a worksheet similar to the tournament worksheet shown on the following page.

In the tournament, each of the four students at table #3 represents a different team. Tom comes from the Giants, Carla is one of the Dodgers, Joe a Cub, and Lisa one of the Red Sox. What these students have in common is that they are all students who have had trouble with English. All of them earned very low "C's" for the first marking period. Each tournament table in Mr. Pillemer's class is set up this way: the students each represent a different team, but they are all approximately at the same achievement level.

WORKSHEET

Directions: Identify each statement as one of the five thought patterns answers.

1. On our vacation in Ecuador we visited a marketplace, a small rural village, a cathedral and an ancient Indian ruin.

2. We enjoyed our vacation in Southern France because the people were so friendly and gracious.

3. Tornadoes occur mostly in the spring, whereas hurricanes usually occur in August and September.

4. Pepsi-Cola has a dry, bubbly taste while Coca-Cola is very sweet tasting.

5. Put 8 ounces of sour cream in a bowl; then add 2 tablespoons of mayonnaise. Mix in dill seed and onion salt to taste. Finally, chill mixture in the refrigerator for one hour before serving.

6. In 1972 a woman who used to live in Bay Head was not allowed to go on the beach because she had moved across the street into another town.

7. Bill, a tall, slim basketball player, is considered talkative, whereas Luke, who is somewhat shorter and huskier, is extremely quiet.

8. Last Saturday, the Sunday School picnic included a balloon launch, a clown act, a male versus female volleyball game, and a parachute jump.

9. Under the old contract, the workers, including cooks, dishwashers, chambermaids, handymen, bellhops, doormen, and the like, earned an average of $315 a week.

10. You'll enjoy washing you hair with Shammy. First wet your hair well, then lather and feel your hair come alive. After shampooing, rinse carefully and dry. Your hair will have a new bounce and shine.

11. Ruth has planted a vegetable garden which included tomatoes, carrots, peas, zucchini, corn, lettuce, and squash.

12. The rhinoceros and hippopotamus appear similar at first glance, but they are quite different. The rhino's skin is loose dry and grayish, while the hippo's is tight, oily and pinkish. The hippo has curved front tusks while the rhino has a horn.

13. The Chinese have played marbles for 5,000 years. Moses may have played marbles as a child in the Pharaoh's palace around 1300 B.C. Marbles that children played with in ancient Greece, circa 400 B.C., are now in museums. In America, circa 500 to 1400 A.D., the Mound Builders left marbles of flint and beautifully marked clay.

14. The winning of independence from England by the American colonies had many permanent effects. Inherited titles were done away with. Voting rights were broadened. A republic with a central government and separate state governments was established.

15. During the Revolutionary War important battles occurred at Bunker Hill in 1775, Trenton in 1776, Brandywine and Saratoga in 1777, Monmouth in 1778, and Yorktown in 1781.

16. In the internal combustion engine fuel is burned inside a cylinder. The hot gases produced by this burning process expand in a controlled explosion and drive a piston or rotor which in turn moves the crankshaft.

Tom holds the question sheet and has the first turn. Each team has a deck of cards numbered 1 to 16, since there are sixteen questions, and an answer sheet. The student to Tom's right, Carla, holds the answer sheet. Tom picks the top card from the shuffled deck, and reads aloud the number "12." After reading aloud the question about the rhinoceros and hippopotamus, Tom decides that the paragraph demonstrates the "Compare and Contrast" thought pattern. Carla looks to Tom's left to see if Joe wants to challenge. He doesn't so Carla checks the answer sheet. Tom is correct. He keeps the "12" card until the end of the game. Tom passes the question sheet to Carla for her turn. Carla hands the answer sheet to Lisa.

Tom listens intently to Carla as she chooses the top card, and says the number "1", and reads the sentence about Ecuador aloud. If Tom disagrees with Carla's answer, he can challenge it since he is sitting to her immediate left. If he is right and she is wrong, he will get her card. If he is wrong, though, he must put his one card back at the bottom of the deck, regardless of whether Carla is also wrong. The winner of this four-person game will take the maximum, six points, back to his heterogeneously grouped team. Tom has won for the Giants against other opponents before; he intends to win again.

The Team Games Tournament Strategy

The Team Games Tournament Strategy is an instructional process developed by David de Vries and his colleagues at the Center for Social Organization of Schools at Johns Hopkins University (Slavin, 1976). The strategy involves small groups, instructional practice in a games setting, and tournaments. TGT complements regular instruction in elementary, middle, and high school classrooms. TGT actively involves all students in the teaching and learning process, and consistently provides positive reinforcement for successful performance. During study teams' time, students help one another learn ways to remember the content.

In TGT, students are placed in heterogenous teams and engage in academic tournaments with students from other teams. The teams are composed of four or five students, a high achiever, a low achiever, and two or three average achievers. Teams should be mixed with respect to sex and race. Each week the teacher introduces new material, perhaps in a lecture or through discussion. The teacher prepares a set of short objective questions and answers which cover the material students are expected to master. The teams then study the materials together, assisting and supporting each other in their practice.

At least once a week, the members of each team compete with members of other teams in simple academic games to gain points for their team. This competition, the Game Tournament, takes place between students of equal achievement, thus allowing each student

Let me explain the roles of Doer, Challenger and Observer to you.

	Rank	Team
High-Achieving Students	1	A
	2	B
	3	V
	4	D
	5	E
	6	F
	7	G
	8	H
Average-Achieving Students	9	H
	10	G
	11	F
	12	E
	13	D
	14	C
	15	B
	16	A
	17	
	18	
	19	A
	20	B
	21	C

Newsletter

It was a great
Chipmunks w[...]
top score i[...]
league. [...]
place t[...]
relat[...]

an approximately equal chance to contribute to the team total. To clarify the procedure, imagine only three teams, Yellow, Red, and Green, each team with a high achiever, a low achiever, and three average achievers. The Yellow Team meets to study together, to practice and help each other master the assigned material (times tables, perhaps, or chemical symbols). The Red Team and the Green Team do likewise. On Tournament day, the Yellow Team's high achiever competes against the Red Team's and the Green Team's high achievers. The Yellow Team's low achiever competes against the Red Team's and the Green Team's low achievers. The Yellow Team's average achiever #1 competes against the Red Team's and the Green Team's average achiever #1, and so on. Students score points for first, second, and third place, which they report to their team captain who adds them together to determine the team total. It is possible for the Yellow Team, having put maximum effort into practicing the material, to sweep the first places; in other words, each student on the Yellow Team has an equal chance to win against the students from the Red and Green Teams and to contribute the maximum number of points to the Yellow Team's total score.

A teacher-prepared weekly newsletter may be used to reinforce student participation by recognizing successful teams as well as those individuals who have contributed in an outstanding way to their team's scores.

Research studies by the developers of TGT indicate that the use of this strategy has an immediate and positive effect on student academic achievement, student attitudes toward the class and the subject matter, and working relationships among the students. The TGT structure promotes peer group rewards for academic achievement by altering the social organization of the classroom in two ways: by creating an interdependence among students which reinforces students' need to help each other learn, and by making it possible for students with different learning rates to have an equal chance to succeed at an academic task. An extra point contributed to a team score is just as useful coming from a low achiever as from a high achiever. As a result, achieving students gain in status among their peers, and less academically motivated students succeed because they also realized that they have something important to contribute.

The Team Games Tournament Strategy is a flexible technique that works effectively with students of differing learning rates and styles. TGT capitalizes on the possibilities of learning in small groups. It provides group identity, which is especially important to feeling-type learners. It promotes peer tutoring and concern for each other's success with academic tasks—two things not often found in traditional classrooms. The high level of student interaction and the motivational nature of instructional games appeal to the sensing-type learner's need for action. The game component provides instant feedback and positive reinforcement via the answer sheet. The task orientation of TGT is also appealing to sensing-type students. The competitive spirit of the tournaments appeals to the thinking-type learner's need to compete.

The intuitive-type students will also enjoy this strategy, but once the novelty of the games has worn off, they may be less comfortable with the knowledge and skills orientation of the games. Variations of the TGT strategy which require students to research their own topics and write their own tournament questions may prove more rewarding for intuitive-type students.

The Team Games Tournament Strategy has demonstrated very positive effects in teaching topics which have quantifiable and behaviorally stated objectives, and which involve relatively simple or concrete skills. TGT is not an effective way to teach skills such as writing or analytical or logical thinking.

The goals of the Team Games Tournament Strategy are:

1. To produce an immediate and positive effect on student academic achievement;

2. To produce positive changes in student attitudes toward the class and the subject matter;

3. To foster positive working relationships among students by creating interdependence;

4. To make it possible for students with different learning rates to have an equal chance to succeed at an academic task; and

5. To help students learn how to learn.

The steps in the Team Games Tournament Strategy are:

1. Place students in heterogeneous learning teams;

2. Prepare the content to be learned;

3. Organize the tournament;

4. Prepare materials to be used in the practice sessions and in the tournament;

5. Conduct the practice and tournament sessions; and

6. Arrange for publication of tournament outcomes.

How to Plan Lessons Using the Team Games Tournament Strategy

The Team Games Tournament Strategy is useful not only for helping students to learn any material which much be practiced, but also for teaching students how to study and for providing tangible evidence that effective study pays off. TGT allows more students to be content-successful within a cooperative atmosphere.

Your students must be taught how TGT works before they begin to use it. Once taught, however, they will be able to follow its procedures for any topic. Your first step is to plan a clear presentation of the Team Games Tournament Strategy itself, which might be a visual organizer such as the one given on the following page.

Young children have trouble, at first, understanding that they will practice with their team, then leave their team to compete against members of other teams, then return bearing points to add to this team's score. Your class will enjoy a lesson in which you provide selected students with colored signs and have them act out the flow of TGT: practice together in your own team (children with the same color cards sit together in groups); compete with someone from another team (colors are mixed); bring your points back to your own team (children return to meet with those having the same color cards).

Once you have designed your lesson to explain TGT to your class, consider your students. How many do you have? Can they be divided into groups of four, five, or six? In theory, you should be able to make groups of three, but the theoretical classroom doesn't exist. Rather than deprive your students of a worthwhile activity that all will enjoy, play with the numbers until you get a set-up that works. Again, once you have determined how to divide your class(es), you will be able to use the same organization whenever you use TGT.

TGT TEAMS

Yellow	Green	Red
Y#1	G#1	R#1
Y#2	G#2	R#2
Y#3	G#3	R#3
Yellow practices together	Green practices together	Red practices together

TOURNAMENT

Game 1	Game 2	Game 3
Y#1	Y#2	Y#3
G#1	G#2	G#3
R#1	R#2	R#3

WINNERS: POINTS

1st	G#1	R#2	Y#3	6
2nd	Y#1	G#2	G#3	4
3rd	R#1	Y#2	R#3	2

Each team meets to record the team's total score:

Yellow	Green	Red
Y#1 = 4pts	G#1 = 6pts	R#1 = 2pts
Y#2 = 2pts	G#2 = 4pts	R#2 = 6pts
Y#3 = 6pts	G#3 = 4pts	R#3 = 2pts
12 pts	14pts	10 pts
Yellow is in 2nd place	Green is in 1st place	Red is in 3rd place

In selecting the learning teams, you should rank the learning according to past academic achievement in the topic to be learned. For a new topic, you might wish to devise a pretest. Plan for four, five, six, seven, eight, or nine member teams balanced according to sex, race, and ethnicity. This division scheme works for classes of 18, 20, 21, 24, 25, 27, 28, 30, 32, and so on. Assign a color or letter to each student to designate that student's team. For example, in a class of 32, there would be eight teams of four students each—red, orange, yellow, green, blue, purple, pink, brown. List your students in order, highest-achieving to lowest-achieving. Assign colors starting with red at the top and at the bottom of the student list, and continuing toward the middle in both directions. When the last color is used, begin to assign the colors in the opposite order, using brown first and continuing to work toward the middle (See diagram on next page).

NAME	RANK	TEAM
H	1	Red
I	2	Orange
G	3	Yellow
H	4	Green
	5	Blue
	6	Purple
	7	Pink
	8	Brown
A	9	Brown
V	10	Pink
E	11	Purple
R	12	Blue
A	13	Green
G	14	Yellow
E	15	Orange
	16	Red
	17	Red
	18	Orange
	19	Yellow
	20	Green
	21	Blue
	22	Purple
	23	Pink
	24	Brown
L	25	Brown
O	26	Pink
W	27	Purple
	28	Blue
	29	Green
	30	Yellow
	31	Orange
	32	Red

Each tournament team should include no fewer than four students. A class of 22 or 26 can be divided into two equal teams. If you have a class that just won't divide, such as 19 or 31, consider setting up an "extra person" rotation that will allow all of the students to practice and compete. Alternatively, assign one of your high-achieving students to assist you, and rotate that responsibility among students.

After you have assigned students to teams, prepare a summary list of team assignments.

To prepare a TGT competition, select a topic which is "gameable;" i.e., which lends itself to short objective questions which have only one correct answer. To be useful in a tutoring situation, a skill area must be one that children can teach to each other. You will need to prepare 25 to 40 questions for each tournament. The number of questions must be sufficient to cover the main points of the content. The style of the questions should demonstrate genuine learner understanding, rather than memorization. For example, the following geography questions ask students to translate what they have been taught about geological formations in the form of riddles. Answering questions in the form of riddles demonstrates understanding as well as memory skills; i.e.,:

I am a strip of land that sticks far out into the water. On most maps I look like a crooked finger.
(Peninsula)

I am land that is higher than the land around me. You can call me by one name if I am small, and by another is I am large. Tell my two names.
(Mesa, plateau)

In preparing questions, consider the appropriate level for the wording of the questions, and be aware of any reading level difficulties. Pictures or illustrations are helpful.

Once you have prepared the questions you wish to use in the tournament itself, prepare practice items. These should consist of sample tournament questions and parallel items which are not part of the tournament. The best results are attained when there is a 50% overlap between the practice questions and the tournament questions. Prepare answer sheets indicating the correct answer for both tournament questions and practice questions.

Establish a schedule which includes your introductory lesson on the Team Games Tournament Strategy, guided practice, team practice, and the tournament itself. Decide on team practice areas in your classroom, perhaps numbering tables and assigning each team to a particular practice table.

Advance organization is the key to making this strategy work. The more students know about what to do and how to do it, the more success and enjoyment they will get from participation.

Putting the Team Games Tournament Strategy to Work in Your Classroom

The Team Games Tournament Strategy consists of two phases: the practice session(s) and the tournament itself. Consider using what students know about how teams work effectively in sports, the roles of team players and coaches in team practice, and the importance of each player's contributions to the outcome. During the practice session(s), introduce your purpose for using TGT and the collaborative learning process. Emphasize the importance of the team structure and the role of team members in helping each other master the material presented in class. Explain that teammates will have a chance to work together to practice and help each other get ready to participate in the weekly tournament; that in these tournaments each student represents the team and earns points for the team. Identify the goals and objectives of the lesson; demonstrate the task or content to be learned; make students aware of your expectations as to quantity or quality of their learning this particular content; i.e., how many, how well.

During practice sessions, students work with their team in their designated practice areas and help each member of the team learn the content to be covered for the tournament. Students must decide how they will practice as a team. They may choose to break up into pairs and use the Reciprocal Learning Strategy, work on the practice questions independently, or complete the practice questions as a group. During practice sessions, you must be available to answer questions, gather information about learner and team performance, and offer feedback to learners and teams. As in the Reciprocal Learning Strategy, you should not give feedback to students regarding subject matter. Subject matter feedback is the responsibility of the team. You should however, answer any requests for clarification. Actively encourage group participation to guarantee team practice sessions; remind students that each have a "best" way of learning material and suggest that they try to help each other accordingly. Identify students or groups needing extra help by monitoring the number of questions learned.

At the start of the tournament, remind the students that the tournament provides a chance for each student to show how much was learned in the team. Explain that each student will play against members from other teams, and that any points won in the tournament are points toward the team total. Groups can play the game as long as time permits; to play another round, students simply record their scores for the first round and reshuffle the deck of cards. Be sure that students understand that they do not receive the same number of points as questions they have answered correctly; rather, they receive points based on whether they are in first, second, or third place.

GAME SCORE SHEET			
Table #____ Date _____ Round #____			
Player's Name	Team Name	Game Score Day's Total	Tournament Points

Students add up the cards they have won in each game and fill in their day's total on the game score sheet. Students calculate tournament points for three-player and four-player games as indicated below.

For a Four-Player Game

Player	No Ties	Tie for Top	Tie for Middle	Tie for Low	3-Way Tie For Top	3-Way Tie For Low	4-Way Tie	Tie for Low & High
Top Scorer	6 points	5	6	6	5	6	4	5
High Middle Scorer	4 points	5	4	4	5	3	4	5
Low Middle Scorer	3 points	3	4	3	5	3	4	3
Low Scorer	2 points	2	2	3	2	3	4	3

For a Three-Player Game

Player	No Ties	Tie for Top	Tie for Low	3-Way Tie
Top Scorer	6 points	5	6	4
Middle Scorer	4 points	5	3	4
Low Scorer	2 points	2	3	4

Your role in the tournament is first to assign students to tournament tables. Optimally, there will be three or four competitors at each table; remember that each competitor at a table must come from a different team, but not every team needs to be represented at each table. Distribute a deck of numbered cards, a game sheet with numbered questions, an answer sheet, and a game score sheet. Move from group to group to answer questions for clarification, and to be sure that each tournament is being played correctly. As timekeeper, signal the students at ten and five minutes before the tournament ends. The students should complete their final round within the last five minutes.

The rules of play are as follows:

1. Shuffle the deck of cards and place five down on the table. Decide which player will begin to play. The person to the left of the player is the challenger, the person to the right holds the answer key. Play goes clockwise around the table. As play moves from person to person, the answer key follows; the checker is always the person to the player's immediate right; the challenger always the person to the player's immediate left. In this fashion, each person is in turn player, checker, and challenger.

2. The player takes the top card from the deck, reads the number aloud; and answers the question. The challenger then has a chance to challenge the correctness of the answer. If there is no challenge from the challenger, then the person to the right indicates if the answer is correct or incorrect according to the answer sheet. If incorrect, the correct answer is read aloud, and the card is returned to the bottom of the deck. If correct, the player holds the card until the end of the round so that a count total can be determined.

3. If the player's answer is believed to be incorrect, and the other challenger can give the correct answer, then the card is given to the challenger. If the challenger's answer is incorrect, the challenger must surrender one of the cards already won. That card then goes back to the deck and not to any of the players. The correct answer is then read aloud from the answer sheet.

4. When there are no more cards in the deck, the players count up the number of cards they have and record this number as their individual score. The player with the most cards received the first place points, and points for the other places are determined accordingly.

In the first tournament, you will assign tournament tables based on past performance. The top three or four students, all from different teams, are assigned to table one, the next three or four to table two, and so on. After the first tournament, however, students change tables based on their tournament performance. The winner at each table is bumped to the next higher table, the second highest scorer remains, and the lowest scorer is bumped down. (In moving students, be sure that students competing against each other at a table are always from different teams.) In this way, students get a change of opponents from week to week. Such rotation also maintains more balance in skills at each table.

The TGT classroom newsletter provides the primary means for rewarding teams and individual students for their performance. Each week you should prepare a newsletter to announce the outcomes of the previous tournament. The newsletter should also recognize individual table winners and keep a record of cumulative standings.

How to Evaluate The Team Games Tournament Strategy

In the formative evaluation phase, you and the students should look for evidence of changed student attitudes toward the class and the subject matter. Having students write about how they feel about the class and the subject matter before TGT is initiated and then occasionally asking them to respond to the same question during the course of using TGT will provide some feedback.

Look for changes in the working relationships of your students. As you monitor practice and tournament sessions, carry a pocket notebook or some index cards on which to note evidence of supportive techniques and comments as well as of interdependence among students.

Finally, look for evidence of positive effects on student academic achievement. Give pretests and post-tests for each topic, and compare individual student progress with general measures of achievement such as past grades and test scores.

The following examples may be used to record each team's summary counts and to record the total tournament scores needed for student assignment to the next tournament round.

TOURNAMENT SCORE SHEET

Date_____   Round # _____

Table #	Players Name	Team Name	Game Score Day's Total	Tournament Points	Table Assignment for Next Round

TEAM SUMMARY SHEET

Team Name _____

Team Members	Tournament Points											FINAL POINTS
	Date											

Points rec'd this round / Total Points to date

Summary

When to use it:

When you want students to develop collaborative and competitive skills while practicing previously taught knowledge and skills.

How to use it:

1. Prepare short answer objective questions and answer sheets for practice session and tournament play;

2. Assign students to practice teams of three or four members (balance teams academically);

3. Assign one member from each team to participate at a tournament table (no more than four students with equal ability);

4. Explain tournament roles: Doer, Challenger, and Checker; enforce tournament rules; and

5. Collect game score and team summary sheets, validate results, and prepare newsletter.

How to evaluate it:

1. Are students able to practice in collaboration?

2. Are students able to compete appropriately in tournament play?

3. Are students learning and enjoying themselves?

Things to remember:

1. Select material which is gameable (objective questions);

2. Select a skill which students can teach to each other in a tutoring session; and

3. Establish practice teams with equal ability; i.e., one high achiever, two moderate achievers, and one low achiever.

Sample Lesson I: Elementary School/Geographical Terms

Objective: To define land and water terms

Procedures:

1. I am land that is higher than the land around me. You can call me by one name if I am small and by another if I am large. Tell me my two names.
2. I am an area of land completely surrounded by water. There are even small continents that are called my name.
3. I am a low area of land that is between hills or mountains.
4. I am the name of the largest bodies of land on the Earth. There are seven in my family.
5. I am a sand-covered area of land which has very little rainfall and where it gets very hot. Few things grow on me.
6. I am a large mass of ice which flows down the slopes of mountains. I move very slowly and I am strong enough to break land.
7. I am a deep valley with steep, jagged sides. I am very famous in Colorado.
8. I am land which is wet and muddy. Strange plants grow on me. I have two names.
9. I am the land which borders a sea or ocean. Either of my names will do.
10. I am a narrow strip of land which connects two larger pieces of land.
11. I am an area of high land that is flat like a table. I am sometimes called a tableland.
12. I am a steep-sided hill that is flat on top. I am quite tall.
13. I am a steep-sided hill that is flat on top, but I am smaller than my sister who has a Spanish name.
14. I am a high, steep face of rock. I could be the wall of a canyon or the side of a mountain.
15. I am a body of water that flows in one direction. I have a current. I always flow into an ocean or sea or other large body of water.
16. I am a body of water that is completely surrounded by land. I can be large or small.
17. I am a strip of land that sticks far into the water. On most maps, I look like a crooked finger.
18. I am part of an ocean or lake that fills in a curve of land.
19. I am the largest body of water on Earth. I am very salty. I have four brothers.
20. I am another name for an ocean. I can also be a very large lake with salt water.
21. I am the place where a river begins.
22. I am the place where a river ends and flows into another body of water.
23. I am a deep, narrow valley of water. I was caused by a glacier that split the land.
24. I am the ocean that is east of the United States.

Answers:

1. Hill or Mountain	9. Coast or Shoreline	17. Peninsula
2. Island	10. Isthmus	18. Bay
3. Valley	11. Plateau	19. Ocean
4. Continents	12. Mesa	20. Sea
5. Desert	13. Butte	21. Source
6. Glacier	14. Cliff	22. Mouth
7. Canyon	15. River	23. Fjord
8. Swamp or Marsh	16. Lake	24. Atlantic Ocean

Sample Lesson II: Let's Go on a Mission

Objective:

To use the TGT Strategy to answer trivia-style questions.

Procedures:

Your teacher will divide the students in your class into balanced teams of four to six people. Each team should select someone to act as "team leader." Your team will be given a designated amount of study time in which you will work together to review the material that has already been presented to you. It is important that everyone participates in the review, because each member will have to go on a "mission" to prove how much you have learned. On the mission, you will score points that represent the success of your learning during the unit. When the missions have been completed, each member of the team will report a score to the team leader. The team leader will add the scores of the individual members to obtain a "team total." He or she will then report the team total to the teacher, who will record the score. Scores from other teams will be recorded as well, and the team with the highest score will be the winner.

Let's go on a mission...

1. Each team should count off. Start at "one" and keep going until everyone in the team has a number. Remember your number because it will determine the mission group to which you belong.

2. Your teacher will then arrange you in the classroom so that all of the "ones", all of the "twos", etc., sit together. There should be a table or desk in the center of each mission group. You are now ready to begin.

3. On your group's table, there should be a sheet of questions and answers and a paper cup. Cut the answer section off and place it aside. Next, cut the questions into strips. Place all of the question strips into the cup. Fold them in half if they don't fit.

4. Decide which player will begin. The person to the left of the player is the challenger. The person to the right should hold the answer key. Play goes clockwise around the table.

5. The first player should take a question strip from the cup, read it aloud, and give an answer. He then should turn to the challenger and ask if they wish to "challenge" the given answer. If there is no challenge, the person to the right of the player indicates whether or not the answer was correct. If correct, the player gets to keep the strip in their hand. If incorrect, the correct answer is given and the strip is returned to the cup.

6. If the challenger challenges the player's answer, the challenger must answer the question. If the challenger is correct, they get to keep the strip. If incorrect, they must surrender one of the strips they've already won. If neither player not the challenger answers the question correctly, the answer should be read aloud. The strip is then returned to the cup.

7. Play should continue until there are no more questions left in the cup. When this happens, your mission is completed. Count the number of strips you have in your hand and report your score to the team leader.

LETS GO ON A MISSION...

1. The class of animals that dominates the small land-living species is _____.
2. A creature whose body temperature is dependent on the environment is _____.
3. An organism that maintains a constant body temperature is _____.
4. When a reptile is cold, its activity level _____.
5. Most reptiles blend in with their environment. This is called _____.
6. Some snakes kill their prey by injecting them with a poison called _____.
7. The best defense a turtle has is its _____.
8. The reptile's legs supply support on land and flexibility in water due to _____.
9. Reptiles don't move often, but when they do they move _____.
10. The egg of a reptile is protected by a _____.
11. The outer covering of reptiles is made up of _____.
12. The senses of taste and smell are joined together on the snake's _____.
13. Because of their shelled eggs, reptiles can lay their eggs away from _____.
14. Reptiles can be more active than amphibians due to improved _____.
15. Some scientists think dinosaurs became extinct due to _____.
16. Are most reptiles carnivores or herbivores?
17. What kind of snake kills its prey by squeezing it?
18. The gila monster is one of only two lizards that is _____.
19. In viviparous reptiles, the offspring are _____.
20. Reptile eggs are fertilized _____.
21. To compensate for high offspring mortality, the number of reptile eggs is _____.
22. As a defense mechanism, the tail of a glass snake will _____.
23. The reptile kidney is adapted to reabsorb more _____.
24. The main enemies of reptiles are large _____.
25. Alligators are exceptional because they protect their _____.

Answers:

1. reptiles
2. cold-blooded
3. warm-blooded
4. decreases
5. camouflage
6. venom
7. shell
8. bent-knee design
9. quickly
10. leathery shell
11. scales
12. Jacobson's Organ
13. water
14. heart and lungs
15. meteorites (check with your teacher if your answer is different)
16. carnivores
17. constrictor
18. venomous
19. born alive
20. internally
21. large
22. break off
23. water
24. mammals
25. offspring

Sample Lesson III:
Teaming up for the Restaurant Game

Objective:
To use the TGT Strategy to learn order of operations techniques utilizing mock restaurant checks.

Anticipatory Set:
If you are really at a restaurant, you will want to be able to check the bill in your head rather quickly. This next activity will give you some practice.

Procedures:
Your teacher will divide the students in your class into balanced groups of four to six individuals. Each team should select someone to act as "team leader." Your team will be given a designated amount of time to review the skills that you have already learned in this unit. Pay particular attention to your recipe cards and to any information that explains how to quickly estimate the total of a restaurant check. It is important that every group member participates in the review because each member will have to out on a "food run" to see how well they can estimate costs. You will receive points according to how well you do, and will report your score to the team leader when you return from the food run. The team leader will add the individual scores of the group members together for a "group total." They will then report the group total to the teacher, who will record the score. Scores from other teams will be recorded as well, and the team with the highest score will be the winner.

Let's go on a food run...
1. Each team should count off. Start at "one" and keep going until everyone in the team has a number. Remember your number because it will determine which restaurant you will go to and with whom you will go.

2. Your teacher will then arrange you in the classroom so that all of the "ones", all of the "twos", etc., sit together. Each restaurant group should have a table or desk at the center of it. When you have arranged yourselves and found a supply of pencils and scrap paper, you are ready to begin.

3. On your group's table, there should be a paper cup and several sheets of restaurant checks. Cut each of the checks out and place them in the cup. If the checks don't fit, fold them in half.

4. There should be an answer sheet on the table as well. Cut and fold the strips down so that the answers are not showing. Label the tops of the strips that you have folded down so that you will be able to "flip-up" the appropriate strip and look at the answer when the time comes. When you are done preparing the answer sheet, place it aside.

5. Decide which player will begin. The person to the left of the player is the challenger; the person to the right should hold the answer key. Play goes clockwise around the restaurant table.

6. The first player should take one of the checks from the cup and place it on the table between himself and the challenger. Both the player and the challenger should estimate the total cost of the check in front of them. The player reads his answer aloud whenever he is done calculating. He then turns to the challenger and asks if he/she plans to challenge. If there is no challenge, the person with the answer key indicates whether the given answer is correct or incorrect. They should also announce the actual total to show how accurate a good estimate can be. If the player's answer was correct, the player holds the strip in their hand. If incorrect, the player should discard the strip.

7. If the challenger disagreed with the player's answer and wished to challenge, they would then have had to announce the answer they believed to be correct. If the challenger was correct, they get to keep the check. If incorrect, they would have to give up one of their own checks. If neither player nor the challenger were correct, the correct answer would still be read aloud. The check would then be discarded.

8. Play should continue until there are no more checks in the cup. When this happens, you should count the number of checks in your hand and report your score to the team leader. Each check counts as one point. Checks that were discarded are worth nothing.

9. Your team leader will tally the scores of all the group members and see how successful your group was.

LET'S GO ON A FOOD RUN...

2 banana splits	$2.11 each	2 chicken sandwiches	$4.89 each	2 clam chowders	$2.38 each
4 cokes	$1.02 each	1 egg salad	$2.25 each	1 salad bar	$6.75 each
1 ice cream	$0.99 each	3 milkshakes	$1.79 each	2 seltzer waters	$0.98 each
Total:		**Total:**		**Total:**	

3 poached eggs	$2.12 each	2 chicken nuggets	$3.84 each	1 large pizza add pepperoni	$6.89 each $0.59 each
2 hash browns	$1.02 each	1 french fry	$1.04 each	2 pitchers soda	$1.89 each
2 lg. orange juices	$0.99 each	1 chocolate shake	$1.02 each		
Total:		**Total:**		**Total:**	

2 chili dogs	$0.99 each	2 macaroni & cheese	$4.75 each	2 burgers	$3.95 each
3 cups soup	$1.10 each	1 broccoli quiche	$3.99 each	2 onion rings	$1.56 each
2 milks	$0.95 each	2 iced teas	$1.04 each	2 cokes	$1.10 each
Total:		**Total:**		**Total:**	

2 pancakes	$3.95 each	2 spaghetti	$3.99 each	1 bologna & cheese	$2.95 each
1 waffle add ice cream	$3.95 each $1.00 each	1 garlic bread	$1.80 each	2 peanut butter & jelly	$2.55 each
2 sm. orange juices	$1.00 each	2 lemonades	$1.02 each	1 fruit punch	$0.95 each
				1 order nachos	$2.25 each
Total:		**Total:**		**Total:**	

ANSWER SHEET

Estimate:

2 x $2 + 4 x $1 = $9.00

✂ CUT

1. Actual Total:
$9.29

✂ CUT

7

---

2 x $5 + $2 + 3 x $2 = $18.00

2. Actual Total:
$17.40

✂ CUT

8

---

2 x $2 + $7 + 2 x $1 = $13.00

3. Actual Total:
$13.47

✂ CUT

9

---

3 x $2 + 2 x $1 + 2 x $1 = $10.00

4. Actual Total:
$10.38

✂ CUT

10

---

2 x $4 + $1 + $1 = $10.00

5. Actual Total:
$9.74

✂ CUT

11

$7 + $2 + 2 x $2 = $13.00

6. Actual Total:
$12.26

12

ANSWER SHEET

✂ CUT

1

(2 x $1) + (3 x $1) + (2 x $1) = $7.00

7. Actual Total: $7.18

✂ CUT

✂ CUT

2

(2 x $5) + $4 + (2 x $1) = $16.00

8. Actual Total: $15.57

✂ CUT

3

(2 x $4) + (2 x $2) + (2 x $1) = $14.00

9. Actual Total: $13.22

✂ CUT

4

(2 x $4) + $4 + $1 + (2 x $1) = $15.00

10. Actual Total: $15.15

✂ CUT

5

(2 x $4) + $2 + (2 x $1) = $12.00

11. Actual Total: $11.82

✂ CUT

6

$3 + (2 x $3) + $1 + $2 = $12.00

12. Actual Total: $11.25

JIGSAW STRATEGY
(The Experts Strategy)

Jigsaw is a gaming technique designed to increase students' sense of responsibility for their learning by making them "experts" in one part of an instructional unit. This sense of responsibility is reinforced by having each "expert" teach that part of the unit to the others on the larger team.

The Strategy at Work

To introduce the main parts of speech—noun, verb, adjective, and adverb—to her fourth graders, Ms. McPherson has decided to use the Jigsaw Strategy as part of the planning process, she has collected information, and made similar small packets about each part of speech. The noun packet, for example, consists of a cartoon about nouns, a definition of a noun, a descriptive paragraph about nouns, some examples of nouns in sentences with explanations below each, and a one-page workbook-type exercise to practice finding nouns in sentences.

Ms. McPherson has organized her class of twenty students into Jigsaw Teams of four members each. She uses the Jigsaw Strategy frequently, but she makes sure to vary team membership each time, and to make Jigsaw Teams heterogeneous in terms of achievement level. Each of the four students in a Jigsaw Team will receive a packet on a different part of speech. The students will be responsible for learning about their part of speech, meeting with an Expert Team to design a lesson on their part of speech, and returning to their Jigsaw Team to teach the other three team members about their part of speech. Each team member's success is crucial to the team's success since all team members will be tested on all four parts of speech, and the individual scores will be added to make up the team's score.

Today Karen is sitting with her Jigsaw Team. Ms. McPherson has placed four part-of-speech cards face down on the desk they are using as a table. Each team member draws a card. Karen will be responsible for learning about verbs; Rachel for nouns; Manuel for adjectives; and Waheed for adverbs. Ms. McPherson distributes the appropriate packets to each student, and Karen begins to read silently and think about the material. She knows that when she meets with the Expert Group, she will be expected to know something about verbs, and to have some ideas about how to teach them.

Ms. McPherson expects that all of her students will finish working independently on their packets today, including doing the workbook-type exercise and self-correcting it with the posted answer sheets.

Tomorrow Karen will meet with the students from the four other teams who also drew verbs; she and the other four students make up the Verb Expert Team. They will discuss the main ideas about verbs, and determine the best way to teach verbs to their teammates. Together they will develop a lesson plan and five suggested test questions. Again, each student's success is crucial to their team's success; the Verb-Expert Team's score will be determined by adding up the points for all of the verb questions answered correctly by everyone in the class. If the class as a whole answers more verb questions correctly than noun or adjective or adverb questions, then the Verb Expert Team will have won the Superteacher Award for this unit. At the end of this session, Ms. McPherson collects the test questions from the Expert Groups. She will use two or three from each Expert Group on the final test.

The next day Karen will return to her team and take her turn to show her expertise. When Rachel, Manuel, and Waheed are also done with their teaching, the Jigsaw Team may practice together until Ms. McPherson says that the time is up.

The final step for Ms. McPherson, prior to test day, is to lead a whole class discussion of nouns, verbs, adjectives, and adverbs in which she will stress the most important things to remember. The test she will administer is broken down for ease of scoring into four sections, one for each part of speech, with five questions in each section. Jigsaw Teams figure their total scores by adding the scores of their teammates; Ms. McPherson checks the totaling. She figures Expert Team totals by keeping a running tally for each section as she grades the tests. The winning Jigsaw Team gets to wear large medals made of construction paper which say, "Top Team;" for the winning Expert Team, the medals say "Superteacher."

The Jigsaw Strategy

In the Jigsaw Strategy, the teacher organizes the group into Jigsaw Teams to study and learn about a particular topic. Each Jigsaw Team member is assigned a subtopic. Then members from each Jigsaw Team, who are working on the same subtopic, meet as an Expert Group to investigate their subtopic, and to plan, design, and construct the lesson and activities that they will take back to their respective Jigsaw Teams. When the lessons and activities have been finished, experts return to their Jigsaw Teams and take turns teaching their subtopics. When the teams hear the presentations of their experts, the teacher conducts a follow-up lesson with the class as a whole, in which experts are called on to act as leaders in a discussion designed to emphasize the most important concepts. The teacher plans an evaluation instrument consisting of sub-tests covering all of the assigned subtopics (as much as half of the evaluation may be planned by the Expert Group responsible for teaching the subtopic.) Scores of Jigsaw Team members will be added and compared so that teams can see which Jigsaw Team did the best job of learning the material; pertinent sub-test scores will be added and compared to determine which of the Expert Groups was most successful in teaching the material.

The goals of the Jigsaw Strategy are:
1. To help students increase their sense of responsibility for their learning;
2. To help students learn how to learn;
3. To help students improve their social and interactive skills in a work situation;
4. To foster improved attitudes toward academic achievement, the subject matter, and peers; and
5. To increase student academic achievement.

The steps in the Jigsaw Strategy are to:
1. Select a topic which students will be able to study, learn, and teach to others;
2. Develop a set of focused materials for each subtopic;
3. Prepare an "Expert Sheet" for each subtopic to tell students what they should concentrate on while reading and/or working with hands-on materials;
4. Assign the students to Jigsaw Teams, and give each student a subtopic for which they are responsible;
5. Have the students read or work with the day's material independently, focusing on the specifications of their Expert Sheet, then review the material to develop questions that they think might be appropriate for a quiz;
6. Have students from each Jigsaw Team who have worked on the same subtopic meet together in an "Expert Group" to discuss the subtopic they share, identify main ideas and important details, develop a set of questions to be used on a quiz, and plan together effective ways of presenting the information to their Jigsaw Teams;
7. Have students return to their Jigsaw Teams to teach their subtopics;
8. Lead a class discussion to focus on important concepts; and
9. Test all students, using both expert-prepared and teacher-prepared questions, and compute total team scores (based on all questions) and total expert group scores (based on all questions for each subtopic).

How to Plan Lessons Using the Jigsaw Strategy

You need to think about the class of students for whom this strategy is planned. How much background information do they have? How adept are they at working independently? How adept are they at working together? How much can they reasonably be expected to cover? A class that has already demonstrated strong positive working relationships, supportive attitudes towards each other, and good independent work habits will be enthusiastic about studying a sophisticated, challenging topic. A class that is lacking in one or more of these areas will respond better to a carefully chosen topic with ample opportunity for you to model appropriate interaction among students. Choose the topic to be covered based on these considerations.

You need to think about the number of students in the class, and how that number is divisible. Should the Jigsaw Teams be composed of five members? Four members? Three? A Jigsaw Team of three members can cover only three subtopics; a team of four can cover either four subtopics or two subtopics (if team members are paired); and so on. How will the number of students on a team affect the way you split up the instructional unit into sections to be studied?

You need to think about the materials that will be available to Expert Groups for learning about their subtopic, and then be made available for their use in planning, designing, and constructing lessons and activities to teach their subtopic to their Jigsaw Teams. Materials for each Expert Group need to be assembled and made available in much the same way that they would be if the teacher were designing a learning center on the subtopic.

In deciding on Jigsaw Team membership and assigning subtopics, you need to consider the particular strengths of individuals. The Expert Group for each subtopic should end up including the individuals who bring different talents to the learning and planning process.

Will each Expert Group include someone good at conceptualizing? Someone who can easily determine main ideas? Someone who has a creative approach? Someone who is artistic? Someone who is good at details and is well-organized? Will the Expert Groups work well together? Are the Jigsaw Teams fairly evenly matched? Are the Expert Groups fairly and evenly matched?

Jigsaw with a class of twelve students, divided into three Jigsaw Teams, and assigned to investigate and teach four subtopics, would look like this:

JIGSAW TEAM A
Expert A #1
Expert A #2
Expert A #3
Expert A #4

JIGSAW TEAM B
Expert B #1
Expert B #2
Expert B #3
Expert B #4

JIGSAW TEAM C
Expert C #1
Expert C #2
Expert C #3
Expert C #4

Jigsaw Teams A, B, and C would meet so that each member could be assigned a subtopic (perhaps by lottery) which that member will be responsible for learning about and then teaching. Then, after an initial meeting to allow Jigsaw Team members to study and learn the material provided for their subtopics, the Jigsaw Team members would regroup, then meet as Expert Groups. For example, the experts from A, B, and C assigned to investigate, plan, and teach subtopic #1 would meet to work together.

EXPERT GROUP #1
Expert A #1
Expert B #1
Expert C #1

EXPERT GROUP #2
Expert A #2
Expert B #2
Expert C #2

EXPERT GROUP #3
Expert A #3
Expert B #3
Expert C #3

EXPERT GROUP #4
Expert A #4
Expert B #4
Expert C #4

Thus, when experts from these four groups return to teach their Jigsaw Team, they will all teach from the same lesson plan and use the same activities.

When you have arranged your groups, selected your topic and divided it into the appropriate number of manageable subtopics, and assembled materials, you will need to devise an Expert Sheet for each subtopic. This Expert Sheet will tell students concentrating on a particular subtopic what the focus of their study should be.

Putting the Jigsaw Strategy to Work in Your Classroom

Explain to students that they will each become part of a Jigsaw Team, and that each member of the team will become an expert on a specific aspect of the topic. They will then be responsible for teaching the members of their team about their area of expertise. Make sure students are clear about the procedures of this strategy: meet in Jigsaw Teams to get assignments and work independently; meet in Expert Groups made up of members from all of the Jigsaw Teams working on the same subtopic to learn about the subtopic and plan together how to teach it; return to Jigsaw Teams to teach the subtopic.

Spend some time discussing the responsibilities of the Expert Groups. They need to understand that they are to "teach" themselves as much as they can about the subtopic by using the materials which you have provided, and they should be sure to clarify difficult points by asking you for help. They should think about and discuss the subtopic in the Expert Group: what do their "students" need to know about the subtopic?; what will be easiest for them to remember? They need to think of an interesting way to teach the subtopic to their "students". They need to design an organizer which their "students" will be able to fill in with notes as they teach, so that their "students" will have a study sheet to keep. They need to design a practice activity so that their "students" will be able to practice their new skill (Think: how

will this practice activity be corrected?). They need to plan a review activity so that, after their Jigsaw Team has worked on all of the subtopics, the Jigsaw Team will have the opportunity to see the material once again before being tested on it. They need to plan a way of testing their "students" to see if they have really learned the material.

Jigsaw Teams need to work together to help the expert by listening carefully and participating actively. They need to help their Jigsaw Team work together to practice the material so that they all learn it. When it is a Jigsaw Team member's turn to be the expert, that member must present the material as clearly, carefully, completely, and patiently as possible; must give team members a chance to ask questions, and must help them understand and learn the material being taught.

When you have set up your Jigsaw Teams, assigned subtopics, and assembled materials, your students are ready to begin. Throughout the learning and planning phase, circulate to all of the Expert Groups, helping to focus learning, clarifying information, challenging experts on facts and understandings, and offering encouragement. When your experts are teaching their Jigsaw Team colleagues, circulate to all of the Jigsaw Teams to help focus, clarify, and encourage, as needed.

Before your students begin to teach the lessons they have developed in their Expert Groups, collect from each Expert Group the questions they have written for their subtopic. Using these and questions of your own, design an evaluation instrument consisting of sub-tests for each subtopic; for example, a test on a topic broken into four subtopics might have five questions in each of four subsections. Administer the test when the Experts have finished presenting their lessons to their respective Jigsaw Teams. Compile the results of the evaluation, and "publish" standings for Jigsaw Teams (based on the total of test scores for each team separately), and for Expert Groups (based on the total of the whole class's sub-test scores for each subtopic).

How to Evaluate the Jigsaw Strategy

As with the Team Games Tournament Strategy, it is important for you to monitor improvement in social skills and working relationships by gathering evidence about the types of student interactions. Making brief notes in a pocket notebook or an index card as you circulate from group to group is a good way to track improvement in student attitudes toward academic achievement, the subject matter, and peers.

To assess student academic improvement, you may wish to use pretests to provide a point of comparison with post-tests. Monitor progress to see if learning continues to increase with new topics as students become more familiar with the Jigsaw Strategy, and with ways to support each other in their learning.

In addition, engage your students in a discussion of how they learn. One of the most important aspects of a strategy like Jigsaw is its hidden goal: helping students **learn how to learn**. You can use a combination of strategies, such as Write to Learn and Circle, to lead your students in an exploration of questions like the following:

1. What did you like best about this project? Why?

2. What did you like least about this project? Why?

3. Why do you think different people like different things about this project?

4. What kinds of information did you find easy to remember?

5. What information was hard for you to remember?

6. What kinds of things did the "Expert" do that helped you to remember?

7. What kinds of things did <u>you</u> do that helped you to remember?

8. If you need to learn something else, what kinds of things can <u>you</u> do to increase <u>your</u> ability to remember? What works for <u>you</u>?

Summary

When to use it:

When you want to increase student participation and develop cooperative research skills (in a selected content area).

How to use it:

1. Divide students into heterogeneous groups or practice teams of about five people;

2. Develop an expert group sheet stating guidelines for subtopic research;

3. Assign each student in a practice team to a different expert group;

4. Distribute appropriate subtopic expert sheets to each student;

5. Have students conduct research on their subtopic and then assemble in expert groups to review, discuss, and determine the most important concepts;

6. Have expert group draft questions to use on a unit test;

7. Collect questions;

8. Have each expert report and share with his practice team;

9. Have students use note-taking sheet to record information from each Expert;

10. Lead class in question and answer session covering entire topic;

11. Ask questions related directly to guideline sheets; and

12. Develop a quiz based on the sample questions submitted by expert groups.

How to evaluate it:

1. Did the students do a thorough job of researching subtopics? (This may take several days.)

2. Did they really come up with the most important concepts?

3. Did students work cooperatively in their groups, contributing to the best of their ability and level?

Things to remember:

1. It is important to have low, average, and high achievers in each group;

2. Students may need to add to guideline sheet for uniformity of information; and

3. The quiz questions should contain the same number of questions from each subtopic.

Sample Lesson I: Mathematics

Mr. Rotberg wanted to provide his sixth grade students with the opportunity to develop conceptual understandings, and to learn and practice arithmetic skills related to measurement topics such as perimeter, area, surface area, and volume.

Objectives:

Mr. Rotberg's students will work together to develop conceptual understandings, and will learn and practice arithmetic skills related to measurement topics such as perimeter, area, surface area, and volume.

Anticipatory Set:

To introduce the Jigsaw Strategy to his class, Mr. Rotberg has always chosen a student in the group who had expertise in a high interest topic such as magic, origami, construction of paper airplanes, etc., to teach the group how to do one of these. This year, the student chosen was Jamie, who agreed to show the class how to do several coin tricks. Mr. Rotberg provided a bowl of pennies so that everyone could participate.

After the lesson, Mr. Rotberg pointed out that Jamie was an EXPERT. "What is an expert?" he asked. "How did you become an expert, Jamie? Did you learn from someone else? From a book? Did you just watch someone? Just read about it? Did you have to practice? Did someone coach you while you were practicing?"

Mr. Rotberg then asked his students if they were experts in something. Had they ever taught something they were good at to someone else? He asked, "How does it feel to teach something you know well to someone else?"

Procedures:

Mr. Rotberg explained to his students that they would each become part of a Jigsaw Team, and that each member of the team would become an expert on a measurement topic. Then they would be responsible for teaching members of their team about their area of expertise.

Each of Mr. Rotberg's teams consisted of four members. The four members drew lots to determine which one would be responsible for learning about perimeter, area, surface area, and volume. Each team member received an appropriate learning packet to read and work through individually, prior to meeting with Expert Groups.

After the Jigsaw Teams had time to go through the packet of materials individually, Mr. Rotberg discussed the functions of Expert Groups. He provided each student with a copy of directions for working in an Expert Group, and discussed and clarified the directions:

Tasks for the EXPERT GROUPS to work on together:

1. "Teach" yourselves as much as you can about the topic by researching the topic; be sure to clarify difficult points by asking for help from the teacher;

2. Think about and discuss the topic: what do your "students" need to know?; what will be easiest for them to remember?;

3. Think of an interesting way to teach the topic to your "students;"

4. Design an organizer which your "students" will be able to fill in as you "teach," so that your "students" will have a study sheet to keep;

5. Design a practice activity so that your "students" will be able to practice their new skill (Think: how will this practice activity be corrected?);

6. Plan a review activity so that, after your JIGSAW group has worked on all of the topics, your "students" will have the opportunity to see the material once again before being tested on it; and

7. Plan a way of testing your "students" to see if they have really learned the material.

Mr. Rotberg then called together his Measurement Expert Teams:

Expert Group #1: Perimeter of polygon: understand concept of perimeter; MEASURE SIDES, using customary and metric measure, find perimeter by measuring; find perimeter by adding; develop and solve perimeter word problems.

Expert Group #2: Area: understanding concept of area: find area by counting covering squares: MEASURE SIDES, using customary and metric measure, to find the area of a square or a rectangle by multiplication; develop and solve area word problems.

Expert Group #3: Volume—understand concept of volume; find the volume of concrete objects such as empty boxes by filling them with cubes, and blocks by building matching shapes out of cubes; find the volume of concrete objects such as blocks by MEASURING SIDES, using customary and metric measure, and computing the volume; find the volume of cubes and rectangular prisms; develop and solve volume word problems.

Expert Group #4: Surface area—understand concept of surface area; find surface area of concrete objects such as blocks by counting covering squares; find the surface area of concrete objects such as blocks by MEASURING SIDES, using customary and metric measure, and computing areas of faces; find the surface area of a rectangular prism; develop and solve surface area word problems.

Throughout the research and planning phase, Mr. Rotberg circulated to all of the Expert Groups, helping to focus research, clarifying information, challenging experts on facts and understandings, and offering encouragement.

After the Expert Groups had worked together in Mr. Rotberg's hands-on learning centers for each topic, Mr. Rotberg collected their proposed questions. He also established

a conference time for each Expert Team in which he used his copy of the guide for Expert Teams to discuss the group's work and to make sure that each Expert Team had completed the assignment.

Before allowing the experts to teach to the Jigsaw Teams, Mr. Rotberg distributed and led a discussion on a copy of directions for Jigsaw Teams:

Tasks for the Jigsaw Teams to work on together:

1. Help the expert by listening carefully and participating actively in learning the material which is being presented to you by your expert;

2. Help your Jigsaw Team work together to practice the materials so that you all will learn it; and

3. When it is your turn to be the expert, present your material as clearly, carefully, completely, and patiently as possible; give your team members a chance to ask you questions and do your best to help them understand and learn the material you are teaching.

Throughout the teaching phase, Mr. Rotberg circulated to all of the Jigsaw Teams to help focus, clarify and encourage, as needed.

When all of the Jigsaw Teams had finished their work, Mr. Rotberg taught four summary lessons, one on each topic, which summed up the main concepts, provided additional examples, and reviewed the material. In each of these lessons the appropriate Expert Group was spotlighted.

The final assessment for this measurement unit consisted of an evaluation instrument designed and administered by Mr. Rotberg. The instrument consisted of four sub-tests, one for each topic. Mr. Rotberg included two questions submitted by each Expert Team, together with two questions he had devised. In addition, each Expert Team had suggested testing students with hands-on activities from these activities. Mr. Rotberg selected one per sub-test, compiled the results of the evaluation, and "published" standings for Jigsaw Teams (based on total of test scores for each team separately) and for Expert Groups (based on total of the whole class's sub-test scores for each topic).

Sample LessonII: Science-Reptiles

Mr. Carrozza decided to use the Jigsaw Strategy with his seventh grade class for his students to learn about reptiles as part of a unit he was teaching called "A Second Chance for Cold-Bloods." He wanted his students to address two essential questions: What kinds of reptiles are there; and How do they adapt to their environment?

Objectives:

Students will work together using the Jigsaw Strategy to develop an understanding of the different kinds of reptiles and how they adapt to their environments.

Anticipatory Set:

Mr. Carrozza explained that the class Reptilia has several subgroupings like lizards, snakes, turtles, and crocodiles. While they all share certain common characteristics, each possesses unique characteristics of their own. Since there is a large amount of information to acquire about each of these different reptiles and how they adapt to their environment, Mr. Carrozza explained that they would be using the Jigsaw Strategy to acquire all they needed to know.

Procedures:

To ensure the interdependence and positive interaction among the team members, Mr. Carrozza decided to make his students experts in one of the ways the four types of reptiles adapt. Therefore, every student had to read about each of the four types of reptiles, but still had to focus on one aspect.

Types / Adaption Expertise	Lizards	Snakes	Turtles	Crocodiles and Alligators
Food				
Child Rearing				
Temperature and Water				
Survival				

Mr. Carrozza provided his students with the following directions: "To begin, you must first join a study group of four students. Your classmates should do this, too. Once your group gets together, you will each have to take on a specialty. Decide who is to be the Food Expert, the Child Rearing Expert, the Temperature and Water Expert, and the Survival Expert for your study group.

The study groups then split up for a while. All the Food Experts from the different groups sit together in their designated area of the room; the same hold true for the experts in Child Rearing, Temperature and Water, and Survival. Each group will need a blank organizer designed specifically for them, as well as the passage which describes their topic.

Each of the members of each Expert Group is to study the passage and help to complete the organizer. Each group should become familiar with the information and should discuss how they will present it to their groups.

When all the expert groups are ready, everyone will return to his or her original study group. All experts should take turns sharing what they have learned about their special topics. Team members should take notes on the remaining organizers that refer to each specific topic.

When finished, you should have completed notes and an understanding of reptilian feeding, child rearing, temperature and water management, and adaptations for survival."

FOOD EXPERTS:	**CHILD REARING EXPERTS:**
What kind of food is eaten and how is it caught?	What are the patterns of reproduction, nesting, and child care?
Lizards:	Lizards:
Snakes:	Snakes:
Turtles:	Turtles:
Crocodiles/Alligators:	Crocodiles/Alligators:
TEMPERATURE AND WATER EXPERTS:	**SURVIVAL EXPERTS:**
How are reptiles adapted to life on land? How do reptiles react and/or adapt to temperature variances?	What kind of defense is used by each type of reptile for survival?
Lizards:	Lizards:
Snakes:	Snakes:
Turtles:	Turtles:
Crocodiles/Alligators:	Crocodiles/Alligators:

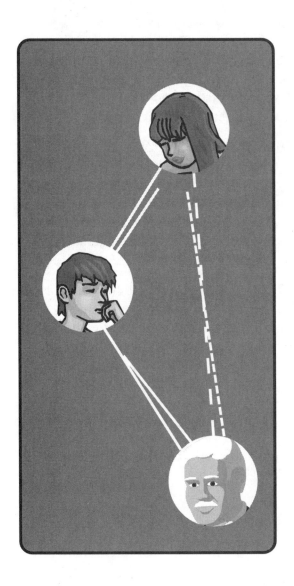

RECIPROCAL LEARNING
(Peers Coaching Peers)

The Reciprocal Learning Strategy (Reciprocal Learning) is a unique partnership that is forged between pairs of students working together to practice previously presented skills and information, to increase reading comprehension of information-rich texts, and to develop the thinking processes needed to become competent problem solvers. Through using the Reciprocal Learning Strategy, students will master important skills needed to be effective in a helping relationship, learn how to be active listeners and how to provide constructive feedback, and develop patience and the ability to praise.

The Strategy at Work

For her seventh grade social studies class, in their study of the ancient kingdom of Kush, Ms. Kuechle wanted to use some original sources, but she knew that the reading would be too difficult for many of her students. She decided to use the Peer Reading variation of the Reciprocal Learning Strategy. For her class, she prepared and led a discussion of the following work sheet. When she was satisfied that her students understood both the procedures for the Peer Reading Strategy and what the required products were, she distributed the accompanying short piece, a translation from Herodotus, for the students to summarize.

Reciprocal Learning as a Reading Strategy

Sometimes you are asked to read a piece that has a lot of information in it for you to understand and remember. When you read about the location of Kush, you will be practicing a helpful strategy that you can use whenever you are studying material that you find hard to learn.

Here is the way this reading/learning strategy works:

1. You need a partner.

2. Sit with your partner. Each of you will read the story about travel to Kush silently to yourselves.

3. Before you begin to read silently, think about the fact that you will be asked to summarize what you read **without looking back**! Will it help you to take notes? Will you remember better if you underline key ideas? Should you stop after each paragraph, close your eyes, and try to "see" the main points?

4. When you have your plan in mind, begin to read the passage. Don't rush, but don't read too slowly either. Don't try to remember everything; concentrate on the main ideas.

5. When you and your partner have both finished reading the whole passage, decide how to divide it in two. For example, the passage about travel to Kush can be divided in the middle of the page where the quote from Herodotus begins. Decide who will summarize the first section.

6. The person summarizing the first section must put the paper away. The person listening should look at the paper and listen carefully to the summary. The listener should ask helping questions where needed: How long did the overland journey take? What did the nobleman take with him for his journey? And so on.

7. Switch jobs: let the listener summarize the second section with the help of the person who summarized the first part.

8. Evaluate your learning:

I really understood the story about travel to Kush.
Agree -------------------------------------- Disagree

I was able to give a good summary of the main idea.
Agree -------------------------------------- Disagree

I was able to help my partner give a good summary.
Agree -------------------------------------- Disagree

My partner was able to help me give a good summary.
Agree -------------------------------------- Disagree

For your portfolio, write a brief summary of the story about travel to Kush.

CAN YOU GET THERE FROM HERE? TRAVEL TO KUSH

We believe that there must have been regular trade and travel between the kingdom of Kush and other places of power such as Egypt, Greece, and Rome, but there are few written records to support this idea. A nobleman from Elephantine (Aswan), around 2340 B.C., caused to be written on his tomb the story of four journeys to Kush, all of which took seven or eight months. He traveled over land with three hundred good donkeys—one hundred carrying goods, one hundred carrying forage (food for the donkeys), and one hundred carrying water. He brought back to the Pharaoh gifts of ebony, ivory, and frankincense.

Much later, around 430 B.C., the famous Greek historian Herodotus came to visit Egypt and to find out as much as he could about the Egyptians because he believed that the Greeks had taken a great deal from them, especially in religion. He became very interested in the rest of Africa while he was in Egypt, saying, for example, "as between the Egyptians and the (Kushites), I should not like to say which learned from the other..." Herodotus made up his mind to travel to Kush to see for himself.

Continued on next page

Continued from previous page

"I went as far as Elephantine (Aswan) to see what I could with my own eyes, but for the country still further south I had to be content with what I was told in answer to my questions. The most I could learn was that beyond Elephantine the country rises steeply; and in that part of the river, boats have to be hauled along by ropes—one rope on each side—much as one drags an ox. If the rope parts, the boat is gone in a moment, carried away by the force of the stream. These conditions last over four days' journey, the river all the time winding greatly, like the Meander (a river in Greece), and the distance to be covered amounting to (about 120 kilometers). After this, one reaches a level plain, where the river is divided by an island named Tachompso.

"South of Elephantine the country is inhabited by (Kushites) who also possess half of Tachompso, the other half being occupied by Egyptians. Beyond the island is a great lake, and round its shores live nomadic tribes of (Kushites). After crossing the lake, one comes again to the stream of the Nile, which flows into it. At this point, one must land and travel along the bank of the river for forty days, because sharp rocks, some showing above the water and many just awash, make the river impracticable for boats. After the forty days' journey on land, one takes another boat and, in twelve days, reaches a big city named Meroe (possibly Napata?), said to be the capital city of the (Kushites)."

The Reciprocal Learning Strategy

The Reciprocal Learning Strategy is often used when you want your students to develop helping skills while practicing previously taught information. In the Reciprocal Learning Strategy, students work together in pairs, using uniquely designed interdependent worksheets that develop their mastery of skills and information. At the same time, by providing a framework in which students of differing achievement levels can work together to improve their knowledge of the content, the worksheets help students learn how to become active listeners and how to provide constructive feedback. The Reciprocal Learning Strategy can also play a significant role in helping students learn how to read difficult passages in their texts, and to become more adept at solving non-routine problems.

The Reciprocal Learning Strategy is based on four key principles of helping relationships:
1. The principle of peer relationships—Students learn from each other as peers because they share a common experience as learners;

2. The principle of clear roles—Students need clearly defined roles when working cooperatively as peer partners;

3. The principle of mutual learning—Students learn from being doers as well as guides in peer relationships; and

4. The principle of effective help—Students learn best when they receive immediate feedback and have to figure out answers for themselves with clues rather than by being told the answer.

The goals of the Reciprocal Learning Strategy are:

1. To improve student self-concept by giving students a framework within which they are able to work with and help someone else;

2. To increase student decision-making responsibility;

3. To make students less dependent on teacher feedback;

4. To add to the number of people providing feedback and evaluating each student's performance;

5. To modify and widen the patterns of social interaction in the classroom;

6. To create a classroom structure within which all students, not only the best, can provide support for any others; and

7. To increase student academic achievement by creating situations in which students learn both by doing the task themselves and by actively observing the task being performed by another.

The steps in the Reciprocal Learning Strategy are:

1. Select or design the practice exercises to be used;

2. Provide answers, and include hints or other forms of helping information to be used by the guides;

3. Arrange students into pairs randomly;

4. Review briefly the kind of work students will be doing;

5. Model and review roles students will play and teach the cooperative skills necessary to be successful as doer and guide;

6. Help the guide, not the doer, if a partnership is experiencing difficulty; and

7. Help students to process the doer-guide encounter by discussing positively what happened in the partnerships.

How to Plan Lessons Using the Reciprocal Learning Strategy

The first step in planning your lesson using this strategy is to select or design your practice exercises. The Reciprocal Learning Strategy works best in practice situations where there are clear right or wrong answers. For this reason, it is ideally suited to the practice of such skills as applying spelling and grammar rules and memorizing vocabulary meanings (both in English and in a foreign language), learning scientific and historical facts, and learning arithmetic facts and methods of solving algebraic equations. This strategy can be used to practice skills at almost any grade level and to review important information in almost any content from science to industrial arts to shorthand.

Often you create exercises for your lessons by simply copying exercises out of your textbook. At other times you will want to create exercises of your own. In all cases make sure that all of the work being practiced is parallel and at the same level of difficulty.

When creating Reciprocal Learning exercises, divide each worksheet in two. On one half, write the questions the doer is to answer. On the other half, write the partner's answers and helpful hints for getting the answers.

Worksheet for Partner A;	
QUESTIONS FOR DOER	ANSWERS AND HINTS FOR PARTNER'S QUESTIONS
(Task A)	(Answers for Task B)
Worksheet for Partner B:	
QUESTIONS FOR DOER	ANSWERS AND HINTS FOR PARTNER'S QUESTIONS
(Task B)	(Answers for Task A)

Sample Lesson I: Forming Contractions

TASK A

Directions: Form a contraction from the two words.

1. she will
2. we will
3. is not
4. you will
5. he will
6. did not
7. I will
8. have not

ANSWERS TO TASK B

Directions: Check to see that the right letters have been thrown away and the apostrophe has been added.

1. I'll — I will
2. didn't — did not
3. we'll — we will
4. she'll — she will
5. isn't — is not
6. haven't — have not
7. you'll — you will
8. he'll — he will

TASK B

Directions: Form a contraction from the two words.

1. I will
2. did not
3. we will
4. she will
5. is not
6. have not
7. you will
8. he will

ANSWERS TO TASK A

Directions: Check to see that the right letters have been thrown away and the apostrophe has been added.

1. she'll — she will
2. we'll — we will
3. isn't — is not
4. you'll — you will
5. he'll — he will
6. didn't — did not
7. I'll — I will
8. haven't — have not

Some General Considerations

A leading question, a riddle, an alternative definition, or a page citation to a relevant explanation in the text can also be provided on the guide's answer sheet for use as a clue which will prompt the doer to recall the answer. You may wish the guide to refer your students to their notes.

Establish partnerships randomly, but plan to change partners frequently. This establishes a clear message about your expectations for cooperation; i.e., that in your class everyone works together. Random assignment of partners goes a long way toward eliminating the problem of "isolates" and "segregates"—students who for non-educational reasons may not be selected as partners.

Plan to rearrange seating so that partners can sit next to each other. Students feel more like members of a team when they sit side by side, and the guide is in a better position to observe clearly the partner's work. If students sit opposite each other, the atmosphere seems more adverse, and the doer is more likely to feel that the guide is correcting rather than coaching.

Plan to help partners to get to know each other. Design a warm-up question—"What foreign country would you most like to visit?" or "If you had to choose one of these, which career would you pursue: automobile mechanic or college professor?" We sometimes assume students know each other just because they are members of the same class. In fact there is a great deal that even close friends do not know about each other, let alone students from opposite ends of town or different social groups.

Plan an introduction to the Reciprocal Learning Strategy and its procedures. As part of this preparation lesson, plan to model and teach cooperative skills. For instance, plan to lead a class discussion about what guides might do when then doer is right about an answer, what guides might do when the doer is wrong about an answer, how to recognize when someone is stuck, and what to do when the doer is making a lot of errors. In addition to discussing these issues in a large group, encourage partners to explore these questions with each other.

Your students will work at different rates. In general, most peer sessions last from 15 to 20 minutes. Because of the support partners give each other, there is rarely more than five minutes between the finishing time of the first and last pairs. However, some partnerships will finish their work before others. For these students, assign another question to be solved cooperatively without answering or coaching clues; or have them reflect on their partnership and discuss what went well; or have them develop additional examples with answers and clues for other students to try; or make sure they have a reading book for free time reading. There is nothing wrong with setting reasonable time limits for the last groups based on the finishing times of the first groups.

Putting the Reciprocal Learning Strategy to Work in Your Classroom

There are three phases to your lessons using the Reciprocal Learning Strategy: preparing your students, having them work together as partners, and processing the partnerships.

The goal of the preparation phase is to get your students ready to work together as partners. In this phase, you first need to review the kind of work your students will be doing. It is generally a good idea for you to take two or three minutes to review the skills or information the doer will be practicing; it is not advisable to use the strategy on brand new material, or as class work that will be graded.

Next, put your students into pairs. Make it clear that you will rotate partnerships each time the Reciprocal Learning Strategy is used so that everyone has the opportunity to learn from everyone else. Stress that development of the skills essential to being an effective helper requires working with different people.

Finally, before setting your students to work on the Reciprocal Learning exercise, model the roles that students will play and the cooperative skills they will need to be successful as a doer and a guide; i.e., active listening, attentiveness, giving clues, "talking it through," and positive feedback. The first time you use the strategy, it is imperative that you do more than just explain the strategy. You need to model it is as well. An effective way to do this is to have two students role play doer and guide. Ask your students to observe the first half of the exercise, when one student plays the doer and the other the guide, and to list the things both participants did which they thought were beneficial to learning. Then have the role players switch roles to complete the Reciprocal Learning exercise, and again ask your students to look for positive interactions. In future sessions, you will only need to review the roles briefly, so the time before students move into partnerships can be used very effectively for mini-lessons (three to seven minutes) on key skills such as active listening, constructive feedback, and open and encouraging body language.

How it works

When your students move into their working pairs, doers read the question on their Reciprocal Learning exercise sheet (which has their set of questions, and, for later use, the answers and hints for their partner's set of questions), and do the task out loud so their guides can hear their thinking. Guides use the answers on their Reciprocal Learning exercise sheet (which has the answers and hints for their partner's questions, and, for later use, their set of questions), to determine whether the doer's answer is correct or incorrect. If correct, guides provide praise; if incorrect, guides use the hints on the Reciprocal Learning exercise sheet to provide clues which are designed to lead doers to get the correct answer. After doers have completed their task, and have gotten feedback after each item, doers switch roles with guides and repeat the process. During this phase, circulate around the room, observing and recording what happens. Provide encouragement, feedback, and assistance to guides wherever requested. Do not help doers since this subverts the guides' role. Guide the guides. Help the guides find new ways to make the doers stronger learners.

The first five or six times you use the strategy, make sure you remain active. Circulate. Observe how students are working together. Note examples of good working relationships. Identify cooperative skills that need development.

Carry a small notebook or some index cards for jotting down ideas you want to talk about. One good way to use your notebook is to record errors or problems in the Reciprocal Learning exercises. Jotting down what you see often lets you spot patterns of error or common trouble spots. Then, after the Reciprocal Learning session is completed, you can intervene to address the problem rather than intervening many times during the session.

When both students in all of the partnerships have completed the work, call the class together and lead a discussion on key questions:

1. What happened in the partnerships? What did guides and doers do to make the partnership successful?
2. What questions or problems on the Reciprocal Learning exercise sheet caused the most difficulty?

The first question enables you and your students to discuss and refine partnership skills. The second question helps you and your students identify content skills and information that need work.

Discuss positively what happened in the partnerships. For instance, ask students what guides did that was helpful to doers. To help develop independence in the partnerships, record ideas on poster board or newsprint for display. If a particular technique works well, have the students practice in role playing situations. Often people are ineffective at giving or receiving help, not out of unwillingness, but because they haven't had an opportunity to practice the necessary skills. Discuss how to ask for help when you're a doer, what to do when a doer moves too fast and the guide feels left out, and how to use questions to help doers find answers and to develop sound thinking practices.

How to Evaluate the Reciprocal Learning Strategy

To evaluate lessons using this strategy, look for the following elements: parallel worksheets; appropriate level of difficulty for guided practice; helping information available on both worksheets. When you establish student partners, make sure that you explain or review the purpose of that strategy, and that the roles of doer and guide are modeled or reviewed.

As you circulate during the session, note whether guides were able to provide sufficient help to the doers to ensure successful completion of the task. Observe whether the guides were able to make effective use of the helping information provided on the exercise sheets.

As you help students process their experiences in the Reciprocal Learning lesson, pay particular attention to the students' reports of what they had learned, both about the subject matter and about the partnerships. Note students' progress in understanding and practicing cooperative learning skills.

RECIPROCAL LEARNING AND READING

The strategy applied to reading can play a significant role in helping students learn how to read difficult passages in their textbooks. Many students who read textbook prose feel overwhelmed. They have trouble figuring out what details to focus on and how to arrange them into a pattern that makes sense. If you try to solve this problem by lecturing, your students will not only have little motivation to read the textbook, but they will not acquire the skills necessary to do the reading. The Reciprocal Learning Strategy can help your students to develop these skills.

The steps in the strategy are:
1. Select a passage that presents some difficulties;
2. Arrange students into pairs and ask both students to read the passage silently to themselves;
3. Ask one student to summarize the passage while the other helps; in initial uses, provide the guide with sample summarizing questions with which to aid the doer;
4. To help doer and guide work together effectively, have the doer close the textbook, but let the guide keep the textbook open; and
5. When the doer has finished summarizing the first half, the partners should reverse roles. Now the second student closes the textbook and attempts to summarize the second half of the passage while the first opens the textbook and helps.

Reciprocal Learning and Reading Summary

When to use it:
When you want your students to work cooperatively reading and digesting a text to increase their knowledge and understanding of the piece.

How to use it:

1. Select a passage that presents some difficulties;

2. Arrange students into pairs and ask both students to read the passage silently to themselves;

3. Ask one student to summarize the passage while the other helps to elicit a summary by asking probing questions or providing input;

4. To help the doer and guide work together effectively, have the doer close the book, but let the guide keep the book open; and

5. When the doer has finished, the students reverse roles. Now the helper closes the book and attempts to summarize the second half of the passage. The new helper keeps the book open and helps the doer make an effective summary.

How to evaluate it:

1. Are students better able to comprehend and understand why they have read?

2. Are students able to work in collaboration and support each other in their learning?

Things to remember:

1. Use the strategy with content that is information rich, requiring students to learn and understand the data;

2. Provide guidelines with questions that help to coach readers in discussing the content;

3. Encourage students to take notes and, where appropriate, to underline key ideas while reading in order to prepare their summaries;

4. Have students first summarize the gist of the reading, and then give details of who, when, where, what, and why; and

5. Rotate peer partners regularly.

Peer Problem Solving

Arthur Whimby and Jack Lockhead (1980) have created a variation of the Reciprocal Learning Strategy called Peer Problem Solving. Here students once again work in pairs, but both the task and the roles have been altered significantly. The task is a non-routine problem such as:

**Peer Problem Solving
Student A**

YOUR PROBLEM

A farmer has some land which was to be divided equally among his four children in to four parcels. His land is shown below. The parcels must be the same shape and size. Draw the four parcels on the figure below.

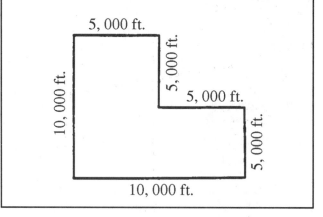

Your Partner's Answers & Hints

Hints:

A. Suggest that your partner consider dividing the property into three equal parts.

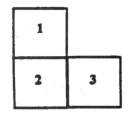

B. Then, divide each of three parcels into four smaller parts.

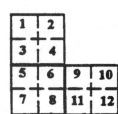

C. Have your partner count the total number of smaller parts (there should be twelve). Next, tell him to divide the twelve parts by four since there are four children.

D. Finally, have your partner arrange the groups of three little parts in such a way that all of the children receive a parcel of the same shape.

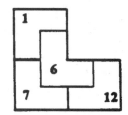

Peer Problem Solving
Student B

YOUR PROBLEM

You have eight balls, all of which look exactly the same. Seven of them weigh the same, but one is slightly lighter than the others. You have a scale to balance the balls. How can you find out which is the lighter ball in only two weighings?

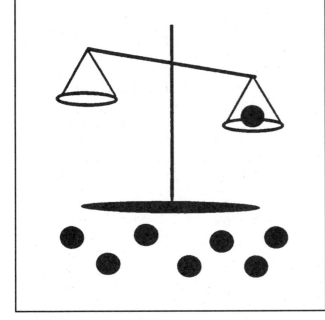

Your Partner's Answers & Hints

Hints:

1. Most people try to weigh all eight balls at once.

2. How can you figure out which is lightest if you only have three balls?

Answer:

1. Weigh six balls (three on each side)

2. If they weigh the same, then the lighter ball must be one of the two balls that wasn't weighed. Weigh the remaining two balls to see which is lighter.

3. If they are of different weights, weigh two of the three balls that were on the lighter side. If they weigh the same, the ball that is left is the lighter ball. If one weighs less, you have found the lighter ball.

One student is the problem solver. The problem solver's job is to solve the problem and to constantly verbalize the thinking processes used. The other student is the listener. The listener's job is to keep the problem solver talking, listen to what the problem solver says, check the work, and help clarify the thinking. Roles are reversed for the next problem.

This strategy can be a useful tool in helping students develop their abilities as problem solvers, but demands a high degree of sophistication in the listener. Use the Reciprocal Learning Strategy to help students develop these sophisticated process skills. Introduce students to problem solving with a series of more routine problems presented in a Reciprocal Learning exercise sheet. After they have developed some facility with problems presented in the Reciprocal Learning format, include for each student one non-routine problem and tips on how to solve it. Working together in this structured way, your students can begin to develop the more sophisticated skills necessary for Whimby and Lockhead's Peer Problem Solving. Once these skills are in place, the move into full-fledged Peer Problem Solving can be made smoothly and with greater likelihood of early success—not just at solving the problem, but at helping and listening as well.

Summary

When to use it:

When you want students to develop helping skills while practicing previously taught information.

How to use it:

1. Prepare parallel options for students;

2. Set up Reciprocal Learning Partners "doers" and "guides;"

3. Describe the role of the "doers" and "guides."

Doer:

Does the task aloud

Communicates with the guide

Changes role

Guide:

Observes and listens to the doer's performance

Compares and contrasts against criteria

Concludes and communicates with the doer; and

4. Teacher communicates only with guides.

How to evaluate it:

1. Are students able to function as peer partners?

2. Are students able to understand and use criteria sheet for guiding partners?

3. Are students able to perform the task correctly?

Things to remember:

1. Criteria for evaluation must demonstrate how the answer was derived;

2. Criteria for evaluation must be self-explanatory;

3. Rotate peer partners regularly; and

4. Train students in how to give positive feedback and how to guide partners.

Sample Lesson I: Homonyms

TASK A

Directions: Write the correct word in the blank to complete the sentence.

1. He _____ the sandwiches at _____ o'clock.   (eight, ate)

2. He looked _____ when he saw what was in the _____.   (pail, pale)

3. The _____ reason the horse won the contest was his beautiful _____. (main, mane)

4. He _____ the boat so that the _____ could not carry it away. (tied, tide)

5. He took a _____ at what was in the lunch box when we reached the mountain _____.   (peek, peak)

TASK B

Directions: Write the correct word in the blank to complete the sentence.

1. It was a cold and dark _____ when the _____ arrived.   (knight, night)

2. He recalled the happy moments from his _____ when he _____ by the house.   (past, passed)

3. He _____ the ball _____ the window.   (threw, through)

4. The king's _____ was marked by forty years of _____ from the skies. (rain, reign)

5. The lion in the _____ had a long _____.   (tail, tale)

ANSWERS TO TASK B

1. night (meaning evening)
   knight (meaning soldier)

2. past (meaning time gone by)
   passed (meaning moved by)

3. threw (meaning to propel something)
   through (meaning to go between)

4. reign (meaning rule)
   rain (meaning water from clouds)

5. tale (meaning story)
   tail (meaning a part of an animal)

ANSWERS TO TASK A

1. ate (meaning to eat)
   eight (the number)

2. pale (meaning without much color)
   pail (meaning a bucket)

3. main (meaning most important)
   mane (meaning long neck of hair of a horse, lion)

4. tied (meaning to tie a knot)
   tide (meaning the flow of the sea)

5. peek (meaning look)
   peak (meaning top)

Sample Lesson II: Mathematical Terms

TASK A

Directions: Answer the following questions:

1. a whole number greater than 1 that has exactly two factors, one and itself   _____
2. a whole number that divides another number exactly, leaving a zero remainder   _____
3. counting numbers beginning with one   _____
4. a composite number expressed as a product of primes   _____
5. the largest factor by which you can divide two or more given numbers   _____
6. a numeral in which the decimal digits follow an endless repeating pattern   _____
7. a fraction whose numerator is larger than its denominator   _____
8. a whole number that is not a multiple of two   _____
9. for any real number a, a x 1 = a   _____
10. for any real numbers a, b and c, ax(b + c) = (a x b) + (a x c)   _____

TASK B

Directions: Answer the following questions:

1. the smallest non-zero product that two or more numbers have in common   _____
2. the whole numbers and their opposites   _____
3. a decimal in which the division operation results in a remainder of zero   _____
4. the product of a number and a whole number   _____
5. a whole number that has more than two factors   _____
6. a fraction whose numerator is smaller than the denominator   _____
7. counting numbers including zero   _____
8. a whole number that is a multiple of two   _____
9. for all real numbers, a, b, and c (a x b) x c = (a x b) x c   _____
10. for all real numbers a and b, a + b = b + a   _____

ANSWERS TO TASK A

1. prime number
2. factor
3. natural numbers
4. prime factorization
5. greatest common factor
6. repeating decimal
7. improper fraction
8. odd number
9. multiplication property of one
10. distributive property of multiplication over addition

ANSWERS TO TASK B

1. least common multiple
2. integers
3. terminating decimal
4. multiple
5. composite number
6. proper fraction
7. whole numbers
8. even number
9. associative property of multiplication
10. commutative property of addition

CIRCLE STRATEGY

The Circle Strategy emphasizes the development of awareness of self and others, communication skills, interpersonal discussion through group interaction, and the sharing of personal experiences and problems.

The Strategy at Work

In a lesson she called "Looking at My Many Selves," adapted from the Junior High Interchange Human Development Training Institute, and incorporating information on Lakota name-giving, Mrs. Lansky used the Circle Strategy to give her eighth grade students an opportunity to focus on an important aspect of self-identification—how they are known, and how they would like to be known.

After asking her students to sit with her in a circle, Mrs. Lansky explained that most people at some point in their lives have gone through a lot of changes about their names. One little girl named Catty decided when she was two years old that her name was really Mary, and she would answer only to that name for almost one year. Others, she said, have gone to fantastic lengths to change their names, sometimes going to court to change them. A Native American tribe who call themselves "Lakota" or "friends" (but who are more commonly known by the nasty name "Sioux" or "snakes/enemies"), consider names valuable property. They believe that names have magical qualities. Because names are considered property, the Lakota may sell them or pawn them, or give them away. Lakota boys were usually given a new name when they reached manhood. Lakota names were sometimes earned because of a great deed; for example, the famous Lakota chief, Crazy (connoting "enchanted") Horse, received his name as a gift from his father, Crazy Horse, when he showed exceptional courage in his first battle, and his father then took a new name to replace the one he had given his son.

Mrs. Lansky asked her students to close their eyes and think of the name they would have chosen for themselves if they could have picked their own name. After a silent wait, she said, "Now say that name to yourself slowly and thoughtfully. What kind of feeling do you get from that name?" After another silent wait, Mrs. Lansky explained that she would go around the circle so that each person could say what kind of feeling the chosen name gave. She reminded her students that, in the circle, each person gets an equal chance and time to share, that an individual may choose not to take a turn, and that everyone must listen actively to the person who is sharing.

After each person who wanted to had shared feelings, Mrs. Lansky asked the circle to consider and respond to the following questions: what similarities did you notice in the reasons we had for picking these names? Did the names we picked have to do more with our real selves, or did they go with some secret, fantasy selves? Why do you think names are so important to so many people?

The Circle Strategy

The Circle Strategy, adapted from the work of Geraldine Bell and V.H. Malomares (Bell, 1977), gives students the opportunity to share their ideas, concepts, values, and feelings in relation to a particular discussion topic. By sharing and listening in an accepting atmosphere students have the opportunity to learn from one another. In the Circle Strategy, students are made aware of the universality of emotions, and of how students are similar in terms of their wants and needs. Students also learn how unique they are, and the importance of becoming aware of the differences between them. Self-awareness tends to lead to increased self-confidence and improved social interaction skills.

In the Circle Strategy, the teacher must establish a climate in which students feel comfortable, and are enabled to learn to think aloud, to get reactions from peers, and to respond to the ideas of peers. For such an atmosphere to exist, students must be able to express themselves without fear of correction or restatement from the teacher or negative remarks from peers. The teacher's role is to build a climate of trust.

The Circle Strategy is founded on the belief that an important goal of education is to help students learn about themselves, who they are, how they function, and how they relate to others. The strategy also helps students understand that feelings, thoughts, and behavior are all interrelated and must be so considered when working for self-understanding and growth. The Circle Strategy emphasizes that intellectual growth requires the expression of feeling if desired behavioral change is to follow.

In the Circle Strategy, students and teacher sit in a small circle and participate as peers, discussing a topic presented by the teacher, or on one selected by the students. Circle seating is used because in such an arrangement there is no leader; everyone faces one another; and all can hear and be heard. This is conducive to the sharing and listening that needs to take place. Each student is given a moment to share thoughts and feelings about the topic. Students may choose not to share if they wish, but everyone is expected to listen attentively to the person who is sharing. During the discussion, there should be no interruptions, probing, or put-downs. Everyone should have an equal chance to participate. After the discussion phase, the group reviews what has been shared, and looks for similarities and differences in student perspectives. Conclusions are drawn and students are asked to share what they have learned from the discussion.

The goals of the Circle Strategy are:

1. To help students learn to share and listen;

2. To help students become aware of their similarities and differences; and

3. To help students increase their self-confidence and expand their social interaction skills through improved self-awareness.

The steps in the Circle Strategy are:

1. Set up the circle;

2. Review the ground rules;

3. State or select the topic;

4. Discuss the topic;

5. Review what was shared;

6. Analyze the responses; and

7. End the Circle Strategy discussion with statements of participants' conclusions.

How to Plan Lessons Using the Circle Strategy

In the planning phase, you need to determine the time and location for the circle, and the number and type of participants to be involved. You must choose the students to be included and select the topic to be discussed.

You will find that circle sessions are approximately twenty to thirty minutes in duration. If student trust levels are low, the initial sessions may be shortened. Once group trust develops, it may be difficult to complete all of the steps in a circle discussion in twenty to thirty minutes.

The circle should be set up in an area where students can be comfortable and where distractions are minimal. The group may choose to use chairs or to sit on the floor. Sessions may also be conducted outdoors with students seated in a quiet, secluded, grassy area.

Circle sessions are creative and unhurried opportunities to focus on individual issues and problems; as such, the group's size needs to be kept relatively small. Any number up to ten works well. Larger groups may be used but time must be allowed for sharing by everyone.

Each group should have as a heterogeneous a make-up as is possible with respect to sex, ability, and racial and ethnic background. Since you will be working with a small group, you must also plan for students not participating in the group.

In the beginning, you may choose to have all students in your small circle group involved in the discussion. As the group becomes more experienced, one part may form an inner circle which responds verbally to the topic, while those in the outer circle serve as observers and provide feedback.

In selecting a topic for discussion, you should begin with a known student interest, experience, or concern. The content must be designed to help students develop insights into themselves and others while simultaneously practicing positive communication skills. Begin with topics which students may share comfortably, and then move on to more challenging areas, which may be harder to talk about. For example, talking about how someone helped you to learn to ride a bicycle is less threatening than talking about bad feelings. Topics that lend themselves to griping, axe grinding, or confrontation should be avoided. Plan for topics that will lead to a discussion or exploration of a variety of feelings within the circle.

Putting the Circle Strategy to Work in Your Classroom

Your role in implementing the Circle Strategy is to present a discussion topic, to establish and maintain an atmosphere of responsible, thoughtful communication, and to become a member of the group. You must help students to be clear about what they are saying; seek clarification without cross-examining or badgering. Students must be helped to assume leadership in conducting the sessions.

The basic teacher behaviors during the implementation phase are focus-setting, structuring, accepting, clarifying, responding to students' data, and teacher silence. The definitions for these behaviors are as follows:

1. **Focus-setting** behavior involves presenting a discussion topic or acknowledging an appropriate student-presented topic; i.e., "One thing we might want to consider about the program is, 'Why does Francois appear to be prejudiced?'"

2. **Structuring behavior** involves discussing any ground rules that seem to be needed for the lesson, including lesson format, student-teacher and student-student roles and relationships; i.e., "Hold on, Chris, everyone here has the right to an opinion," or "Just a minute, Charleston, only one person at a time. We can't hear what's going on."

3. **Accepting behavior** involves recognizing ideas and opinions from a student without valuing them; i.e., "Okay," "Yes," "Could be," or "That's possible."

4. **Clarifying behavior** involves action to clarify or amplify a student's statement or question that seems ambiguous; i.e., "You've talked about several things, Ben. Are you saying that people smoke pot because it's illegal, or are you saying that we need to change the laws concerning marijuana use?"

5. **Responding to the students' data** involves taking action, if feasible, to make it possible for the student to get data requested; i.e., "Ray, according to the information contained in one study, forty-five percent of the students reported they started to smoke because all their friends smoked," or "Billy, I'll make arrangements for you to use the office phone to call Dr. Loggins, as you requested, to get that information on prejudice."

6. **Teacher silence** involves allowing students to decide on a course of action; i.e., remaining silent at decision times in order to let students work through to their own conclusions. Note that teacher silence is used as a response to student silence only to communicate the notion that in the circle discussion it is up to them to take action without prodding, pushing, or cueing by the teacher.

When you use these behaviors appropriately, your students will:

- Present data, ideas, concepts;

- Express opinions, positions, etc.;

- Seek clarification of what other students have said; and

- Influence the structure of the lesson with the boundaries you have established.

Lessons intended to bring about open-ended discussions in the classroom don't just happen. They require a deliberate lesson structure, and a teacher who is able to shape behavior in a way that fosters (rather than impedes) communication.

A basic assumption of the Circle Strategy is that, given the opportunity and training, every student has the ability to lead the group. The transfer of group leadership from the teacher to the student is an important goal for student learning. You can begin training student leaders once group members are comfortable with one another, and circle procedures are familiar. Suggest that students think about volunteering to lead upcoming sessions.

The role of the student in the Circle Strategy is to participate fully in the discussion by sharing, actively listening, paying attention to what's happening to oneself and other group members, and using "I" messages; i.e., speaking only for oneself. Students must also maintain confidentiality of what has been said in the group, and obey the ground rules of the circle session.

How to Evaluate the Circle Strategy

In the Circle Strategy, students participate fully in the evaluation phase. Cognitive summaries; i.e., reviews of what's been said, provide students with an opportunity to synthesize the experience. Key questions serving this purpose are:

1. Have you noticed or learned anything in this session that you would like to comment on?

2. Would anyone like to share something new that was learned during the session (about someone or something)?

3. What are some things you may have noticed that some or all of us have in common?

4. What are some things you noticed about how we respond to different situations, feelings, ideas, or experiences?

The summary must be conducted as an "open forum." Students, exposed to a variety of input, must be free to choose and incorporate ideas that make sense to them. Sometimes discussions relate to morals and values; in such cases, it is particularly important for "respectful sharing" to occur. Lawrence Kohlberg (1973) argues that moral development is fostered when students can listen and respond to the moral statements of others. Remember that students generally "turn off" people who moralize. For these reasons, you should not impose opinions (moral or otherwise) on students, or allow students to impose their beliefs on others.

Summary

When to use it:

When you want students to grow in self-awareness and awareness of others, and when you want to increase their ability to communicate about personal experiences and problems.

How to use it:

1. Select or have students choose a topic for discussion;

2. Review the ground rules for the Circle Strategy;

3. Give each person a turn to speak… if they want to speak;

4. Make no judgments on student responses or sharing;

5. Facilitate clarity in communication by asking open-ended and focusing questions;

6. Conduct reviews of what has been said; paraphrase, acknowledge feelings, and describe behaviors;

7. Use teacher silence at decision times to allow students to work through to their own conclusions; and

8. Conduct a cognitive review focusing on the meaning of the session.

How to evaluate it:

1. Are students active participants in the discussion?

2. Have students progressed in their awareness of other's positions, feelings, and ideas?

3. Are students willing and able to express different points of view?

4. Are students able to seek clarification of what other students have said?

5. Are students willing and able to influence the structure of the lesson within the established bounds?

Things to remember:

1. Students must be free to choose and incorporate ideas that make sense to them;

2. Students must have an equal chance and time to share;

3. Students must participate fully by paying attention, but they may choose not to take a turn to share;

4. Remember that what is discussed in the circle is confidential, and not to be shared outside the circle; and

5. Do not permit interruptions, put-downs, probing, or gossip.

Sample Lesson: Poetry Writing—The Nicest Things

As an introduction to poetry writing in his tenth grade creative writing class, Mr. Hopkins planned to use the Circle Strategy to focus on memory and feeling.

Objectives:

Mr. Hopkins wanted to allow his students to feel again some pleasant feelings from the past that they could draw on for their poetry writing.

Anticipatory Set:

To get his students thinking about memory and feeling, Mr. Hopkins invited his students to move their desks into a circle and listen while he read a translation of the "Petite Madeleine" section from Proust's *Remembrance of Things Past*, in which Proust's action of dipping the Madeleine into his tea evokes a host of deeply joyful emotions and memories.

Procedures:

Mr. Hopkins asked the circle to think about some of their most pleasant memories to focus on. He explained that the memory could be something that happened recently, half and hour ago, something from the past, or an experience they had when they were small.

After a silent wait, Mr. Hopkins asked the students to close their eyes and try to remember everything they could about the events, surroundings, sensory feelings, or other things that make the memory vivid.

After another silent wait, Mr. Hopkins reminded his students that in the circle, each person gets an equal chance and time to share, that an individual may choose not to take a turn, and that everyone must listen actively to the person who is sharing without interrupting. He then set the discussion question: How did you feel inside?

After the sharing, Mr. Hopkins raised the following discussion issues: Did you or anyone who shared seem to actually feel the feelings from the happy memory again? Some memories are thought about and others are felt; how can you tell if you are re-feeling past emotions and not just thinking about them? What did you notice in this sharing that was of special interest to you?

I want you to reflect upon your own personal reactions as well as the thoughts of the character you are going to portray.

ROLE-PLAYING STRATEGY

The Role-Playing Strategy provides for active and emphatic learning when students assume the roles of others and analyze their own thoughts and feelings in these roles. Role-playing assists students to appreciate and understand others by encouraging them to experience the historical, personal, and intellectual constraints of a given character. Roles are often designed to elicit conflict. As such, the strategy has many applications for critical thinking, conflict resolution, and problem solving.

The Strategy at Work

To introduce the study of Hamlet, Dr. Quammen has decided to use the Role-Playing Strategy in a lesson he will call "Family Loyalties." He has asked for four volunteers, two male and two female, from each of the three sections scheduled to begin studying this play.

In class, Dr. Quammen explains that one male student will play the role of the adult son in the family who has just returned from a long trip and discovers the sudden death of his father. One of the female students will play the role of his grieving mother who has quickly remarried. The second male student will play the role of his grieving mother's newly married husband, and the second female student the role of the adult son's fiancée. Dr. Quammen provides written role descriptions for each actor, but the characters and observers do not know the role descriptions of the other players.

The role descriptions are:

The adult son returns from a long trip to discover that his father, a wealthy and respected business executive, has mysteriously died. He discovers that his mother has married another man within weeks of his father's death.

The grieving mother greets the son's return with misgivings. She cannot explain her husband's death. She chooses not to explain her sudden remarriage. Yet she loves her son.

The new husband has taken over the father's business. He is distrustful of the returning son. He wants the son to stay out of his relationship with the mother. He worries about his son's intentions both for gaining control of the company, and for investigating the cause of his father's death.

The fiancée loves the son and wants him as he was before his long trip. She is perplexed by his lack of concern for her, though he professes his love for her. She wants more attention and does not understand his preoccupation with the father's death, nor his distrust of his new stepfather. She is hurt, and a little angry.

After Dr. Quammen has given his actors their role descriptions to read and think about, he reviews the roles for the observers with the rest of the class, and asks them to take notes on the actual behaviors of the characters, including facial expressions, body language, and what they say. He reminds them not to interpret anything at this point, but rather to stick to reporting the facts as they see and hear them.

Dr. Quammen then lists the following on the board:

The Action:

SCENE 1: Son returns home and confronts mother and stepfather.

SCENE 2: Son confides in fiancée.

SCENE 3: Son meets mother alone.

After the role playing, Dr. Quammen asks the role players to discuss their individual understanding of their roles and their feelings while playing the roles. Then he asks the class to provide responses to the roles as played: Were they believable? Were they realistic? What were the relationships between the characters? How did they feel about each of the characters? How did they feel about the interactions?

The homework assignment is to read the first scene of *Hamlet*.

The Role-Playing Strategy

The Role-Playing Strategy is designed to assist students to use improved self-awareness in problem solving. Role playing is an effective learning tool that provides students with insights into the feelings of self and others. In the process of acting as the other person, students' powers of observation, empathy, and understanding are strengthened. Generating and sharing personal feelings elicits appreciation for the thoughts and values of others. Since role plays can be constructed around problem situations or controversial issues, students also become familiar with problem solving, negotiation, and conflict resolution.

The Role-Playing Strategy addresses those aspects of curriculum that require student understanding of interpersonal conflicts, intergroup relations, historical and current problems, and individual dilemmas. Role playing is a useful mechanism for helping students to develop an appreciation of the characters and issues involved in historical events. The high levels of physical and mental activity required contribute to student involvement in and retention of the learning experience. Any content that can be more effectively learned through peer interaction, personal sharing, creativity, or problem solving is a "natural" for the Role-Playing Strategy.

Role playing as a strategy is a model of good teaching. In role playing, the teacher sets up a learning situation for maximum involvement, evokes critical and creative thinking, calls for the expression of personal feelings and values, rehearses the basic facts and concepts of the situation being acted out, and has students reflect on and analyze the learning experience.

The goals of the Role-Playing Strategy are:

1. To experience the historical, personal, and intellectual constraints of a given character;

2. To analyze their own thoughts and feelings, as evoked by roles they have assumed;

3. To learn to empathize with others;

4. To increase their self-awareness; and

5. To heighten student involvement with the content to be learned.

The steps in the Role-Playing Strategy are to:

1. Identify and make explicit the problem or conflict to be role-played;

2. Prepare role descriptions (where needed);

3. Decide on the questions to be answered;

4. Prepare questions for observers;

5. Provide preliminary orientation to role-playing if students are unfamiliar with the strategy;

6. Explain the role-playing situation; and

7. Implement role-play and evaluation.

How to Plan Lesson Using the Role-Playing Strategy

Role playing is a strategy which is useful both on its own and in combination with other strategies such as Dilemma Decision Making and Write to Learn. In planning lessons which use role playing, you must first identify and make explicit the problem or conflict to be role-played. Develop a problem statement or scenario. Create clear role descriptions, and, if appropriate, write conflict situations into role descriptions. Often these role descriptions should be privately shared with each of the volunteer actors, either by giving them written information about a character's personality, beliefs, and emotions, or by conferring separately with the actors.

Think about the questions you would like the class to consider at the conclusion of the role-playing. What are the main ideas you wish to emphasize? The questions you ask should get your students ready to analyze their own thoughts and feelings about the issue or problem under discussion, and should lead them to draw conclusions about the personal and intellectual results of the experience. Prepare questions for the observers which require them to focus on actual behaviors of the characters. Ask observers to take notes on specific things that were said. Have them notice how well the actors stayed in character; i.e., how believable they were in their roles.

If your students are unfamiliar with the strategy, plan to model role-playing behavior. Entertain questions for clarification. Be sure to discuss the roles of observers, and make clear the distinction between observing and interpreting.

Putting the Role-Playing Strategy to Work in Your Classroom

Your role in implementation is to present the problem or conflict situation, to review the rules and roles for role-playing, and to remind your students of the need to reflect inward on their own personal reactions as well as outward on the feelings and thoughts of the character and role being portrayed.

Since a major objective of role-playing, as an Interpersonal Strategy, is to encourage peer learning, the sharing of feelings, and creative thinking, you will need to create an atmosphere that is open and explanatory, and where levels of trust are appropriate for the sharing of feelings and ideas.

As with the Circle Strategy, you need to be available to your students for questions and requests for clarification of roles and purposes. You need to participate as a member of the learning exercise, either as an observer or as an actor. You need to serve as a counselor, facilitating and analyzing each individual's experience, as well as a leader focusing the group on the larger purpose of the role-play itself.

As you encourage discussion and evaluation of the role play, ask questions designed to assist your students to become more astute as observers and recorders of human behavior; i.e., Did the actors accept the constraints and assigned behaviors of the character? Did they stay in character? What were their actual behaviors? What did they say? Help your students to distinguish between making observations and making interpretations, between feeling and thinking; i.e., ask your actors to share their thoughts and feelings first as the character, then to share their personal reflections on the character. Maintain a strong expectation that your students will appreciate a diversity of opinions, feelings, and interpretations.

How to Evaluate the Role-Playing Strategy

Share the evaluation phase of the Role-Playing Strategy with your students. Individually debrief the roles. Examine the conclusions drawn. What has been learned? What new understandings have been gained? What has the class discovered about personal feelings? What changes need to be made?

In subsequent reflection, consider whether the role playing met your cognitive and affective objectives for this particular group of students. Was role playing the most appropriate technique for eliciting feelings? Based on the discussion with your students and your own observations, how would you change your role-playing lesson?

Summary

When to use it:
When you want your students to appreciate, analyze, and understand others by experiencing the historical, personal, and intellectual constraints of a given character.

How to use it:
1. Identify and make explicit the problem or conflict situation to be role-played;
2. Prepare role descriptions (where needed);
3. Decide on the questions to be answered;
4. Prepare questions for observers;
5. Provide preliminary orientation to role-playing if students are unfamiliar with the strategy;
6. Explain the role-playing situation; and
7. Implement role playing and evaluation.

How to evaluate it:
1. Help students to individually debrief roles;
2. Help students to draw conclusions about what has been learned;
3. Use student discussion and teacher observation to determine whether cognitive and affective objectives for the lesson have been met; and
4. Determine whether role playing was the most appropriate technique for eliciting feelings, and consider changes that need to be made.

Things to remember:
1. Require students to accept the constraints and assigned behaviors of the character, and stay in character in the role play;

2. Insist that observers look for actual behaviors, take notes on specific things said, and assess how well the actors stay in character. Observers should not interpret, only report;

3. Ask actors to share their thoughts and feelings as the character, then to share their personal reflections on the character; and

4. Have actors, observers, and teacher work together to interpret the role play, analyze their thoughts and feelings about the issue or problem, and draw conclusions.

Sample Lesson I: Role Playing in Social Studies

Thanksgiving

Mrs. Griswold planned to help her second graders review their study of the daily lives of pilgrims and Native Americans in Massachusetts and to use role playing to develop an understanding of the origins of Thanksgiving.

Objectives:

Mrs. Griswold wanted her students to use role playing to explore the origins of Thanksgiving.

Anticipatory Set:

Mrs. Griswold divided her class in half. One half worked with her to make a list of facts they had learned about the lifestyle of Native Americans. The other half worked with her to make a list of facts they had learned about the lifestyle of the pilgrims. After each half shared their lists with the other, the class worked together to make a list of the problems the pilgrims faced when they first came to this country.

Procedures:

Mrs. Griswold asked each student to bring in a stuffed animal for a Thanksgiving activity. During sharing time, each student told the class a little about the stuffed animal.

At social studies time, Mrs. Griswold asked the students to bring their animals and sit on the floor in a circle. She explained that she wanted the students to take turns acting out a part and that they would need to share their stuffed animals for the play. She asked if anyone objected to sharing their animal. Charles asked if he would get his animal back. "Right away," she assured him.

Next Mrs. Griswold explained that some of the students would act at Native Americans. They would each have two stuffed animals. She asked if anyone could guess why. Janine said, "Because they hunt for food?" Mrs. Griswold said that was correct, and added that, since Native Americans were good hunters, they had more food than they needed. They needed one animal for themselves and their families, she explained, but they had an extra one. She chose five students and asked them to act out the Native American life in the center of the circle.

Mrs. Griswold went on to say that some of the students would be pilgrims coming to the new world of America. She chose five students to join the Native Americans in the center of the circle, and asked them to join in acting out their parts. As she anticipated, after a brief scene in which the pilgrims talked about how hungry they were, the Native Americans gave each pilgrim a stuffed animal.

After having two more groups role-play these scenes, Mrs. Griswold asked the students to share their feelings when they were playing their roles. Then she asked them to tell what it felt like to watch, and what they were talking about when they saw the role-play.

Mrs. Griswald used the following questions as guides for herself in leading the discussion:

1. How would the Native Americans feel about pilgrims coming to their homeland? How would they feel knowing of the needy pilgrims' hunger?

2. How would the pilgrims feel arriving in a strange new home with nothing to help them survive?

3. How did it feel to role-play being a Native American? How did it feel to role-play a pilgrim?

4. How did it feel to be an observer of some of the events of the first Thanksgiving?

5. What do you know about the earliest Thanksgiving celebrations that the pilgrims and Native Americans shared?

6. How do you and your family celebrate Thanksgiving?

6

CHAPTER SIX

Meta-Strategies

OVERVIEW OF THE META-STRATEGIES
(Strategies for "Four"-Thought)

Meta-strategies are teaching interventions that address all the styles either simultaneously or in sequence. Meta, the Greek prefix for moving something from one place to another, literally means moving the student through some content across each of the four learning styles. Meta-strategies have as their overall purpose the learning of content on both a broader and deeper level. Meta-strategies work toward balancing both breadth and depth of understanding. Questing (not included in this volume because of its comprehensiveness) is the sina qua non of meta-strategies as it rotates questioning around each of the demands of thinking required by the four styles. (See Questioning Styles and Strategies, 1985.)

The Meta-strategies described include: *Write to Learn, Creative Problem-Solving, Knowledge by Design, and Task Rotation.*

In the *Write to Learn Strategy*, students use writing as a means of learning about content, organizing ideas, explaining and justifying positions, solving problems, and thinking critically. The purpose is to make visible the inner conversations through which they make discoveries and develop what they know. The teacher's role is to focus students on the content or topic, to provide a central question, and to give students time for writing and sharing responses in a supportive environment.

In the *Creative Problem-Solving Strategy*, students are engaged in a four step process for working through a problem. The strategy is a delicate balance between convergent analytical thinking and divergent creative expression. The Creative Problem-Solving Strategy emphasizes all four teaching/learning styles. The mastery style is involved in collecting data, the synthesis style in generating possibilities, the understanding style in analyzing alternatives, and the involvement style in choosing themost desirable solution. The

teacher's role in this strategy is to explain the four-step process, to ask questions, and to provide constructive feedback.

In the *Knowledge by Design Strategy*, students participate in a four-step process aimed at unlocking the design characteristics of a concept or object. As in the Creative Problem Solving Strategy, both convergent analytical thinking and divergent creative expression are required. The Knowledge by Design Strategy uses the mastery style to identify and describe the structure of a concept or object; the interpersonal style to define the purpose; the understanding style to develop arguments for and against; and the self-expressive style to generate modifications and alternatives. The students' role is to engage in the creative process used in designing a new product. The teacher's role is to select a concept or object for consideration, to challenge students to use the four-step process to pry open the structure of a concept or object to examine its unique components and properties, and to encourage students to think divergently to invent a product.

The *Task Rotation Strategy* is a deliberate four-step approach to an aspect of the curriculum. In the *Task Rotation Strategy*, the teacher plans to provide students with a broad frame of reference which results in seeing and interacting with the given content from four specific orientations. Within this four-step process, students are asked to master basic factual material, mediate the content through critical and analytical thinking, synthesize the new information through application, and explore ways in which the content builds on what students already know and contributes to what students discover in their own personal experience. The result is a richly satisfying approach to learning that is specifically designed to be responsive to students' needs and learning styles. The teacher's role is to determine objectives, establish activities and focusing questions in each of the four positions, and assist students in articulating relationships between and among tasks to deepen and broaden understanding of the given content.

WRITE TO LEARN STRATEGY (Learning Logs)

The Write to Learn Strategy is designed to help students discover, create, and develop their ideas fully. Students will use writing as a means of learning about content, examining evidence, solving problems, and thinking critically.

The Strategy at Work

Mr. Miscia has decided to use the Write to Learn Strategy to introduce a unit on poetry to his eleventh grade Advanced Placement English class. He begins the lesson by asking his students to spend five minutes writing down everything they know about poetry. Next, he asks his students to share their writing with a neighbor or in groups of three. In the sharing which follows, students help him list information about poetry based on their writing.

Once the class list has been made, Mr. Miscia asks his students to choose one item from the class list to write about in detail. He tells them that they may choose any item they feel comfortable writing about, and tells them to write as much as they can within a ten-minute time limit.

Mr. Miscia again asks his students to share their writing with a neighbor or in groups of three, but this time he wants someone else in the group to paraphrase what they have learned for the whole class.

From this sharing, Mr. Miscia and his students make a class list of questions about poetry to use in investigation of the topic.

The Write to Learn Strategy

Writing is basic to thinking about knowledge in all subjects. Writing is also crucial to processing and assimilating information. Through writing, students make visible the inner conversations which they use to discover what they know. When students write to develop and organize their ideas, to explain or justify a position, or to brainstorm about a topic, they are engaged in exploring and shaping their thoughts. Rereading, revising, and reconstructing their writing helps students make sense of their schooling. Sharing their writing, receiving feedback, and providing feedback on the writing of their peers engages students in disciplined discussion of their learning, and teaches them to value their personal reflections and observations.

The Write to Learn Strategy provides students with regular practice in writing at length. Frequent use of a learning log or journal in the course of instruction encourages students to internally manipulate what is presented through lecture, discussion, and reading. The learning log allows students to take a whole chunk of information, largely undigested, and wrestle with it, consider it, explain it, summarize it, accept or reject it, question or debate it, justify it, talk to themselves about it.

The goals of the Write to Learn Strategy are:
1. To use writing as a means of learning;
2. To write to discover, create, and develop ideas about learning;
3. To write to examine evidence and to solve problems;
4. To use writing as a framework for disciplined discussion of what is being learned; and
5. To write to communicate learned information.

The steps in the Write to Learn Strategy are to:
1. Focus the students on the content or topic, and provide a central question;
2. Have students generate and share what they know about the content or topic; and
3. Provide time for writing and sharing responses.

Kindling writing is used to get students to generate ideas necessary to start the fire of imaginative thought. When doing kindling writing, students are asked to generate ideas in response to a provocative question. When a question is posed, students are given time to internalize it and to explore some possible responses. Students write their ideas in a Learning Log and share with a partner prior to group discussion.

Building writing is used to get students to integrate ideas into an organized piece of writing. Again, a question is posed, and students are given time to internalize and then generate responses. After sharing and discussing, students synthesize their ideas as they shape them into a paragraph or essay. They inspect their writing, share it with fellow students in pairs or small groups, and receive feedback. Finally, they summarize their insights.

How to Plan Lessons Using the Write to Learn Strategy

Since the Write to Learn Strategy is useful primarily as an ongoing activity, you need to consider how to introduce the Learning Log to students. For kindling writing, younger students may need to be provided with a composition book or stapled packet, perhaps in a folder, in which to write and/or draw responses, while older students may wish to control the choice of a notebook—spiral, bound, or loose-leaf, medium-sized or large. In addition, younger students may use the Learning Log only in the classroom, while older students may be asked to use the log not only to respond to your teaching, but also on an almost daily basis for both kindling and building writing as they do home assignments. Decide whether you wish to have students use a learning log for reflecting on academic topics and a separate journal for daily personal writing, or whether you prefer that your students use their logs for both purposes. Be clear in your own mind about how you plan to evaluate this type of writing.

In addition to providing students with a procedural framework, your introductory lesson should include discussion of the variety of purposes for writing. You may ask students to reflect on the questions, "Why do people write? Why do you write? Why do your parents write? Why do other adults write?" Students may suggest some of the following: to help me remember something, to thank someone, to summarize what I need to study, to protest a political decision, to persuade someone to do something, or to make complaints. Planning a discussion of the functions of writing will allow you to emphasize to students the benefits of writing for personal reflection and observation, for free expression of their questions and hypotheses, for speculation, and for generation and expansion of ideas and emotions.

As you plan for the regular use of Learning Logs, consider these questions:

1. In this particular lesson, what is your purpose in having students write? Do you want your students to generate ideas, analyze, synthesize, judge, recall, anticipate, or defend?

2. How can you best phrase your question to elicit responses that will be useful in achieving your purpose?

3. When is the optimum time for students to respond to your question: the night before the lesson, at the beginning of the lesson, somewhere in the middle, at the end, the night after the lesson?

4. What might the responses look like: a list, a diagram, doodles or sketches, brainstorming or free writing, questions or predictions, a summary, an opinion, data obtained by physical observation or interviewing or reading, an explanation or clarification?

5. What is the most useful way for students to share their writing with each other: initially, not at all, with a neighbor, with a formally established peer group, with the whole class, as a written dialogue with a peer or with you?

6. Will this particular response be used as part of the ongoing process of learning; i.e., as kindling writing, or is it intended to form a base for the development of a polished product; i.e., as building writing?

7. Will you need to build an opportunity for students to reflect on and rethink what they have originally written?

Putting the Write to Learn Strategy to Work in Your Classroom

Provide frequent opportunities for your students to write freely in their learning logs so that they have regular practice in thinking and articulating their thoughts. As they write silently in response to your questions, they will generate ideas, begin to take risks, and become personally engaged in their learning.

To introduce a lesson, have students write for five minutes on what they know about a topic, or ask them to reflect on an appropriate quote. Writing prior to the lesson gives students time to focus and to commit themselves to a hypothesis. Follow this writing with discussion, a lecture, or reading, and then provide time for students to reread what they wrote and to write again.

End a lesson by giving students five minutes to summarize the most important points, to look for a pattern, to develop a logical next step, or to define questions. The sharing of this writing may provide a useful introduction to a lesson the next day, or even weeks later as you ask your students to go back to reread what they have written.

Pose a problem to your students, and ask them to write a solution. Ask your students to explain why the author of a story chose a particular point of view, or what the poet's choice of line breaks does to the rhythm and sense of a poem. Have them rewrite an algebraic word problem in their own words, or write a set of directions for solving an equation. Ask them to write a description of a scientific experiment they have just done or observed.

Stop a lesson in the middle, once or at several intervals, to have students reflect on the ideas that have been discussed. Use this writing to allow students time to summarize complex information, to react personally to the topic, to deal with student's misunderstandings or to sharpen the focus. Such writing pauses, interspersed through a lesson, enable you to ensure broader participation in discussions where otherwise a few students tend to dominate.

Ask students to respond regularly in writing to what they read, to their lab work, and to their field trips. Ask them to record their initial insights when they first read a poem, or listen to a piece of music, or see some examples of an artist's work. Make students aware of the value of their learning logs in preserving their early thinking and allowing them to see the development of their understanding.

When you are using building writing, start by finding a question which will require your students to integrate ideas. Have them generate possible responses, and then assign a shape into which they will fit their writing. Possible shapes include compare and contrast, relate personally, evaluate or appraise, associate, trace or sequence, enumerate, identify, and describe, define, explore and predict, argue a position, and summarize. When writing has been completed, have students inspect what they have written, and exchange ideas with a writing group. Then have them summarize their insights.

How to Evaluate the Write to Learn Strategy

Frequent writing, in a non-judgmental classroom climate, encourages students to trust their own thoughts and opinions and to value honest personal responses from their peers as well as from their teacher. Ideally, students take some risks with their ideas. Their writing is by definition tentative, speculative, messy, vulnerable, and unpredictable.

Evaluation of journal writing needs to communicate to the students that such writing counts for something; on the other hand, the teacher response should convey support and constructive feedback rather than judgment. Here are some possibilities:

1. Set a schedule for reading and responding to journals, for example, every three weeks, period 1 on Monday, period 2 on Tuesday, and so on. Read to find one or two of the most interesting or worthwhile ideas, and write a personal response centered on those.

2. Don't read journals at all. Instead, provide ample opportunities for students to use their journal writing as a base for peer group discussion, whole class presentation, and polished writing assignments. Let students know that you are looking for evidence of effective journal use. From time to time, ask students to meet with you to discuss the ways in which they are using their journal writing.

3. Ask students to reread their journals regularly, and have them choose an entry to share with the class.

4. Each marking period, or semester, have students prepare their journals by adding page numbers, a table of contents for entries they feel have the most significance, an introduction, and a final journal entry in which they evaluate their own journal writing. Read the "publication" material and skim the rest.

5. Use some reasonable combination of these evaluation formats. Set a point system for grades in which credit is given for journal writing. Evaluate according to quantity or quality of writing, or evidence of personal growth.

6. Provide regular opportunities to use journal writing in the preparation of polished writing, such as research papers, book reports, personal opinion papers, formal summaries, essays, and so on. Use such entries to facilitate conferences with students, but formally grade only finished papers.

Summary

When to use it:

When you want students to discover, create and develop their ideas, and/or integrate what they have learned in a written paragraph, essay, or report form.

How to use it:

1. Focus students on the content and the question being asked;

2. Have students generate what they know about the content;

3. Have students analyze the question and use the content to construct an answer to fit the form;

4. Ask students to inspect their response—Is the content correct? Does it answer the question?;

5. Ask students to exchange responses with other students; and

6. Summarize student responses through large group discussion.

How to evaluate it:

1. Are students able to write to fit the form; do they know the criteria for the question they are being asked to answer?

2. Do students have the content knowledge to answer the question?

3. Are students able to share responses and provide feedback to each other?

Things to remember:

1. Before writing, students need to be stimulated to review relevant content to the working memory;

2. Use specific questions for students to answer when they inspect their writing. Have them write about their inspection; i.e., select a title for the piece, circle the most powerful word, etc.;

3. The teacher should write and share his/her responses with students; and

4. Read a few responses; do not always grade, but comment in writing and note in public ideas students have expressed in their writing. This will motivate students to write and to have their writing read.

Sample Lesson I: Social Studies—Day to Day in Ancient Egypt

Mrs. Stoeckel wanted her sixth grade social studies students to use writing as a means of learning about the daily life of ancient Egypt. She was interested in having her students explore content, examine evidence, and think critically about the ways in which archeologists learn about the lives of ancient peoples.

Objectives:

Mrs. Stoeckel wanted her students to use Write to Learn as a way to explore and shape their thoughts about daily life in ancient Egypt, to brainstorm about the possibilities, and to develop and organize their ideas. By asking them to share their writing, she planned to engage them in disciplined discussion of their learning.

Getting Started:

Mrs. Stoeckel introduced her lesson on the daily life of ancient Egyptians by saying, "Often when we look at ancient Egypt, we focus on the pharaohs and their lives because the evidence we have found tells us so much about them. But what about the ordinary people who lived and worked and played in ancient Egypt? What information do we have about them?"

"What did the ordinary people of ancient Egypt look like?"

"How did they dress?"

"What kinds of jobs did they have?"

"What were their talents?"

"What did they do for entertainment?"

"What were their beliefs?"

"I have some photographs and sketches of statues and wall paintings found in ancient tombs and temples. I'd like you to look at them. What do these pieces of art tell you about ancient Egyptians?"

Procedures:

Mrs. Stoeckel went on to explain that she had made copies of her questions for each student, but that she first wanted them to look carefully at the artwork.

"Make some lists; just jot down 'stuff' you notice," she told the class.

After five minutes, Mrs. Stoeckel asked the class to form groups of three to compare lists and to share ideas.

Next Mrs. Stoeckel said, "When your lists are completed, examine them to see what ideas go together. Have you noticed a lot about one thing? Does something you look at particularly interest you? Decide what aspect of the life of ancient Egyptians you would like to write about. Go back through the photographs and sketches once more to see if there's anything about your topic that you missed. Then write your piece."

"When you have finished writing your piece, re-read it carefully. Underline the sentence you think is the best one. Put a circle around three to five words you think are very important to the main idea of your piece. Then write a new title for your piece."

"When you are finished, you will have a chance to share your draft with your group of three. Listen carefully to the questions your group asks about what you have written. Listen to what the others have written. You may get some ideas about ways to improve your piece."

"Add to, change, and cross out on your draft until you are satisfied that it expresses your thoughts clearly."

"Proofread your draft. Make a good copy for your portfolio. (Put your drafts and lists in your portfolio, too!) Be ready to discuss what you have learned by Monday."

Mrs. Stoeckel's students have used the Write to Learn Strategy and peer conferences since the beginning of the semester. When the individual pieces of writing are shared, they will form the basis for the examination of daily life in ancient Egypt.

CREATIVE PROBLEM-SOLVING STRATEGY

The Creative Problem-Solving Strategy involves students in a systematic problem-solving process which requires both convergent and analytical thinking and divergent expression. The strategy requires students to define the problem, generate alternative solutions, evaluate alternative solutions against appropriate criteria, decide which solution is most desirable, and, where possible, test the chosen solution by implementing it.

The Strategy at Work

Mrs. Hernandez has had her ninth grade students read the first two acts of Shakespeare's *Romeo and Juliet*. To deepen their understanding of the play, and to engage their imaginations, she has decided to devote several periods to a creative problem-solving exercise based on the situation in which Romeo and Juliet find themselves. She has divided her class into small groups, and has set them to work to answer the following questions:

1. What is the problem faced by the two lovers? Gather data from the first two acts to help you to define the problem. Then make a list of the possible causes of the problem, and the possible effects of the problem on the people in the play.

2. What are the possible alternatives? Consider not only what the two lovers should do if they proceed with their plan to be secretly married, but what other actions they might take to be united in their love. List as many possibilities as you can; don't impose any limits on your imagination. Don't settle for the obvious; try to move from the usual ideas to unusual ones.

Before proceeding, Mrs. Hernandez will have each group report their definition and description of the problem so that discrepancies in interpretation can be brought to light and discussed. Then, together with the groups, she will make a master list of alternative solutions which each of the groups may consider.

Since this is the first time this class has used the Creative Problem-Solving Strategy, Mrs. Hernandez will take time to discuss the need to weigh alternative solutions against specific criteria, and the class will work together to develop a list of criteria which they can agree will produce a list of solutions acceptable to them. Then the class will resume working in the original small groups to consider:

1. Which solutions are feasible? Which solutions should be eliminated from consideration because they appear on their face to be irrelevant or unworkable? Which ones should be grouped together as variations of one basic solution? Which ones best fit the criteria? Which ones come close to fitting the criteria? Do they deviate from the criteria in important ways? Make a list of the ones you agree should be considered as feasible.

2. Which solution is most desirable? Which solution "feels good" to you? What makes you choose this particular solution over all the rest?

Again Mrs. Hernandez plans to have the groups share their results in discussion. After reading the rest of the play and discussing the results Romeo and Juliet achieved by implementing their solution to the problem, the class will speculate on the changes which would have occurred (still assuming the slaying of Mercutio by Tybalt, the vengeance of Romeo against Tybalt, and the subsequent banishment of Romeo) had their desired solution been in place.

The Creative Problem-Solving Strategy

What is a problem? One way to define a problem is to think of it as a discrepancy between an actual state of affairs and some ideal or desired state. Every personal and professional problem can be viewed as the gap between what exists, and what is wanted. The resulting dissonance results in a challenge to search for a solution. Problem-solving requires the application of existing knowledge and skills in fresh and unconventional ways in the struggle to close the gap between the actual and the desired state.

Every problem provides an opportunity to devise a creative solution. The Creative Problem-Solving Strategy involves students in compiling facts, defining views of the problem, imagining solutions, recognizing and/or developing criteria, and finding ways of ensuring successful implementation. The process requires both convergent analytical thinking and divergent expression. Students will need to work in all four teaching/learning styles. When collecting facts and describing the problem, students are working in the

What could the animal hide be used for?

How are we going to survive here?!

Mastery style. To generate alternatives, students need to work in the Self-Expressive style to break their mindset and think in new and different ways. The Understanding style is used when students analyze alternatives and determine cause and effect. When students exercise their personal preferences to determine the most desirable solution, they are working in the Interpersonal style.

Problem-solving involves both facts and analysis. To be effective, students must maintain a dynamic balance between the two. Idea production requires students to defer judgment in order to go beyond their self-imposed limits; discrimination among alternatives to determine the relative potential cost and effectiveness requires focus and judgment, and is essential for choosing the idea with the best chance of success. The teacher challenges students to stretch beyond their normal limits in both of these stages.

The goals of the Creative Problem-Solving Strategy are:

1. To help students identify, define, clarify, and analyze the problem (ST);

2. To help students use divergent thinking to generate alternative approaches to the resolution of the problem (NF);

3 To help students use convergent thinking to analyze, evaluate, and select solutions which fit appropriate criteria (NT); and

4. To help students to accept one of the solutions as most desirable to them as individuals, or as a group, and where possible, to become committed to implementing it (SF).

The questions to be addressed in the problem-solving process are:

1. What is the problem?

2. What are the possible solutions?

3. What are the feasible solutions?

4. Which of the feasible solutions is desirable?

How to Plan Lessons Which Use the Creative Problem-Solving Strategy

You need to design a challenge or problem which will engage your students in the creative problem-solving process. In selecting and designing this challenge, consider whether students have sufficient background knowledge to deal effectively with the subject. The problem can be of two types: an historical problem for which there is adequate information as to cause and resolution, or a current problem to be walked through the four stages. Do they need background information, or can they rely primarily on personal experience, as they would if asked to develop alternative endings to a novel prior to reading the author's own conclusion? Can they rely primarily on personal experience, as they might if asked to develop alternative ways of improving their class record of punctually completed homework assignments? If students have insufficient specialized information or background knowledge to define the problem accurately, what resources and materials will be needed, and how will you make them available? Will your students work individually to solve the problem, or in small groups? Will the class as a whole address the problem? Do you want to have students work in a sequence—first independently, then as part of a small group, then with the whole class—on parts or all of the problem?

As you consider the necessary resources and materials which will be needed, and the manner in which students will work on the problem, consider also the element of time. Students tend to vary dramatically in the amount of time needed for solving problems. This is so even when the problems selected are of comparable difficulty, or when all of the students are working on the same problem. You must consider ways of providing for flexible use of time, and may also need to plan ways to support and enhance efficient student interaction in groups.

Putting the Creative Problem-Solving Strategy to Work in Your Classroom

The creative problem-solving process is open-ended; in the search for verification and feedback, the role of the student is expanded. Students are involved in all of the subject matter implementation and evaluation phases. Your role shifts from "sage on the stage" to "guide on the side."

Before presenting a problem to your class, explain the problem-solving process. Discuss each step, and help your students to understand the distinctions between possible solutions, feasible solutions, and desirable solutions. Take time to develop clear expectations of the ways student roles change in each phase of the problem-solving process:

1. First, students collect and verify facts about the problem and use these to define the problem, and analyze its possible causes and effects. Students need to organize themselves to gather data from available resources and materials in an efficient manner. They need to share the data and develop a definition of the problem which fits it. Then they need to analyze and list the problem's possible causes and effects.

2. Next, students generate possible solutions to the problem (see Divergent Thinking Strategy) by emphasizing fluent, flexible, and original thinking skills. Here, students need to focus on new and unconventional ways of looking at the problem, and to generate many ideas. Students need to understand the importance of withholding evaluation during this phase of problem-solving.

3. In the third phase, students must develop a set of specific criteria against which to measure their solutions. Feasibility criteria may include considerations of time, cost, manpower, correctness of fit, and so on. At this stage, students should list their alternatives, eliminate those which appear irrelevant or unfeasible, and group solutions which appear similar. Students will then examine each alternative solution against the selected criteria.

4. The last step is to determine desirability. At this step, students will select the solution which seems best to them. Their decision about desirability should consciously reflect cultural mores, personal belief, morality, legality, and beauty.

Your role will also change as student roles change in each phase of the problem-solving process. In the first phase, you will facilitate the process of gathering and analyzing data by providing or suggesting resources and materials, by asking appropriate focusing questions, and by assisting students and/or groups which need help. In the second phase, you will help students feel comfortable by suspending the evaluation of ideas, by encouraging them to move from the usual to the unusual, and by stimulating them to search for a variety of solutions and insights rather than to settle for a few seemingly "correct" responses. In the third phase, you will encourage students to develop a working list of criteria against which solutions can be weighed, and to add to it as important insights occur to them. In the final phase, you need to encourage students to examine and articulate their reasons for backing a particular solution, especially when the solution must reflect a group decision. Throughout the process, you need to observe individual students to learn how they perceive and engage in the problem-solving process, how they propose and examine solutions, and how they interact with others.

How to Evaluate the Problem-Solving Strategy

Evaluate a solution to a problem by developing a plan of action, carrying it out where possible, and determining its effectiveness. In addition, focus on the process involved. With your guidance, students need to examine and evaluate their participation in each stage of the creative problem-solving process. Students need to be actively involved in this evaluation in order to enhance their own problem-solving skills. A formative evaluation which occurs as students work through each phase allows students an opportunity to rethink their decisions. You need to assist students to identify criteria to serve as a framework for evaluation; for example, you may suggest that students derive criteria for evaluating the phase in which they generated alternatives by reviewing the elements of divergent thinking—fluency, flexibility, elaboration, and originality. When you ask students to work in a group, you should also encourage them to evaluate such group process issues as leadership, listening, consensus, decision-making, participation, and working toward quality.

Summary

When to use it:

When you want your students to follow a systematic process for solving a problem.

How to use it:

1. Select or design a problem for students to address;

2. Describe what it is; Have students define the nature and details of the problem in concrete terms; Generate what is possible; Have the students generate alternative solutions to the problem; Consider all possible ways of attacking the issue;

3. Analyze what is feasible; Have the students develop criteria to analyze the alternatives;

4. Select what is desirable; Have the students select the solution which is most desirable and which they would be willing to implement; and

5. Develop a plan of action.

How to evaluate it:

1. Was the problem described clearly, accurately, and completely?

2. Were multiple solutions generated?

3. Was the criteria list appropriate for analyzing the alternatives?

4. Was a workable solution selected?

Things to remember:

1. A problem is a discrepant event; It represents a gap between an actual state of affairs and some ideal or desired state;

2. Use Divergent Thinking to generate alternatives; Have students work for fluency, flexibility, originality and coherence; and

3. Problem-solving involves both gathering facts and making analyses; It requires sensing for describing what is, intuition for generating possibilities, thinking for analyzing alternatives, and feeling for selecting what you believe to be the best decision.

Sample Lesson I: Science—Improving the Environment

Dr. Chu wanted her ninth grade Earth Science students to use creative problem-solving to write a convincing descriptive essay recommending action on an environmental problem they had researched and analyzed.

Objectives:

Dr. Chu wanted her students to investigate an environmental problem, using various sources of information. She wanted them to develop a list of possible solutions, analyze their alternatives, and make and justify a recommendation for action. While she intended students to work together to investigate a problem and to develop and justify a solution, she held each student responsible for writing an essay describing the environmental problem, analyzing alternative solutions, and proposing a course of action.

Getting Started:

Dr. Chu asked students to imagine that they had just been appointed chief scientific advisor to the President of the United States, and invited them to make a list of major scientific concerns affecting the future of our country. After they had shared ideas with a neighbor, she led a class discussion, and recorded suggestions, marking environmental topics as the discussion proceeded.

Procedures:

Dr. Chu divided the class into groups of four students, with each group responsible for investigating a different environmental topic. She then explained the problem-solving process to the class, emphasizing that they needed to carefully assemble material to answer the following questions:

1. What is the problem situation?

2. What can be done to change the situation for the better?

3. Of the alternatives generated, which are feasible and why? Which are desirable, and why?

4. Which alternative is the best choice? How can you justify this choice?

Dr. Chu planned several class periods in the library for groups to work together to gather information to answer the first question, "What is the situation?" The librarian reviewed how to use the Readers' Guide to Periodical Literature, and provided access to library resources. Dr. Chu encouraged the collection of relevant articles from daily newspapers and magazines, and furnished names and addresses of environmental action groups to be contacted for up-to-the-minute information. Groups worked together, in and out of school, to build comprehensive lists of important facts about their environmental problem; then as individuals, students wrote their paragraph(s) describing "what is."

After drafts of the first paragraphs were written, Dr. Chu led a brief class discussion of peer group conferences, emphasizing ways in which students could help each other improve their written expression. She asked the groups to listen as each member read aloud in turn, and to write down what they recalled as the strongest sentence in each paragraph, to comment briefly on clarity, and to identify a sequence of ideas. She directed students to hand these written responses without further elucidation to the person who had read. In another brief discussion at the end of this class period, some students pointed out that they had heard good ideas and "wished (they) had said that." Dr. Chu urged her students to incorporate these good ideas from other students' papers into their second drafts.

While students worked at home on second drafts, Dr. Chu had them work in class to generate possible solutions to their environmental problem. The students brainstormed in independent groups after being reminded to select one student in their group to monitor the process to make sure that no possible solutions were evaluated in this phase.

Dr. Chu then asked the groups to put similar solutions together and to discuss their feasibility and desirability. As they examined their solutions, they kept a record of the good and bad points of each solution.

Lastly, Dr. Chu had each group consider which of their solutions was their best choice, and to develop arguments to justify that choice. Since each student was writing an independent essay, there was no need for group members to agree on one solution. Groups were encouraged to work together to define the benefits and drawbacks of each of the preferred solutions within the group, and to help each other develop strong arguments in favor of their chosen solutions.

Since feedback is more helpful if peer readers have specific tasks, Dr. Chu asked students to confer again on first drafts of this section, commenting on clarity and summarizing the main idea of each draft. Then students worked on second drafts; peer readers looked for the best reason in the argument.

When final versions were due, Dr. Chu arranged for an opportunity to publish the essays for a simulated scientific conference for the presentation of environmental papers.

Sample Lesson II: Mathematics—Understanding the Concept of Area

Mr. Luppino wanted to help his sixth grade students develop a better understanding of the idea of area. He found that, while his students were usually able to memorize the formulas for determining the areas of various shapes—rectangle, triangle, parallelogram, trapezoid, and circle, many of them become confused as to when to apply a formula to find the area and when to apply a formula to find the perimeter. He planned to help his students to explore the concept of area by asking them to analyze and solve a problem.

Objectives:

Mr. Luppino wanted his students to develop an understanding of the concept of area. He wanted them to explore the idea by investigating a problem in which they were required to find an area of a figure. To find the area of this figure, they needed to generate possible methods of computing area, analyze the effectiveness of the alternatives they had generated, and justify their choice of method. Mr. Luppino wanted them to evaluate the effectiveness of their method by actually using it to try to determine the area of the figure, and by comparing their results with those of their classmates.

Getting Started:

To introduce the problem-solving tasks, Mr. Luppino asked his students to imagine that they lived in an ancient city ruled by a mean, nasty king. This king, he told them, had ordered five identical life-size human figures to be drawn on the floor of the palace courtyard. He had issued a proclamation to all who live in the city: someone must find a good way of measuring the area of one of these figures before sunset, or all of his subjects will suffer the consequences of his displeasure.

Procedures:

Mr. Luppino divided the class into five groups of students. He had already prepared identical outlines of a life-sized human figure drawn on mural paper, and now provided one for each group. He explained that the groups were to work together to find the area of their life-sized human figure. Because feedback and sharing is essential to the problem-solving process, Mr. Luppino encouraged the students to work collaboratively.

Before allowing the groups to begin working, Mr. Luppino explained the problem-solving process to the class. Together with the class, he made a worksheet for the groups to use to record answers to the following questions:

1. What is the problem? What has the group been asked to do?

2. What can we do to solve the problem? What are the possible ways in which the area can be determined?

3. Of the alternatives generated, which are feasible and why? Which are desirable, and why?

4. Which alternative is the best choice? How can we justify this choice?

In this session, Mr. Luppino planned time for his groups to work together to gather information to answer the first question, "What is the problem? What has the group been asked to do?" When all groups had a chance to define the problem, he asked each group to share their understanding of the task with the whole class, and to discuss their objectives.

When the first question had been discussed, Mr. Luppino had students work to generate possible solutions. Since his students were not used to brainstorming in independent groups, Mr. Luppino moved from group to group providing leadership and guidance. On several occasions, he reminded his students not to evaluate any suggested solutions, just to record them. Since all groups were working on the same problem, Mr. Luppino had them brainstorm as separate groups, share ideas as a class, and then brainstorm some more.

Lastly, Mr. Luppino encouraged students in each group to define their best choice, and to develop strong arguments in favor of their preferred solution. Since each group was working independently, there was no need for groups to agree on one solution; however, Mr. Luppino made it clear that acceptable solutions must eventually provide for ways of comparing answers.

As soon as each group decided on a method of finding the area, they began to "solve the problem." Mr. Luppino's groups used the following methods:

1. Measure the area in terms of hand area.

2. Use one person's shoe sole area as the unit of measure. (This group traced the shoe in different positions to fill the figure, and estimated how many little pieces in between would make additional "shoes.")

3. Cut out a square and place it on the figure to determine how many squares or parts of squares will fit into the figure. (Two groups used this method, but one made a square by measuring ten centimeters on a side with a ruler, while the other used a folded paper method to make an unmeasured square).

4. Cut pieces of centimeter graph paper to fit inside the outline, paste the paper on cover the whole shape, and then count the squares. (This group first tried counting, then numbering the squares. When they became bewildered, they resorted to making sets of 100 squares and outlining these sets with different colors so that they wouldn't confuse what they had counted already with what remained).

When the groups had all determined answers, Levon asked Mr. Luppino which group was correct. Mr. Luppino told the class that, since all of the answers were figured out using different units of measure, he could not compare them. He asked them to develop a method of making the answers of the group comparable.

After discussion, the class decided to find out what the areas would be if all of the groups had used square centimeters as their unit of measure. Each group, except the one that had used centimeter graph paper, traced its unit of measure onto centimeter graph paper to find out how many square centimeters each unit was worth. Mr. Luppino had the students use calculators for multiplying to determine the whole area in terms of the standard square unit. Mr. Luppino then asked the class to think about and discuss the methods they used, the accuracy or inaccuracy of the work, and the advantages and disadvantages of the processes they used. For homework, the students wrote a brief summary of the problem and its solution.

KNOWLEDGE BY DESIGN STRATEGY

The Knowledge by Design Strategy engages students in the creative process used in designing a new product. The strategy requires students to inspect structures or concepts by identifying their characteristics, defining their purpose, listing their positive and negative attributes, and generating ways in which they might be modified or recreated.

The Strategy at Work

Ms. Oscina wants her tenth grade biology class to focus on the reasons for natural variation as her students consider the adaptation of organisms. She has posed the question: Why do we find animals that attach themselves to surfaces under the water, but not on the land? Her students respond by first writing in their Response Journals, then sharing ideas. Several students enumerate difficulties for an animal in finding food on land if it were attached to one spot. This leads to questions about how animals attached to one location in water "find food." Is it possible that the water carried food to these animals, they ask? What about reproduction? How do these animals reproduce? Animals that can move about escape their enemies by hiding, by running or flying away, or through camouflage. How do animals attached to one location in water escape their enemies? Ms. Oscina records all of the hypothetical statements offered, as well as the students' questions.

Using the Knowledge by Design Strategy, Ms. Oscina asks her students to consider first what the structure of an organism attached to one location in water would have to be. Discussion of this question leads to agreement that such organisms would have to have some structure that would facilitate fastening themselves to a surface; examples proposed and described by her students include sea urchins, barnacles, mussels, corals, and sponges.

Next, Ms. Oscina asked her students to consider what might be the purpose of "fastening on." Here, her students suggest that the structure of these organisms do not permit easy movement; they have no legs or wings, so fastening on keeps them out of unsafe areas from which they could not escape.

Ms. Oscina then asks her students to list the advantages and disadvantages of being fastened to one location. The finished list looks like this:

Advantages
- Cannot be moved into unsafe areas
- Will reproduce and grow mainly in areas where food is plentiful
- May be able to grow heavy protective covering because it doesn't have to move around
- May be aided in food gathering, protection or reproduction by being part of a colony or group

Disadvantages
- Cannot run away from danger
- Cannot move to another location if food supply is diminished
- Food must come to it because it cannot move to food
- Must have some method of reproduction that does not require moving to find a mate
- Cannot move away from harmful conditions such as pollution

For a brief report on sessile animals, Ms. Oscina then asked her students to investigate, using their text and other resources, the questions under discussion, and to add to (and, if necessary, correct) the proposed answers. Her guidelines for the report include:

- What is the structure of these animals? Describe their characteristics. Name, describe, and draw (or provide pictures of) representative classes.
- What is the purpose of these animals' ability to fasten on?

- What properties or characteristics allow these animals to survive? What are the dangers these animals face?

- Finally—If you were able to design ways to improve these animals by modifying or changing their structures, what would your proposal look like? Choose one animal to modify, or describe changes which would affect all sessile animals. Justify your proposal.

The Knowledge by Design Strategy

Knowledge can be thought of as a kind of design, as information placed within a structure for a purpose.

The Knowledge by Design Strategy allows students to pry open the structure to examine its unique components and properties. It provides students with a framework for probing structure and purpose, and for determining how an object, theory or idea works.

Newton's laws, the Bill of Rights, and the science of ecology are all examples of knowledge; i.e., numerous bits of data embedded in a design which helps to explain and illuminate. The Knowledge by Design Strategy permits students to take apart and put together such designs in order to increase understanding. In this sequence, students start with abstract knowledge—Darwin's theory of natural selection, the organization of a paragraph, rate x time = distance, etc., and use the four positions which enhance critical and creative thinking about the topic.

Alternatively, students may examine a concrete example—a screwdriver, a traffic light, a deceptive advertisement, a piece of equipment, the legislative or legal process—as a means to develop an abstract understanding. The close inspection of such cases allows students to discover the underlying design and how it works, and to form appropriate arguments to explain, evaluate, and defend it.

The goals of the Knowledge by Design Strategy are:
1. To help students select the design of a concept or idea to be examined across the four positions (SF);
2. To help students focus on developing a careful and exacting description of the attributes of an object or concept (ST);
3. To help students discover the purposes and/or value of an object or concept (NT/SF);
4. To help students perceive the advantages and disadvantages of the object or concept (NT); and
5. To help students think divergently to generate modifications and changes to the object or concept (NF).

The steps in the Knowledge by Design Strategy are to:
1. Select a concept or object for students to consider;
2. Ask students to formulate a precise description of the concept or object;
3. Ask students to consider the purposes of the concept or object;
4. Ask students to envision and articulate the possible arguments for and against the concept or object; and
5. Ask students to explore and invent ways to modify or change the concept or object.

How to Plan Lessons Using the Knowledge by Design Strategy

Knowledge is a kind of abstract design which we have devised to join together disparate pieces of information. The Knowledge by Design Strategy helps students to take apart the design to see what we have constructed. Instead of simply expecting your students to accumulate sets of data, you want to use this strategy to make your students aware of the design characteristics of a concept or object. Choose a concept or object for your students to examine. Base your choice on the need to break a familiar frame of reference, to increase understanding, or to enhance critical and creative thinking. When you first use this strategy, choose a concrete example to model the process, then move to more abstract cases.

Once you have chosen a concept or object to explore, you want your students to consider four questions:

- What is the structure? What are its components, of what is it made, what properties and characteristics does it have? What are some model cases: draw, show, demonstrate, make it work.
- What is its purpose? Why have it?
- What are the arguments for this? What are the arguments against this? What are its pro and con arguments?
- How can it be improved? How can it be made more useful or better?

Start with a concrete design and work toward an abstract understanding; i.e., the close examination of a spring scale will lead to an understanding of principles of physics. Or start with abstract knowledge; i.e., Darwin's theory of natural selection, to discover a way of explaining the enormous and confusing variety of adaptations found in nature.

Putting the Knowledge by Design Strategy to Work in Your Classroom

When you are ready to introduce the Knowledge by Design Strategy in your classroom, remember that it will be easier for your students to understand the process if you choose a simple example as a model. A biology teacher might choose to investigate the sponge, an English teacher quotation marks, or a history teacher the time line. These choices limit and focus discussion, and make it easier for students to see how the strategy illuminates their work. Teaching students first how to use the strategy will make it easier for them to tackle complex cases such as the double helix, the essay, or the political movement toward oblivion of slavery. Remember, however, that examination of "simpler" cases may provide your students with insights that are just as valid, and sometimes more teachable, than the more theoretical ones.

The Knowledge by Design Strategy leads naturally to the development of a product. That product may be an invention, a model, a piece of writing, some sort of artwork, an illustrative chart or graph, preparation for a debate or discussion. Your objective will have a direct tie to the product you require. Consider what sort of product will be most profitable as a learning experience.

Consider how students should work, and what form their responses should take. Do you want to allot class time for this investigation? Do you want students to work independently, as pairs, or in small groups? Do you want the work done outside of school? Do you want the class to work on one topic; i.e., the long division algorithm, or gravity? Or do you want to set groups working on different topics related to a theme; i.e., the question mark, quotation marks, the period, the comma, the apostrophe, and so on, with the goal of sharing insights about punctuation? How should students record their responses? Written responses for all four questions, journal entries, participation in class discussion, completion of a project, model, or chart? How will you share the work and the results?

How to Evaluate the Knowledge By Design Strategy

Were students able to describe the attributes of the concept or object? Students should be able to list and describe (or show) model cases. They should be able to demonstrate how the concept or object works. How precise and complete were their recorded observations?

Were students able to state the purpose of the concept or object? Students should be able to explain the reason, value, or usefulness of the concept or object.

Were students able to list both the advantages and disadvantages of the concept or object? Students should be able to delineate the properties or characteristics that make the concept or object effective. They should be able to develop pro and con arguments related to the concept or object. They should be able to evaluate it.

Were students able to think divergently to generate modifications and alterations? Students should demonstrate the ability to go beyond the known and mundane in the search for changes and improvements that are other-worldly, unconventional, useful, and fun.

Summary

When to use it:

When you want students to inspect the design of a particular concept, idea, object, machine, or organization and generate ways in which to modify and change it.

How to use it:

1. Select the concept to be examined;

2. Have students first describe the concept;

3. Explain the purposes of the strategy;

4. Analyze the arguments for the existence of the concept as well as arguments against the concept; and

5. Have students explore modifications or changes in the concept and the results of their inspection.

How to evaluate it:

1. Were students able to examine the concept for its attributes, purposes, disadvantages, and advantages?

2. Were students able to think divergently to generate modifications and alterations?

Things to remember:

1. Select a concrete example to model the process; and

2. Have the students examine the cause and effect relationships suggested by the inspection by having them relate the description of the design to the disadvantages and advantages.

Sample Lesson I: Social Studies— In My Own Neighborhood

Mrs. O'Malley wanted her first graders to review and extend their knowledge of neighborhoods prior to studying neighborhoods in other parts of the world.

Objectives:

Mrs. O'Malley wanted her students to be able to identify the characteristics of a neighborhood, its purpose, its advantages and disadvantages, and its possibilities.

Getting Started:

Mrs. O'Malley introduced her lesson on neighborhoods by having them look again at the photographs she had taken on their walk around the school neighborhood. She encouraged the children to show the neighborhood pictures they had drawn and to restate why they thought their picture showed something important about their neighborhood.

Procedures:

Mrs. O'Malley posted a large piece of mural paper divided into quadrants. She asked the children to close their eyes and think about what they knew about neighborhoods. What makes a place a neighborhood? As the children responded, she wrote their answers down.

Next, Mrs. O'Malley asked the children if they knew what the purpose of a neighborhood was. Then she had them consider what were the arguments for and against having neighborhoods. Was there anything especially good about having neighborhoods? Might there be something bad about having a neighborhood? At this point in the discussion, Mrs. O'Malley's record of responses looked like this:

• What makes a place a neighborhood? People live there. People are close together in a neighborhood. People are near things. Lots of different people live in a neighborhood. My church is in my neighborhood. We have stores to shop in. We have a park—we play there with our friends.	• What is the purpose of a neighborhood? People can be close to things in a neighborhood. They don't want to go far. People help one another in a neighborhood. People in a neighborhood share. People in a neighborhood can work together.
• What are the arguments for having neighborhoods? People feel safe. People are close to things they use, like parks and schools. People make friends. • What are the arguments against neighborhoods: People can't be private. Everybody knows when I get in trouble. People don't always agree. My next-door neighbors are fighting with my mom.	Mrs. O'Malley explained that this section of the chart was for the children's pictures and stories. "I want you to imagine what a neighborhood of the future might look like. How would you change your neighborhood? What would your new neighborhood of the future have in it? I want you to draw a picture of your neighborhood of the future. When you are done, I will help you write about it."

When the children's pictures had been completed, Mrs. O'Malley had them share their ideas.

Sample Lesson II:
Science—The Reptilian Egg

Ms. Johnson wanted her students to understand the impact of the reptilian egg in order for animals to live on land full-time. She decided to use the Knowledge by Design Strategy so her students would understand the structure of the reptile egg and its importance for the reptile's survival.

Objectives:

Students will be able to describe the parts of a reptile egg, to assess the value of its structure for land survival, to point out its advantages and disadvantages, and finally to redesign the reptilian egg to fit two different environmental scenarios.

Getting Started:

Ms. Johnson introduced her lesson by explaining that everything in nature is designed to serve life's functions and purposes and that the reptilian egg was a significant innovation which allowed reptiles to leave the swamps and survive out of water.

Procedures:

Ms. Johnson provided her students with a reading on the reptilian egg. She asked them to examine the information carefully and to use it to help fill in their organizers.

After the Knowledge by Design activity, she had her students read a piece on a spaceship. After they completed the reading, they had to use the Metaphoric Expression Strategy to compare how a reptilian egg is like a spaceship. The metaphoric activity demonstrated her students' knowledge and understanding of the reptilian egg as well as their ability to think metaphorically.

A MIGHTY METAPHOR
How is an egg like a spaceship?

Directions: Consider the question, "How is a reptile egg like a spaceship?"

- In the first space below, write down what you know about spaceships.

- In the next space, write down what you know about reptile eggs.

- Next, close your eyes and visualize an astronaut in a space capsule.
  Then visualize an embryo inside an egg.

- In the last space provided, write about any connections you can make about the two.
  It's okay to be creative or even a bit weird!

Spaceship   Reptile Egg

_____   _____

_____   _____

_____   _____

_____   _____

_____   _____

_____   _____

_____   _____

_____   _____

_____   _____

How is an egg like a
spaceship?

_____

_____

_____

TASK ROTATION STRATEGY

The Task Rotation Strategy promotes depth and breadth in student thinking while encouraging teachers to identify forgotten parts of the curriculum, focus on the needs of underachieving learners, and exercise under-used aspects of their own teaching selves or styles.

The Strategy at Work

Mr. Anderson wanted his third graders to be able to describe what a noun is, and to be able to recognize nouns. He designed a worksheet which looked like this:

Mr. Anderson had decided to have his students work in pairs so that they would be able to discuss each task and provide each other with immediate feedback and support. He required, however, that each student provide a written response for each one of the four tasks. He told his students that, when they had completed all four tasks in writing, they were to read together their written responses and decide what they had learned to answer the two posted objectives: "We want to know what NOUNS are. We want to be able to find NOUNS in sentences." Then they were to design a folder cover showing what they had learned about nouns to hold their responses.

NOUNS	
Nouns are words that name a PERSON, PLACE, or THING. Underline the nouns in the sentences on the attached sheet. Then make a chart listing the nouns in the correct column: PERSON PLACE THING	Ask your mother or father to help you make a list of the first words you ever spoke when you were a baby. Look at your list. What do you notice about your first words?
Are you a good NOUN DETECTIVE? Find the noun hidden in each of these three sentences. Tell what clues you used to find them. 1. Lethargy is not hard to see. 2. Those fallacies are often believed. 3. Did you write those six formulae?	Now try this: write ten sentences that are full of nonsense words like, "My beautiful snagrid won the porfgret." Ask three different people to find the nouns in your sentences. Try including some nonsense words that are not nouns, like this: "My mergly snagrid durled the porfgret." Can your friends still find nouns?

To introduce this Task Rotation, Mr. Anderson wrote on a large sheet of paper to be posted later: "We want to know what NOUNS are. We want to be able to find NOUNS in sentences." After he read this message to his class, he asked his students to explain their job. When he was satisfied that they understood the objective, he distributed the worksheet to his class, and introduced each activity, providing adequate time for restatement of each task, questions, and discussion.

As the student partners worked on this Task Rotation, Mr. Anderson moved about, assisting and clarifying, and observing the way in which his students approached each of the tasks. Two days later, when all of the folders had been completed, he led a discussion based on the sharing of the folder cover designs which tied together what his students had learned about nouns.

After he had recorded his student's observations about nouns and their rules for finding nouns in sentences, Mr. Anderson asked his class to think about which task they enjoyed most. He asked them to write their choice in their Learning Logs, and to explain why that task was their favorite. Sharing this writing allowed the class to become more aware of their own learning preferences and the learning preferences of others in the group. Finally, Mr. Anderson recorded each student's learning styles that he had been keeping since September.

The Task Rotation Strategy

The Task Rotation Strategy contributes to greater depth and breadth of student understanding by deliberately choosing to present aspects of any given content in each of the four learning style positions. The teacher plans a series of tasks which require students to master basic factual material, understand the content through critical and analytical thinking, synthesize the information by applying it in some new way, and explore its contributions and connections to their personal experience. This approach provides both students and teacher with a broader frame of reference for appreciating the topic, and allows them to see and interact with the matter to be studied from four specific orientations. The critical aspects are presented in ways which validate students' own preferred learning styles and which reinforce students' own comfort levels; at the same time, they challenge students to "flex" across each of the other styles. As students identify and experience their preferred learning approach, they also begin to identify and appreciate approaches to learning that differ from theirs.

For teachers, the Task Rotation Strategy allows for the development of insights into the individual learning styles of students. In addition, it is a challenging and rewarding way for teachers to increase their own understanding of the content being taught. Task Rotation permits teachers to plan ways to reinforce factual recall, and to enhance understanding through critical and analytical thinking.

However, this strategy also pushes teachers to go beyond the mastery and understanding goals to devise means through which students are invited to invent unconventional applications, and to explore approaches through which content is made specifically responsive to students' needs.

The goals of the Task Rotation Strategy are:
1. To help students master basic factual material by asking them to recall facts or definitions, use sequences, use categories, and/or use procedures (ST);

2. To help students increase understanding by asking them to compare and contrast, summarize, prove, and/or establish cause and effect (NT);

3. To help students reorganize content by asking them to hypothesis, imagine and elaborate, use metaphors, and/or synthesize (NF); and

4. To help students relate personally to the content by asking them to describe feelings, empathize, express a preference or make a value judgment, and/or reflect on decisions and outcomes (SF).

The steps in the Task Rotation Strategy are:
1. Determine the objective(s);

2. Design four activities or questions which represent the four positions;

3. Provide information to students on their roles;

4. Tie tasks and activities together to provide for depth of understanding through the identification of relationships and meanings; and

5. Have students discuss their learning preferences as evidenced by their feelings about the activities or questions in each of the four positions.

How to Plan Lessons Using the Task Rotation Strategy

You need to choose a topic to explore in all four positions. Next, decide whether you will use this strategy to reach one objective or multiple objectives relative to the topic. Look over the work which you might plan to cover in a particular subject in the next week or two. What objectives do you wish your students to achieve in that time? Select objectives that can be viewed as a whole, and write them down. Objectives must be written down in order to be clarified by the students. Objectives must be clearly expressed as a result of student questioning.

Next, you need to establish activities and focusing questions for each of the four positions. There should be one clear and specific task for each position: *mastery* (ST); *understanding* (NT); *self-expressive* (NF); and *interpersonal* (SF).

Mastery tasks include observing, memorizing, sequencing, and categorizing. When you ask students to observe, you want them to identify the properties of a particular item, happening or concept. You may ask questions designed around the following:

1. What did you see, hear, touch, taste, or smell?

2. Describe the facts.

3. What did you observe?

4. Describe the characteristics and properties of…

When you wish students to memorize, you want them to recognize and recall information such as facts, definitions, concepts, values and skills. You may ask questions designed around the following:

1. Who, when, where, was the…?

2. What did they…?

3. How did they…?

When you wish students to sequence, you want them to arrange information in a logical order according to chronology, quantity, quality or location. You may ask questions such as:

1. What do you do first?

2. Sequence the following events.

3. What happened first? second? third?

4. Which is the smallest? the next largest? the largest?

When you ask students to categorize, you require them to place objects, ideas, and phenomena into categories according to specified criteria. You may ask students to separate a list of words into nouns/not nouns or into parts of speech; to listen to several musical pieces and separate them by type; to group a list of numbers into even/odd, prime/composite, abundant/perfect/deficient. Alternatively, you may develop lists of criteria, and then ask students to categorize accordingly.

Understanding tasks include comparing and contrasting, analyzing, and summarizing. When you ask students to compare and contrast, you want them to determine similarities and differences on the basis of some stated or inferred criteria. You may ask questions designed around the following:

1. List the similarities and difference between…

2. Compare and contrast the following…

3. Compare two or more… or contrast…

4. What are the significant similarities (or significant differences) between…

When you ask students to analyze, you want them to break down a concept, problem, pattern, or whole into its component parts systematically or sequentially so that the relations between the parts are expressed explicitly. Questions to use may look like the following:

1. List the parts of a sentence (paragraph, story, poem, machine, compound, etc.) that are essential to understanding…

2. Compare and contrast these… with…

3. What are the essential factors involved in this problem?

4. Analyze the given data, and identify the facts and fallacies.

When you want students to summarize, you are asking them to state briefly the substance of what has been observed, heard, or experienced. Use questions such as:

1. Summarize what you have read.

2. Think of a title for this section.

3. Draw a picture which summarizes what you learned.

4. List the most important points.

5. The salient points of the lecture were…

Self-expressive tasks ask students to reorganize information by associating, hypothesizing, synthesizing, and using metaphors. When you ask students to associate, you want them to relate objects, data, or thoughts as they come to mind so that the discovery of ties between related items may be discovered. Association may be free and unrestricted, controlled by being limited to a given content or area, or linked so that each association becomes the stimulus for the next in a train of associations. Questions which elicit associations follow the form: What do you think of when you hear…? or What words or ideas come to mind when I say…?

When you ask students to hypothesize, you want them to generate assumptions concerning cause and effect relationships. Hypothesizing which asks students to reorganize is elicited by questions such as: What would happen if…? or Suppose… What would be the consequences? Hypothesizing which asks students to employ the suspension of disbelief is elicited by questions such as:

1. How would you best solve this problem if this were the best of all possible worlds and anything you wanted could come true?

2. If you could have anything you wished, real or imaginary, to solve this problem, what would it be?

When you ask students to think self-expressively, you want them to combine and arrange parts or pieces into a whole to establish a pattern or product not present before. Questions that elicit creative thinking or metaphorical response include:

1. Combine the following unrelated words into a meaningful sentence;

2. Combine the following characters from three books or stories, and construct your own story;

3. Develop a plan to achieve a specified purpose given a set of data;

4. Organize information into a meaningful report;

5. Use a personal experience to write a short story or poem conveying what happened, how you felt, etc.;

6. Combine the following lines, shapes, etc. into a pattern;

7. Given the following items, construct a mobile, a collage, a picture, a diorama, etc.;

8. Combine the following arithmetic operations by constructing a problem in which they all must be used;

9. Given the following figures and data, construct a graph; and

10. Combine the following geographical data onto a map.

When you ask students to reorganize information by using metaphors, you want them to establish relationships of likeness between one object or idea and another by using one in place of the other. Through these substitutions, the familiar is connected with the unfamiliar, or a new idea is created from two familiar ideas. Three types of metaphors are: direct analogy, in which two objects or concepts are compared (How is a book like a river?); personal analogy, in which personal involvement through empathic identification is explored (How would you feel if you were an automobile engine?); and compressed conflict, in which paradoxical points of view about an object or idea are combined in order to facilitate seeing the object or idea from two different frames of reference (How is a machine like a smile or a frown?).

Metaphorical questions you might ask may take the form of forced associations: A… is like a… because…, or if I were a…, I would look like a…, or How is… like…. Metaphorical questions may require personal involvement; How would you feel if you were a…? Metaphorical questions may ask for the application of two different frames of reference: How is a revolution both kind and cruel?

Interpersonal tasks ask students to feel, empathize, prefer, or value. Feeling questions require students to use words to describe their feeling state: How do you feel about… or How would you feel if… Empathizing questions ask for an imaginative projection into another person's subjective state of mind: How do you think… feel? Preferring questions ask for a voluntary reply or act as a result of a choice among alternatives: Given a choice, which would you choose? or What would you like to do?

Valuing is a process that involves making choices and decisions. It focuses on how beliefs and behavioral patterns are established. The valuing process involves choosing behaviors freely from among alternatives after thoughtful consideration of consequences. It requires public affirmation and a consistent pattern of action. Eliciting questions may ask students to choose freely, or to choose from alternatives (What else did you consider before you picked this?) Questions may be designed to help students to choose thoughtfully and reflectively (What would be the consequences of each alternative? or What assumptions are involved in your choice?) Activities may be designed to encourage students to affirm and/or act on their choices: Would you prepare to tell us your feelings about that? or What action can you take in support of your choice?

When you have written a clear objective or set of objectives and have established a clear and specific task or activity for each of the four

positions, you must think about the information you will need to provide to your students. How will seating arrangements be determined? May your students work together? If so, how should the work be shared? How will your students gather materials? How should your students record their responses? Your outline should contain explicit answers for these issues.

Putting the Task Rotation Strategy to Work in Your Classroom

To introduce the Task Rotation Strategy, you need to make clear to your students from the outset that you are going to ask them to look at a topic from four distinct perspectives, that you want them to become aware of the tasks with which they feel most comfortable, and that you want them to be able to discuss the relationships between and among the four types of activities after they have finished their assignment.

Distribute to your students a worksheet containing a precise statement of the objective(s) and a description of the four tasks. Encourage your students to discuss and clarify the objective(s). Then introduce each task with a question in that position and aid students to clarify the four assignments. Be sure to discuss student roles and responsibilities, and to address issues related to gathering materials, developing working relationships, and recording student responses for each of the four activities.

When your students have completed the four tasks, provide an opportunity for them to articulate relationships between and among the four types of activities. As they discuss the objective(s), ask them to demonstrate their knowledge of the objective(s) by generating additional examples for each quadrant in turn. In this wrap-up, you want to help your students tie the tasks and activities together to promote a deeper understanding of the objective(s).

When you and your students have completed the discussion of their understanding of the objective(s), take time to encourage them to discuss their experiences in learning the required content. What differences did they notice in their responses to the various tasks? Were there activities which made them feel more comfortable? Did they feel that some types of tasks helped them to learn the content more readily than other types? Was there an activity that they disliked doing? Did they feel that there were advantages and disadvantages to doing tasks that required different types of thinking? Make provisions for recording shared student responses, and survey the students individually to get attitudinal feedback on their preferences. Analyzing student responses to the Task Rotation Strategy will help you to know your students' preferred learning styles, and will enhance your future planning.

How to Evaluate the Task Rotation Strategy

The goal of the Task Rotation Strategy is to present the curriculum more effectively by designing learning tasks that match the learning styles of all students. Evaluation of this strategy requires looking at both the teacher's design and the students' level of success and comfort.

The teacher's design must include clearly stated objectives. Were the students able to restate the objectives readily? Was it apparent from their explanations of what they were expected to learn that they understood the outcome toward which they were to work?

The teacher's design must also contain carefully planned tasks which are reflective of the four learning styles and which serve to illuminate various aspects of the topic. Did observations of the students at work indicate that students found some tasks easier or more to their liking, while other tasks were more challenging or less liked? Was there evidence in the students' approach to the assignment that student reactions reflected differences in learning styles?

If a task was universally liked or disliked, it is probably not because of learning styles; on the other hand, if some students found a particular task exciting while others avoided it until the last possible moment, learning style may be the issue. When the students discussed the relationships between and among the four types of tasks, did they evidence an understanding of the topic, and were they able to articulate the way in which their understanding was advanced by each of the activities?

Because the Task Rotation Strategy often requires students to work independently of teacher direction, management issues are important. Was the classroom atmosphere orderly and purposeful? Were students involved and on task? Were student responses appropriate and useful? Did student responses and subsequent discussion give evidence of student growth in understanding and knowledge?

Summary

When to use it:
When you want students to explore an important learning objective in depth.

How to use it:
1. Identify the learning objective;

2. Design or select four assignments that relate to your objective.

   a. Mastery assignments require students to remember or repeat a learning correctly.

   b. Understanding assignments require students to reason about the learning ideas and to relate them to evidence or proof.

   c. Self-Expressive assignments require students to reorganize or think divergently about a concept or data they have been given.

   d. Interpersonal assignments require students to respond personally to the learning and to find the relevance of the lesson for themselves and what they value; i.e., pertinence and relevance;

3. Encourage students to complete all four assignments; and

4. Explain to students how to share their preferences and results in small groups or with the rest of the class.

How to evaluate it:

1. Are students able to complete the four assignments successfully?

2. Are students able to identify their preferences?

3. Are students able to relate assignments to the learning objective?

Things to remember:

1. Be sure to provide sufficient time to complete all four assignments; and

2. Sometimes students will block or freeze when it comes to a certain style of assignment. Be ready to show them how to complete work in all the types.

Sample Lesson I: English—Robert Frost in the Round

Ms. Bocour wanted her seventh grade students to use the Task Rotation Strategy to approach the study of poetry within a broad frame of reference. She hoped to encourage an appreciation of the topic, as her plan would allow her students to see and interact with a poem from four specific orientations.

Objectives:

Ms. Bocour wanted to introduce her poetry unit by encouraging her students to interact with a selected poem in ways which required them to master basic factual material about the poem, to understand the content of the poem through critical and analytical thinking, to synthesize information about the poem by applying it in some new way, and to explore the poem's contributions and connections to their personal experience.

Getting Started:

To introduce her lesson on Robert Frost's poem, "The Road Not Taken," she told her class how she had wrestled with the problem of choosing between two colleges to which she had been accepted. One college, close enough to home to make it possible for her to see her family at holidays and less expensive, was the choice of two of her best friends. The other, with a very good reputation for its English department, was farther away, and so expensive that she would have to work during the school year as well as during the summer to help her parents pay the costs. After much thought, she chose the college that was farther away. Although lonely at first, she made many good friends, and, in her senior year, met the man who is now her husband. She asked her students to write in their Response Logs their opinion about her choice: Did Ms. Bocour make the right decision? Why do you think so? The subsequent discussion was spirited, producing a variety of opinions based on "what if…" statements.

Procedures:

Ms. Bocour explained that the class would begin its poetry unit by working in groups of four to examine a poem about making a decision. She told the group that she wanted them to be able to restate the meaning of the poem, and to notice the way in which the author used language to convey meaning. She wrote these objectives on the board, and asked several students to restate them so that they would be clear to everyone. Then she asked the class to listen carefully as she read the poem aloud.

Next Ms. Bocour distributed a copy of the poem and a worksheet which looked like this:

Identify the author. Underline any words you don't understand and look them up. Study the rhythm of the poem. Describe it. Memorize the poem.	Think of an important choice you made in your life. Tell how the choice affected you and people around you. Would you make the same choice again? Why?

THE ROAD NOT TAKEN
Robert Frost

Write a prose summary of the poem. Prove this statement by citing particular lines from the poem: *Robert Frost had both positive and negative feelings about his choice.*	How is life like two roads? How is your life like a journey? What else might you compare life to? Why? Write a poem on a topic and a meter of your choosing.

Before dividing the class into workgroups, she discussed each task in turn, clarifying where necessary, and, in particular, focusing on the meaning of "rhythm" and "prose summary." When she asked for individual written responses to each of the tasks, one student asked whether the written response could be a drawing or a cartoon instead of a paragraph. He said, "I'm thinking of the question about making an important choice." Another student commented, "You could do a drawing, or maybe a poem, about something to compare life to." Ms. Bocour agreed that these responses would be acceptable, told the class that they would use the rest of the period, and all of the period on Friday to work on the assignment, and that the completed assignment would be due on Monday. She spent the two class periods assisting, clarifying and observing students as they worked on the different tasks.

On Monday, Ms. Bocour asked the work groups to develop a joint response to the objectives: restate the meaning of the poem, and notice the way in which the author used language to convey meaning. While the students worked, Ms. Bocour moved from group to group to check written responses, noting which ones she wished to have shared. Then she led a discussion, tying together the tasks to identify the relationships among them, and using samples of students' work to illuminate the objectives. At the end of the discussion, she surveyed her students to see which task had been their personal favorite, and briefly discussed what she and they had discovered about the students' learning preferences.

References
and Useful
Resources

REFERENCES

Ausubel, D.P., Educational Psychology: A Cognitive View. New York, NY: Holt, Rinehart, Winston, 1968.

Bloom, Benjamin S., Ed., Taxonomy of Educational Objectives, Handbook 1: Cognitive Domain. New York, NY: David McKay, 1956.

Bruner, J., Toward A Theory of Instruction. New York, NY: Norton, 1968.

deBono, Edward, Lateral Thinking: Creative Thinking Step By Step. New York, NY: Harper and Row, 1973.

Gilligan, J., In A Different Voice. Cambridge, MA: Harvard University Press, 1982.

Gordon, W.J.J., Synectics. New York, NY: Harper and Row, 1961.

Guilford, J.P., The Nature of Human Intelligence. New York, NY: McGraw Hill, 1967.

Hanson-Silver's Learning Styles and Strategies: Manual #1 in the Dealing With Diversity Series. Princeton Jct., NJ: Hanson-Silver & Associates, Inc., Thoughtful Education Press, 1981.

Hanson, Silver, Stong's Questioning Styles and Strategies. Princeton Jct., NJ: Thoughtful Education Press, 1985.

Hunt, Irene, Across Five Aprils. New York, NY: Follet Publishing, 1954.

Hunter, M., "Knowing Teaching and Supervising," In P. Hosford (Ed.) Using What We Know. Alexandria, VA: A.S.C.D., 1984.

Joyce, Bruce and Marsha Weil, Models of Teaching. Englewood Cliffs, NJ: Prentice Hall, Inc., 1972.

Kaplan, Sandra, S.K. Madsen and B.T. Gould, The Big Book of Independent Study. Pacific Palisades, CA: Goodyear Publishing, 1976.

Kohlberg, Lawrence, Ed., Moralization, the Cognitive Developmental Approach. New York, NY: Holt, Rinehart and Winston, Chapter 45, 1973.

Marzano, R.J. and Arredondeo, D.E., Tactics for Thinking. Alexandria, VA: A.S.C.D., 1986.

Meeker, Mary, The Structure of the Intellect: Its Interpretation and Uses. Columbus, OH: Chas. E. Merrill, 1969.

Moston, Muska, Teaching: From Command to Discovery. Belmont, CA: Wadsworth Publishing Co., 1972.

Parnes, Sidney J., Creativity: Unlocking the Human Potential. Buffalo, NY: DOK Publishers, 1972.

Raths, Louis E., Merrill Harmin, and Sidney B. Simon, Values and Teaching. Columbus, OH: Chas. E. Merrill, 1966.

Simon, Sidney B., Leland W. Howe, and Howard Kirshenbaum, Values Clarification: A Handbook of Practical Strategies for Teachers and Students. New York, NY: Hart Publishing, 1972.

Suchman, R., Inquiry Training in the Elementary School. Chicago, IL: SRA, 1960.

Taba, Hilda, Hilda Taba Teaching Strategies Program. Miami, FL: Institute for Staff Development, 1971, Units 1 and 2, Secondary Edition.

Triffinger, D.J., and B.L. Barton, Fostering Independent Learning. G/C/T Magazine, March-April, 1979.

Whimbey, A. and J. Lochhead, Problem Solving and Comprehension. Hillsdale, NJ: Lawrence Erlbaum Assocs., 4th Edition, 1986.

Williams, Frank E., Classroom Ideas for Encouraging Thinking and Feeling. Buffalo, NY: DOK Publishers, 1970.

USEFUL RESOURCES ORGANIZED BY LEARNING STYLES

Interpersonal References

Sensing-Feeling—Self Concept and Socialization

Berne, E., Games People Play. New York, NY: Grove Press.

Canfield, Jack and Wells, Harold, 100 Ways to Enhance Self-Concept in the Classroom. Englewood Cliffs, NJ: Prentice Hall.

Freed, A., T.A. for Kids. Sacremento, CA: Jalmar Press, Inc.

Ginott, Haim G., Teacher and Child. New York, NY: MacMillan, 1972.

Gordon, Thomas, Teacher Effectiveness Training. New York, NY: Peter H. Wyden Publishing Co., 1975.

Harris, T., I'm O.K.–You're O.K. New York, NY: Avon Books.

Hawley R. and Hawley I., A Handbook of Personal Growth Activities for Classroom Use. Amherst, MA: Educational Research Activities.

Howe, Leland, and Howe, Mary M., Personalizing Education. New York, NY: Hart Publishing Co.

Johnson, David W. and Johnson, Rogert T., Learning Together and Alone: Cooperation and Individualization. Englewood Cliffs, NJ: Prentice Hall, 1975.

Lyon, Harold C., Jr., Learning to Feel-Feeling to Learn. Columbus, OH: Charles E. Merrill Publishing Company, 1971.

Moustakas, Clark, The Authentic Teacher-Sensitivity and Awareness in the Classroom. Cambridge, MA: Howard A. Doyle Publishing Company, 1966.

North, M., Body Movement for Children. Boston, MA: Play, Inc.

Powell, Carl R., Freedom to Learn. Columbus, OH: Charles E. Merrill Publishing Company, 1969.

Rubin, Louis J., Facts and Feelings in the Classroom. New York, NY: Walker and Company, 1973.

Schmuch, Richard A. and Patricia A., Group Processes in the Classroom. Dubuque, IA: William C. Brown Company, 1971.

Understanding References

Intuitive-Thinking—Critical Thinking

Bartlett, Sir Frederic, Thinking. New York, NY: Basic Books, Inc., 1958.

Black, Max, Critical Thinking. New York, NY: Prentice Hall, 1946.

Bloom, Benjamin S., Taxonomy of Educational Objectives, Part I Cognitive Domain. New York, NY: Longmans, Green and Company, 1956.

Bruner, Jerome S., The Process of Education. Cambridge, MA: Harvard University Press, 1961.

Bruner, Jerome S., Goodnow, Jacqueline J., and Austin, George A., A Study of Thinking. New York, NY: John Wiley and Sons, Inc. 1961.

Dewey, John, How We Think. Boston, MA: D.O. Heath and Company, 1910.

Frankenstein, Carl, They Think Again: Restoring Cognitive Abilities Through Teaching. New York, NY: Van Nostrand Reinhold Co., 1979.

Gerhard, Muriel, Effective Teaching Strategies with Behavioral Outcomes Approach. West Nyack, NY: Parker Publishing, Inc. 1971.

Guilford, J.P., Intelligence, Creativity and Their Educational Implications. San Diego, CA: Robert E. Knapp Publishing Co., 1968.

Hunkins, Francis P., Involving Students in Questioning. Boston, MA: Allyn and Bacon, Inc., 1976.

Kapfer, Miriam B., <u>Behavioral Objectives in Curriculum Development</u>. Englewood Cliffs, NJ: Educational Technology Publications, 1971.

Keyes, Kenneth S., <u>How to Develop Your Thinking Ability</u>. New York, NY: McGraw Hill, 1950.

Raths, Louis E., Wassermann, Selma, Jonas, Arthur, and Rothstein, Arnold, M., <u>Teaching for Thinking: Theory and Application</u>. Columbus, OH: Charles E. Merrill Publishing Co., 1967.

Sanders, Norris M., <u>Classroom Questions, What Kinds?</u> New York, NY: Harper and Row, 1966.

The University of the State of New York. <u>Critical Thinking and Reasoning</u>: A Project Search Development, 1971-75.

Self-Expressive References

Intuitive-Feeling—Creativity

Bruner, Jerome S., <u>On Knowing: Essays for the Left Hand</u>. Cambridge, MA: Belknap Press, Harvard University, 1962.

Gordon, W.J.J., <u>Synectics</u>. New York, NY: Harper and Row, 1961.

Ornstein, Robert, <u>The Nature of Human Consciousness</u>. New York, NY: Viking, 1974.

Osborn, Alex, <u>Applied Imagination</u>, 3rd ed., New York, NY: Scribners, 1963.

Parnes, Sidney, <u>Guide to Creative Action</u>. New York, NY: Scribners, 1977.

Silvano, Arieto, <u>Creativity: The Magic Synthesis</u>. New York, NY: Basic Books, Inc., 1976.

Torrance, E. Paul, <u>Encouraging Creativity in the Classroom</u>. Dubuque, IA: W.C. Brown, 1970.

Torrance, E. Paul, <u>The Creative Teacher at Work</u>. Lexington, MA: Ginn, 1972.

Self Expressive References

Intuitive-Feeling—Values and Moral Development

Duska, Ronald and Whelan, Mariellen, <u>Moral Development: A Guide to Piaget and Kohlberg</u>. Paulist/New Press, 1975.

Galbraith, Ronald and Johnes, T.M., <u>Moral Reasoning: A Teacher's Handbook for Adapting Kohlberg to the Classroom</u>. Minneapolis, MN: Greenhaven Press, 1976.

Hawley, Robert, <u>Human Values in the Classroom</u>. Amherst, MA: Education Prometheus Books, 1975.

Lickona, Thomas, ed., <u>Moral Development and Behavior: Theory Research and Social Issues</u>. Holt, Rinehart and Winston, 1976.

Harmin, Merrill and Kirschenbaum, H., <u>Clarifying Values Through Subject Matter</u>. Columbus, OH: Merrill Publishing.

Simon, Sydney and Kirschenbaum, H., <u>Readings In Values Clarification</u>. Minneapolis, MN: Winston Press.

RECOMMENDED READINGS

Jungian Psychology and Learning Styles

Bennett, E.A., What Jung Really Said. New York, NY: Schocken Books, 1967.

Clements, S.M., Ed., Abstracts of the Collected Works of C.G. Jung. Rockville, MD: National Institute of Mental Health, 1978.

Hall, C.S. and V.J. Nordby, A Primer of Jungian Psycholgy. New York, NY: Mentor Books, 1973.

Hanson, J.R., Learning Styles and Visual Literacy. Research Monograph Series #1. Moorestown, NJ: Hanson, Silver, Strong & Associates, Inc., 1987. (A)

Learning Styles and Academic Performance. Moorestown, NJ: Hanson, Silver, Strong & Associates, Inc., 1989. (A)

Learning Style Models: Trends, Pitfalls and Needed New Directions. Moorestown, NJ: Hanson, Silver, Strong & Associates, Inc., 1989.

Learning Styles, Types of Intelligence and Students at Risk: An Argument for a Broad Based Curriculum. Moorestown, NJ: Hanson, Silver, Strong & Associates, Inc., 1989.

Learning Styles, Visual Literacies and a Framework for Reading Instruction. Moorestown, NJ: Hanson, Silver, Strong & Associates, Inc., 1989.

The Positive-Negative Stress Index: An Observation Procedure for Making Inferences about Student Learning Preferences. Research Monograph #3. Moorestown, NJ: Hanson, Silver, Strong & Associates, Inc., 1981. (A)

Hanson, J.R., and H.F. Silver, Learning Styles and Strategies. Moorestown, NJ: Hanson, Silver, Strong & Associates, Inc., 1978.

Teaching Styles & Strategies: Manual #2 in the Dealing with Diversity Series. Moorestown, NJ: Hanson, Silver, Strong & Associates, Inc., 1978, 1986 (2nd edition).

Hopcke, R., A Guided Tour of the Collected Works of C.G. Jung. Boston, MA: Shambola Press, 1989.

Jung, C.G., Memories, dreams and reflections. New York, NY: Vintage Books, 1965.

Jung, C.G., Psychological Types. Princeton, NJ: Princeton University Press, Bollingen Series XX, 1971.

Lowen, N., Dichotomies of the Mind. New York, NY: John Wiley and Sons, 1981. (A)

Mattoon, M., Jungian Psychology in Perspective. New York, NY: The Free Press, 1981. (A).

Myers, I., Manual: The Myer-Briggs Type Indicator. Palo Alto, CA: Consulting Psychologist Press, 1962, 1975.

O'Connor, Peter, Understanding Yourself. Mahwah, NJ: Paulist Press, 1985.

Rychlak, J., Introduction to Personality and Psychotherapy: A Theory-Construction Approach. Boston, MA: Houghton Mifflin, 1973.

Samuels, A., Jung and the Post-Jungians. New York, NY: Routledge & Kegan Paul, 1985. (A)

Samuels, A., B. Shorter and F. Plaut, A Critical Dictionary of Jungian Analysis. New York, NY: Routledge & Kegan Paul, 1986.

Sharp, Daryl, C.G. Jung Lexicon: A Primer of Terms and Concepts. Toronto, Canada: Inner City Books, 1991.

Personality Types: Jung's Model of Typology. Toronto, Canada: Inner City Books, 1987.

Spoto, A., Jung's Typology in Perspective. Boston, MA: Sigo Press, 1989.

Storr, A., The Essential Jung. Princeton, NJ: Princeton University Press, 1983.

Additional
Materials

Building Powerful Student Learning Profiles

Do you have the tools you need to address your students' diverse thinking and learning styles?

Introducing... the all new Learning Style Inventory™ for Students

Without a clear understanding of how each student learns, there is little possibility we will be able to raise our standards.

The Learning Style Inventory™ for Students is the most valid, reliable, and practical tool for obtaining this information for all our students.

With the **Learning Style Inventory™ for Students (LSIS),** teachers will learn how each of their students prefers to learn, what motivates each student, which teaching strategies work best, and which are likely to be less than effective.

New Features!
- **Statistically validated questions**
- *Student's Introduction to Learning Styles*
- **Expanded reporting system**
- **Compatible with data management systems**
- **Free access to online resources**

You'll be amazed at the insight you gain into how your students learn! The data from the **LSIS** will provide you with all the information you need to:

- **Develop individual education plans for individuals or classes**
- **Design differentiated instruction and assessment models**
- **Advise parents on homework and learning strategies**
- **Devise varied learning paths to help different students meet the same standard**
- **Link learning style data with student achievement data in your school or district**

The new **Learning Style Inventory™ for Students** is designed to be used with students ages 10 and up.

LSIS01 . . . .**$5.00 each**
(Minimum order 10 (includes computer scoring and reporting)
Call for class, school and district volume discounts!

New! LSIS Training Available!
Learn how to use LSIS data to raise student achievement district-wide! Call for a free consultation.

Learning Styles/Multiple Intelligences Checklist™

Transform your everyday observation of students into a dynamic profiling tool!

The two best models for understanding differences and developing student potentials—multiple intelligences and learning styles—come together in the *Learning Styles/Multiple Intelligences Checklist™*. Simply observe a student and check off the behaviors he or she exhibits to develop a comprehensive learning profile. The observation format of the *LSMIC* is ideal for working with students of all grade and ability levels, including pre-readers and ESL students. The *LSMIC* includes a planning template, guidelines for working effectively with different styles and intelligences, and a handy learning styles and multiple intelligences desk reference chart. A convenient folder design facilitates the collection of student work and ongoing profile development.

#LSMIC1 (K-12) Pack of 10 . . . .**$35.00**
#LSMICR Single review copy **$8.00**

Save $27.00 *Plus get a FREE Portfolio Bag!*

The Learning Styles/ Multiple Intelligences Checklist Kit
Includes:

- **30 *Learning Styles/Multiple Intelligences Checklists***
- ***So Each May Learn: Integrating Learning Styles and Multiple Intelligences*** (see pg. 10)
- 3 learning style/multiple intelligences desk reference charts
- Durable nylon carry-all portfolio

#LSMICK (K-12) **$99.95**

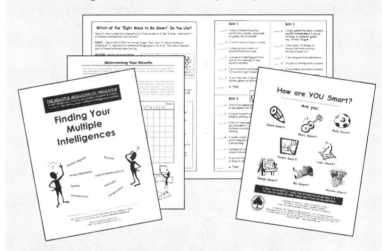